Eye Shadow

Emilio DeGrazia

(Personal Essays)

Rocket Science Press
SHIPWRECKT BOOKS PUBLISHING COMPANY

IN®
DIE

Minnesota

Cover and interior artwork by Dante DeGrazia
Digital mastering and cover design by Shipwreckt Books

This Book Is Dedicated

To my loving and brilliant wife
Monica
who has graciously edited and corrected the text
while catching many of my slips into foolishness,

and to my wonderful children
Emily
Leah
Dante
who over the years have had
the good sense to ignore some of their dad's
advice.

Special thanks to my sister
Aurora Frances
for her encouragement and loving kindness.

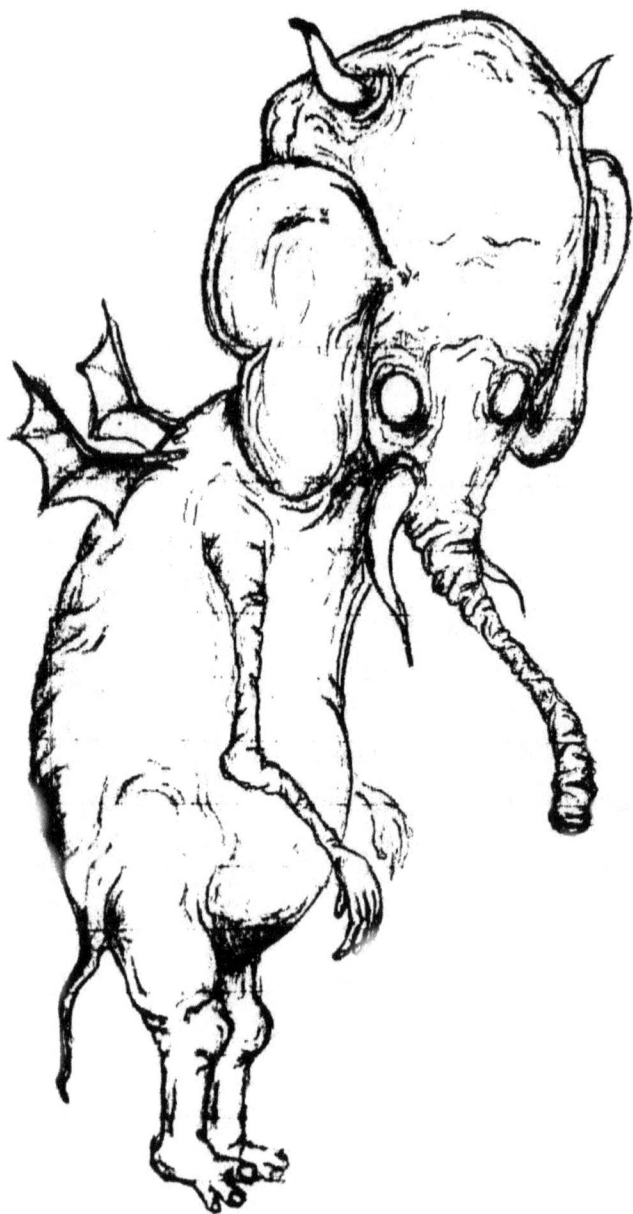

Contents

Fore-words

FEW READERS ARE AWARE of the sinister book called *The Devil's Dictionary*, compiled more than a hundred years ago by a sassy journalist named Ambrose Bierce. Like Bierce, who one day disappeared into Mexico and was never heard from again, his dictionary is virtually defunct, and all those who believe words simply mean what ordinary dictionaries say are happy for the loss.

To improve on both Daniel Webster and Bierce I offer here and there in these pages selections from my own work in progress, **The Oxymoronic Dictionary**. In a good dictionary such as mine we learn that words make sense, and we also are reminded of the obvious: That the word "sophomore" is the offspring of two ancient Greek words, *sophos* ("wisdom") and *moros* ("dull," "stupid," "moronic"), and, therefore, that a "sophomore" is a sophisticated moron.

Since the Greeks decided that their word *oxus* means "sharp" or "keen," we, however, may wonder if the author of an oxymoronic dictionary is a "sharp" and "keen" moron.

How to Pass Your Ph.D. Exams

Inscribe this on the iPad of your mind and keep rewriting it: "Either you will control words, or they will control you."

This will be on all tests.

I.   American Dreams

(from *The Oxymoronic Dictionary*)

Adjective with plural noun.

1. Belief in tax subsidies for railroad companies, but no credit for workers who built the railroad tracks that got the Little Engine That Could to the top of the heap.
2. Visions of a City on a Hill enjoyed by sleepwalkers in a garden that has no snakes or weeds in it. Tall gates to the garden keep trespassers out—especially thoughts about the perks provided by a moderate climate, vast stretches of fertile soil, and protections from world conflicts provided (until 9/11) by two very large oceans.
3. The alluring models in ads that make us feel that our personal role in history is exceptional.
4. In times of war, the nightmares seen too late that are visited from the heavens on foreigners.

Synonym: Hollywood.

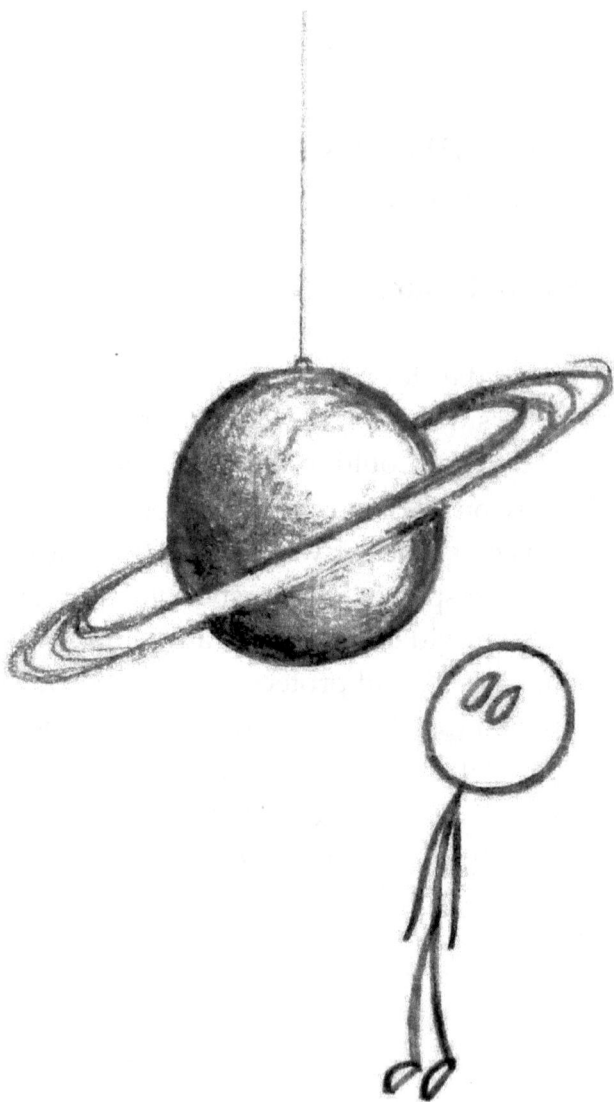

Bikini Parades

The paddlefish in Madison Lake (Minnesota) may need a new hook if they want to keep their hold on the good people of their community. Some women there have decided to convert the Paddlefish Days Parade into the "World's Largest Bikini Parade." I don't know if these enterprising women will display the World's Largest Bikini on a float with apocalyptic dimensions, but if so the poor paddlefish will feel left behind. The Bikini Parade request has raised a row, some eyebrows, and who knows what else. The town's mayor figures the bikini bunch will leave a "black mark" on Madison Lake. But, the good mayor says, "the parade will go on."

Though the Bikini Parade was cheered on loudly by owners of tanning booths, it is being sold as a fund-raiser for breast cancer prevention based on the curative powers of Vitamin D. I think the real inspiration for the event is Wisconsin cheese. Though corn queens are maintaining their cultural weight in small town parades throughout the Midwest, no queen—of apples, watermelons, strawberries, cranberries or pork—can challenge the iconic prestige of Wisconsin dairy queens. The nationwide currency of Dairy Queen franchises doubtless originated in the prototype of the lovely teenage dairy queen adorning, in her white dress, the throne of a float slowly parading itself along some Wisconsin town's Main Street on hot July days. The Madison Lake bikini bunch, which may revolutionize the way Dairy Queen products are marketed everywhere in the world, also may dwarf Wisconsin as a tourist destination.

Downstream in Winona, where I live, we honor steamboats at summer festival time, with a dairy queen or two suffered to trail behind Miss Steamboat Days. Maybe because we haven't figured out how to rig a steamboat to float down the Broadway pavement, we let all sorts of queens from other places in. And because Wisconsin's just across the interstate bridge, the cheese connection runs deep. Winona has two Dairy Queens, one on each end of town, and Winona County's Dairy Princess shows up religiously every year on her very own float.

I prefer to snooze on hot afternoons, but when I see crowds gathering (I live two blocks from the parade route) I decide to see what the fuss is about. Thousands, ritually, turn out for it, with more and more staking out curbside property right claims two days ahead of the parade. It must be a big deal, so I want to be in on it. Everybody loves a parade.

Every year our dear friend Ellen reserves a curbside chair for my wife and me. Family and friends show up for the parade, and for the delicious Sloppy Joes and other goodies Ellen spends hours preparing for everyone. We sit, gab, munch, and wait for whatever's coming by next, maybe a surprise—a good way to live, it seems, thanks to Ellen and the return of parade season.

As the floats begin dragging by I can't help thinking about the Madison Lake bikini bunch. Will their efforts stigmatize the community, or will they increase and multiply the popularity of their parade to the point where it competes with the World Cup? It's consoling to know that bikinis are being put to good use as cancer cures, especially by those running cancer causing tanning booths. If Wisconsin can rightly be proud of its cheese, Madison Lake might become more celebrated than the Mayo Clinic.

Already Minnesota can be proud of women who are above average, good-looking and strong. Madison Lake might push us to unthinkable new limits, and maybe over some new edge.

Since Minnesota's test scores are above the national average I wonder if the bikini wearers are ahead of their times in looking back. History has countless lessons to teach, and maybe the women understand how deeply the ancient Greeks and Romans enjoyed parades. Back then parades were victory processions for imperial conquering hoards, or occasions for fertility gods and goddesses to get the life juices of mortals flowing. In those good old days amazed spectators gawked at the warrior legions showing off their loot, their captive women and boys newly minted into slaves and toys, with lions, giraffes, and great apes in chains to show the world how men were above the animals. The fertility gods and goddesses had their special moments too, ritually. When babies are hard to come by fertility deities are happy to be enablers, so throngs would happily follow them to the wine parties and sacred groves where women would have a decent chance to get pregnant. The players in these ancient parades didn't all become defunct. Bacchus, one of the fertility gods, eventually made his way to New Orleans and Mardi Gras, and most of the goddesses crossed the oceans with the immigrant waves, having conversion experiences that qualified them to show up in our parades as cranberry, strawberry, apple, watermelon, pork, and dairy queens.

This demotion of goddesses to queens is historically understandable, since babies are a lot easier to come by in these modern high tech times. Nowadays we have milk substitutes in the grocery stores, so maybe breasts are not needed any more except to be on parade.

If bikinis were in the Steamboat Days parade, I wonder how it would go over with the teenagers in the marching bands. In the Winona parade the frontrunners seem rather stiff—uniformly overdressed and high-stepping it toward some war we imagine we've won. The local police pass by first, then the state highway patrol, firemen, ambulance corps, VFW, American Legion, Military Order of the Purple Hearts, veterans of Korea, Vietnam and miscellaneous wars, the U.S. Army and Army Reserves—most of them sweating like the kids carrying trombones and tubas in the marching bands. The teenagers in the marching bands perform their duties too, though I doubt many see themselves as budding parts of a war machine. Most of the ones I know can hardly wait to get out of their band uniforms so they can slip into swimsuits and beeline it to a beach. I think of them when I see the float sponsored by the local humane society. I like to think the cats and dogs penned behind bars on that float have a pretty good chance of being rescued if enough people get to see their brown eyes. A couple summers ago, one member of a (nameless) high school marching band, a snare drummer, quietly liberated a bunch of cats while everyone was gawking at the queens.

Players in our Steamboat Days parade keep plodding past, but I can't really say they amount to anything that adds up. I like the Clydesdales and midget ponies, though I'm sure one of those Shriner Motorcycles will run down a stray toddler someday. It's hard not to see most of the entries as thinly disguised commercials—for canoes, boat and stock car racing, banks, cable companies, cars, RV's, furniture, and chains. Religious groups also use the parade to sell themselves, trying to propel people into church or Bible school by throwing Tootsie Rolls at their feet. And politicians are such parade addicts that the Minneapolis *Star/Tribune* is sponsoring an "I Love a Parade" competition. Politicians with the highest parade miles logged in by Labor Day will be declared winners weeks before people go to the actual polls. One politician in my district walked 300 miles running for office in parades.

As the sun bakes the parade route, I start thinking that parades are a national pastime like baseball—that game full of yawns, especially between pitches in the late innings when managers march relievers on and off the mound while commercials on TV have a field day. I keep telling myself there's a difference between what I see in a parade and on TV. I've never seen on TV the Safe and Sober Crash Test Dummies, the Whacky Wheeler of Ready-Mix, the St. Paul Bouncing Team, the Jolly Giant Stiltwalkers, the Twin Cities Unicycle Club, the Zor Fire House Jesters, the Waumandee Lions Pumpkin Cannon, or the Zurah Ho-Ho Classics. Rather bored by the seemingly endless succession of bizarre displays, I still slowly eat it all up, wondering if I have become what I eat.

If parades provide telltale indicators of who we are and what we value, then we shouldn't be surprised by what we see. Parades are untidy events full of diversity and surprises. They invite me to ask a question that's been bothering me a lot, especially in these polarized times when a lot of Americans have taken to disliking, if not hating, other Americans they don't even know: What's "American" about America? It's like asking, "What's Christian about Christianity?" Americans can't seem to agree about what words mean, and the bipolar noise these questions inspire makes the questions not only difficult to answer but also inaudible. This acrimony suggests that our parades are not for everyone.

I don't like everything I see in parades, but then I don't like everyone, especially if I don't know their names. But sometimes, ritually, it's good for me to call time out, mix it up with strangers, and take a look at what's coming down the road. A lot of weird things show up on the parade route, and so many are trying to sell me something I feel like an oddball because I have nothing to sell. But when I look around I see a lot of people like me thoughtfully staring at what's coming our way. I see diversities— different body shapes, skin colors, hairdos, costumes—both in the parade and lining the parade route. This diversity is maybe what defines "America" best, while deepening and expanding the fertile grounds of our national identity and remarkable prosperity. As a nation we, historically, have kept a lot of differences on the move, and as our differences keep getting mixed together a lot of fertile production seems to result from the stews. Process—and the tolerance, inclusiveness, civility and cheesy silliness required to keep things going—is mainly who we are. Though we throw tons of stuff away for someone to pick up after us, we don't like to swallow our chewing gum.

Having Ellen there for our Steamboat Days parade personalizes our family's seasonal ritual on her front lawn. Ellen's a devout Roman Catholic, so I doubt I'll be able to talk her into taking the trip with me to Madison Lake to see next season's World's Largest Bikini Parade. But while I know she has strong beliefs about fertility and hates cancer too, I also know that if the bikinis come to Winona next year she'll still get up early on parade day to make us her Sloppy Joes. People like her maybe frown at what they see, but they're generous enough to know the parade must go on.

Homecoming

"Do you feel any younger?" my wife asked as she set the digital clock of our car an hour back. We had just crossed the Indiana state line into Illinois, returning to Minnesota from my fiftieth homecoming reunion at Albion College in Michigan. Suddenly I had gained an hour, and this got me scheming about how my presence in the Central Time zone might give me one more small chance for an exciting mid-life crisis to kick in. The downside was that we were so trapped in Chicago traffic I didn't see how we'd ever get home from my homecoming.

Even as I crawled bumper to bumper with a long line of trucks my wife's question sent a quiver of hope through my loins. What if? If I had gained an hour by crossing into Illinois, could I gain another by speeding into Colorado's Mountain Time? And if I could gain still another hour past the Rockies, why not keep going far out enough to gain a few months and years, not all of them theoretical? I'm no genius, but what would Einstein say?

As traffic did its slow crawl it gave me plenty of time to think about how time flies, but my thoughts came to a dead stop whenever they were interrupted by a chance to break free and step on the gas.

A fiftieth college reunion does give one pause, especially if one has been absent from the other forty-nine. I'd returned to my beloved Albion College a few times in those fifty years, but I'd mainly waved my greetings over to the campus from I-94 as I sped by on my way to family in Detroit. From the freeway only the steeple of the chapel is visible, so nothing about the place had changed.

A full week before the homecoming event I dusted off my 1963 Albionian Yearbook, and like a good student I did my homework on my old college mates. The faces in the yearbook seemed familiar and fresh, but I had a very hard time getting the yearbook names to stick to my mind. The faces there were like many of my current friends at home— memorized. But the names that go with the faces of current friends are routinely disappearing these days, even when I encounter them on the sidewalk or in the grocery store. Where are well-known names hiding in my declining years, even as the faces that belong to them smile and say hi? If names don't have staying power, what does?

I kept telling my wife my homecoming worries. What if I go blank when I'm shaking hands with one of my best old college friends? What if I can't remember the name of the girl I took to the dance, and what if she remembers mine? "Problem solved," said my wife. "Just tell them you're losing your mind. They'll understand."

I consoled myself with a recent scientific discovery. Astronomers had just seen a galaxy so spaced out it's been dead for thirteen billion years. With 41 of my old classmates already passed away, I saw their yearbook faces in a new light. If that dead galaxy were merely old, it still would be swirling in space, though perhaps more sluggishly than it did in its prime. At the reunion our yearbook faces would not be in their prime, but science was giving us a chance to be something else even if we were dead. In the long view all of us in the class of 1963 would be grayed, wrinkled, and sagging, but we'd also be smiling and bright the way we were when posing for our yearbook photos. We'd all be astonishingly new discoveries, suddenly reborn.

My optimistic spin was also encouraged by evidence suggesting that the history of homecomings was a progress story. In the old days homecomings were celebrations staged for absentee fathers and warrior sons returning from distant battlegrounds. Then festivities featured processions in which the spoils of war stolen by way of killing and pillage were paraded in front of cheering stay-at-home moms, grandmothers, girls and little boys. Nowadays the major homecoming event, the football game, is civilized in comparison. Homecoming features the football team's return after waging football wars on somebody else's campus turf. The parade before the big game mainly shows people off, apparently in order to extend the limits of what a society deems harmlessly ridiculous. Though football is arguably a symbolic subtext for war, the spoils of the game are not put on public display. What originated as a celebration of war's booty has evolved into a party in which fun is had.

It seems proper that so many homecomings, like Halloween, are celebrated in October harvest time. Homecomings are so popular and ritualized they seem like seasonal holidays during which we return to old fields to harvest what we planted years ago. When I arrived I was careful to deck myself out in plain clothes—no fancy suit and tie. But I felt as if I were a character in a Fellini film, one of those caricatures on public parade hoping others would see there was more to me than what they saw. We, members of the class of 1963, approached each other gingerly. Who is who, and is that really you? Who are you now, and where? We asked by indirection—are you liberal, conservative, married, divorced, or gay? Did you like me then? How can I make you like me now? What's your story? Is it true what Mark Twain said—"You tell me where a man gets his corn pone and I'll tell you what his opinions are"—or were our futures and fates shaped by circumstance and chance, or, perhaps, by education and choice?

We're told that education opens windows of opportunity for us, but as my classmates' stories unfolded I began seeing through the windows my college years had put in front of me. We were all characters in Edgar Lee Master's *Spoon River Anthology*, poems I had read as an undergrad about individuals suddenly alive again to tell their tales. The faces of my classmates, fifty years older now, gained the depth and dark clarity I saw in lovely old portraits in museums. I looked at lives through the epic paradigm my old (even then) Albion Professor John Hart had outlined as the shape of a hero's life: Separation, Initiation and Return. We had all left home to encounter experience, some of it in the form of trials, tribulations and monsters, and now here we were again, returning to "the best days of our lives." What had our initiation experiences done to our innocence? What did we bring back with us to our homecoming returns? Had we resigned ourselves to lives of quiet desperation, or committed ourselves to pursuing meaningful lives? Had we become cynical, bored, or wisely creative?

The festivities encouraged certain re-enactments, some of them indicative of how history majors like me love fantasy. One of Albion's graduates, Martin Nesbitt, class of 1985, was honored at a banquet with a Distinguished Alumni Achievement Award. Nesbitt, a friend of President Obama for twenty years, was finance manager for Obama's state and U.S. Senate campaigns, and also his presidential campaign treasurer. Nesbitt also played varsity basketball at Albion. So did I, once upon a time.

I found myself sizing him up as he received his award, asking myself how good he was. I had about twenty-two years on him, but I concluded that difference should not keep him from going nose-to-nose with me in a little game of one-on-one. He seemed to have kept himself in pretty good shape. I squirmed in my seat at the prospect of putting a few jaw-dropping moves on him.

Later, when I went forward to congratulate him for his award, I asked him point-blank: "Can Obama go to his left?" Obama loves basketball too. "You've known him for years, so no doubt you've played The Man one-on-one plenty of times. Can he go to his left?"

"He's left-handed," Nesbitt replied. "He takes a few dribbles right, but he always comes back to his left."

I hoarded the secret to Obama's game, believing it would come in handy someday. For in that moment the past's immediacy gave the future presence too. I saw myself in the old Albion College S.S. Kresge Gymnasium, squared off against the President of the United States in a game of one-on-one, and I, like the quick twenty-two-year-old gazelle I was again, would score easily on him and then easily shut him down because I had inside information about his moves. The game, by the way, was being performed before a standing room only crowd that included the girl I had asked to the dance but whose name I couldn't remember.

So what is it that lures us into these nostalgic journeys back to our college years that we dignify with the status of a place of origins and stability, a "home"? As an English major at Albion College I puzzled over the words in Thomas Wolfe's novel *Look Homeward, Angel*: "You can't go home again." If in Latin the word *educare* means "to go forth," I left home to attend college, and from there way led on to way further away from home. In a mobile society paved over with freeways, it's easy to chase a marriage or job far from parents, family, and old neighborhoods, especially if a college degree greases the wheels. In America, homelessness—absence from the comforts, enduring traditions, and responsibilities inherent in an actual place—is a way of life. Lives, like jazz, are improvised. Here, and increasingly everywhere in the world, home is where the next job is, or it's in cyberspace, or it's where the heart is.

I went to my fifty year Albion College homecoming in search of my youth, lost friends who mattered intensely to me at the time in an actual place, a lovely campus where we, for four fleeting years, did what most of us wanted to do most of our lives—learn about history, science, society, art, religion, philosophy, politics, music and literature, test our limits on level playing fields while learning how to win and lose graciously there, and talk smart to each other like the professors we loved because they had something to profess. All this while we disagreed agreeably, practiced openness, toleration and cooperation, and fumbled our way toward sex, love and marriage as the sap flowing freely through our veins stirred us to test the limits of the permissible and ethical.

What a wonderful model home in a friendly neighborhood, what a wonderful way to live, everywhere, all our lives.

My Kuhl Jak Rabbit #1007

I got something really Kuhl as a Christmas present this year. It's a "Men's Jak Rabbit #1007," a sort of fuzzy-soft jacket sweater with a zipper pocket over the heart area for toting, I suppose, warm feelings about the cell phone I don't own. It's a dream come true.

I'm not sure how much the "Men's Jak Rabbit #1007" cost my lovely daughter, who carefully picked out something she knew I'd adore. The tags that come with my Jak Rabbit #1007 are especially interesting. One tag says that it's "Crazy Soft" and made of "100% polyester Italian fleece." The flip side tells me that it has "Micro fiber faux leather accents for added style," and a "Signature Kuhl thumbloop for added warmth."

I love the thing. It's so fuzzy, smooth and toasty I can't keep my hands off it, though I've become a bit wary about how to preserve the privacy of my virtue when I see others eyeballing it. I'm a rather thrifty guy, but I don't dare ask my daughter how much it cost. I don't want to drop even a tiny hint that she might have been fleeced. I'm content to be wearing it right now, as I write, certain it's giving my literary style a softer touch. That alone makes it worth what she paid for it.

The Kuhl people must be foreigners, maybe German or Swiss, and they take their fleeces seriously. "It's really not even fair for the competition," says one of the Kuhl tags in both English and French, "to put this jacket in the 'fleece' category. The superior quality and ultra-soft hand put the Jak Rabbit in the premium category and at the top of the podium." I'm not sure it belongs at the top of a podium, but to me the Jak Rabbit #1007 feels like a top of the line product, especially for those with good taste in France. What is called "ultra soft" in the English version of the label comes off as "ultra doux" ("ultra sweet") in French. It must be both.

But to tell the truth I admit that my Jak Rabbit #1007 has a special place close to my heart because it's made of "100% polyester *Italian* fleece." Because a tag, in bold letters, informs us that the Jak Rabbit #1007 was "BORN IN THE MOUNTAINS" I can't help thinking that its fleece had its origins in the Italian Alps. Everyone knows that any quest for authenticity involves a search for origins, call them roots. Though my ethnic roots are in southern Italy, a region looked down upon by Italy's righteous Northern League political party, I'm satisfied to know my Jak Rabbit #1007 takes me back both to my European and Italian roots, snow-covered or not. My new fleece makes it clear that my sense of ethnic pride is not skin deep. And the fact that it came from Macy's puts it at the core of the American Dream.

Its American-ness also fits the free-spirited and free-thinking urges at the base of my philosophy of life. The remarkable tag that Kuhl attaches to its product speaks to the worldwide youth movement I still feel in my oldest bones. The Jak Rabbit #1007 is "born," we're informed by the tag, "from our rebellious philosophy to question everything, break the rules, and reject the status quo." I love that line, because I know my Jak Rabbit #1007 will require me to live dangerously, like all Kuhl products, which are said to "resist, defy and oppose the norm. Wearing them tells you they represent not only the freedom of movement, but also freewill."

Since freedom of movement and free will are at the core of what Americans believe, my Jak Rabbit #1007 comfortably fits my patriotic needs.

The philosophical depth of the Jak Rabbit #1007 provides a new high. Experts who keep track of advertisements inform us that Americans, on average, experience 600-625 "exposures" to ads every 24-hour day. If each ad exposure is five seconds long then the average American spends two hours out of each 24-hour day and night exposed to ads. Though it's hard to know how ads affect us while we're asleep, it's obvious that they're participants in the conversations that go on while we work and play. And because so many ads are entertaining and fun, how can we not thank them for influencing our sense of what's true and real?

The tags on my new Jak Rabbit #1007 offer some wonderful educational opportunities for harried teachers in our beleaguered schools. The Kuhl tags make it clear that certain foreign words like "faux" have enormous credibility power these days. The name of the product itself offers shortcuts bad spellers can use to qualify for jobs. Biology teachers stand to gain by engaging students in experiments designed to identify the authenticating qualities of fleeces. And a geography curriculum is waiting to be developed by educators eager to help students find France and Italy on a map, while demystifying them about how a Jak Rabbit—after being "BORN IN THE MOUNTAINS"—leaped across the Atlantic to be manufactured by nameless workers in El Salvador.

Doubtless, some of the educational issues in the Kuhl ad will require the expertise of higher authorities in our colleges and universities. The Kuhl ad might inspire philosophers and scientists, for example, to elevate class discussions of free will to new depths. Departments of psychology could expand their experimental, developmental, and clinical studies of consumer behaviors to include the paranormal. English departments could use Kuhl ads as creative writing models useful to the writing of fiction and poetry, or as examples of a prose style that leads to jobs. Business departments and whole colleges of commerce, currently so frustrated by the economy's failure to benefit from the marketing wisdom passing through their graduation lines, would be able to develop post-doc seminars on the commercial value of the laughable.

One truth remains: I love my daughter much more than I love my Jak Rabbit #1007, however Kuhl it is, and I deeply appreciate her gift. And I mean it when I say that from the 600-625 exposures to ads I experience every day none provides the soft, warm, and fuzzy pleasure I derive from my actual Jak Rabbit #1007. Because the ad for my Kuhl does not draw attention to how truth in advertising affects public discourse and personal integrity, I'm also sure I arrived at that conclusion by way of my own free will. So nothing warms my American dreams like my Kuhl.

Corn in the Commons

Corn, especially when frozen, bagged and then boiled, leaves my palate as flat as an Iowa field. In his book *The Omnivore's Dilemma* Michael Pollan warns that corn, one of our weightiest exports and the primary bloat of our cuisine, gives our nation big waists and waste. When that problem is paired with the poisons in our political air we have something big to worry about, especially if we happened to be on the winning side in a recent election and are inclined to gloat.

But I'll confess in public here: One puff of popcorn makes an addict of me. I also love Garrison Keillor and his *A Prairie Home Companion* radio show, corny as it can be. The popcorn will probably blow me up someday, but I'm convinced Keillor's corn is the right medicine for what ails the U.S.A.

When I turn on Keillor's *A Prairie Home Companion* I end up listening to the kind of stuff that normally turns me off. There's a lot of corny stuff—in the prurient leerings of private eye Guy Noir, or in the sound effects that orchestrate his moves, or in the wailing of some country singer who sounds as if she's got a clothespin holding her nose shut, or in Garrison's plaintive but always sonorous voice putting on like he's the ordinary Lake Woebegoner guy he definitely is not. All this is just right too corny enough for me. And with it we also get regular doses of gospel singers to enspirit us while Keillor's having good clean fun poking good Christian folk, many of whom are not faithful liberal Democrats. The fact that old-time religion tunes and gospel guilt have a regular place on *A Prairie Home Companion* is one thing that makes it All-American mom and pop art.

Let's not fib. Some old-time religious folk are hard to take, especially if their intolerant creeds are voted in. They have so many opinions unclouded by facts they make me feel smart when the only proof I have that I exist is that I'm confused. They get me thinking they're not confused like me, or like me period. They're hung up on or fed up with this or that. They know what the Bible says, though they haven't read most of it in English, let alone Hebrew or Greek. They live in a story-book unreality like the Harry Potter and Star War worlds where impossible things are true—like Noah's ark showing up on a mountaintop in Turkey, or Idaho, or the world coming to a spectacular end like the latest mass destruction scene in an action thriller making millions for Hollywood.

They get me where it hurts. They think scientists shouldn't be believed in like gods, they think professors aren't as smart as they think, and they keep telling me we shouldn't trust the government. This last point is really hard for liberal Democrats to buy, especially after they finally voted some of their people in. These righteous religious zealots, we say, take things out of context. And they do, a fact I keep repeating to myself as I waltz away from them with my own opinions hardening in my skull, unclouded by troubling facts pertinent to the issues bothering me too.

I'll make another public confession here: I routinely take evangelicals, as historical forces, out of context. And if I were Garrison Keillor I'd be tempted to banish their god-awful wonderful gospel music from my show.

Thank goodness Keillor's tent is bigger, and more open-aired, than mine. I find it useful to take our present moment, call it Obamic, forward into history's past. What historical impact did all those various Christian evangelicals have—the Brownists, Independents, Baptists, Lutherans, Familists, Quakers, Shakers, Separatists, Seekers, Puritans, and Ranters—most of whom passionately believed that the right to speak, vote and worship as they pleased was more important than the dictates of land barons, priests and kings? In their Reformation and Enlightenment eras they were not mere liberals; many, not all, were radicals who opposed church authority, the monopolization of knowledge by conservative universities and scientific societies, the oppression of common folk, and the degradation of women by overlords and high churchmen determined to make obedient servants or dead witches of them.

In his engaging history, *A World Without Women: The Christian Clerical Culture of Western Science* (Oxford, 1992), David F. Noble describes early evangelicals as, "drawn primarily from the lower classes," and representing, "a wide diversity of theological opinion," whose revival spirit, belief in direct revelation and passion for change, "swept aside all merely earthly authority, of church, of state, of family." Many of the groups "allowed all members to debate [and] vote," and established "spiritual equality between the sexes" (195). In the nineteenth century some members of evangelical sects led the crusades for workers' and women's rights and for the abolition of slavery. Liberals, even secular ones, owe a lot to them for the difficult battles they fought—and generally won—for, as it turned out, all of us.

This long view of them doesn't make it easy to see eye-to-eye with them. They're pro-life except when it comes to

23

certain wars and capital punishment. They're for God except when He's Muslim too. They're for love and marriage, except for gays. They're okay with science when they're in the doctor's office, but not when it comes to the Shroud of Turin, Darwin, or climate change.

Et cetera. Rather corny way to think about things. Why don't they just go away?

Because they live here too, and have earned their stay. And they will have their say, while deserving it too. The question is who will influence what they say.

In many cases, no one. Evangelicals take their story-lines seriously, while liberals take them as stories, or lack them entirely. So what we call reason, knowledge, science, pragmatism, truth, beauty, and goodness—what we also call "facts"—are mismatched with Belief. But that doesn't keep me from trying to talk with them, and rather enjoying it now and then. I find them listening when I put them in context, explaining that Christianity is large and contains multitudes, here under a large picnic tent that keeps Americans of all colors, persuasions and creeds cool on the Fourth of July. In this tent there is plenty of room for civility and graciousness.

It would be silly to cede passionate believers to right-wingers eager to hijack their votes again. It would be wrong to make aliens of them.

Michael Pollan says that having diverse crops of home-grown corn and other crops would be a lot better for us than millions of square miles of GMOs standing at attention in rows like battalions about to invade somebody else's peaceful cornfields for their own good. There's enough space in this big nation for liberals and evangelicals to stand on wide swaths of common ground, and there should be enough room on that ground for corny Christians and liberal flakes alike.

My best friends are not evangelical old-time religion folk, but some of my relatives are, and it's not just blood we have in common. We both hate war and are committed to abortion decline, but at odds about the government's role and whether the decline is best achieved through educational and social programs. Both camps support underdogs—the oppressed, the ill, the poor. Both camps are deeply skeptical of a bi-polar scientific establishment that can cure diseases and warn us about global warming while giving us drones, nuclear bombs, and genetically engineered corn monopolies. Both camps favor prosperity, affordable health care, safe streets, clean air, peace, mother and apple pie. And who can blame evangelicals for wanting to be born again? That's built right into the American dream. Liberals could enjoy that too now and again.

Socks, Parking, Parables of Hell

When I learned that humans collectively consume a cubic mile of crude oil each year my mental sky did not turn entirely black. I took some consolation from one of William Blake's Parables of Hell. The parable is simple enough: "Enough! Or too much." Over the years Blake has helped shape how I see the world, as have my parents, who believed that waste and excess were sins racing down a wide boulevard leading straight to hell. My heroes—Blake was one—are not like parents. Heroes are never wrong, ever, about anything. But how could I justify Blake's blessing of excess without incurring the wrath of my parents, who recycled handfuls of table scraps long before it was deemed a patriotic act?

It would have been enlightening to have the radical Blake drinking a few too many beers with his radical contemporary Thomas Jefferson, a gentleman and patriot. If too much will do when enough isn't enough, how would Blake respond to Jefferson's "That government is best which governs least"? Blake no doubt would shoot back another of his one-liners: "One Law for the Lion and Ox is Oppression."

Our contemporary oxymorons, radical conservatives, would cheer Blake on: They like the idea of letting lions, oxen, and weasels be themselves, tax-free. The American Revolution, they would insist, was fought to free individuals to be what they imagine they have made of themselves. The pursuit of happiness—be it of corn pone or porn—is a private matter and government should keep its nose clean. In particular, government has no business trying to design the economic future. When we're left to our own devices to design our individual private enterprises, we'll all be equally free to enjoy life, liberty and the pursuit of property. And if some of us become casualties in the attempt, we will freely fall through the cracks, taking consolation from seeing our carnage scattered on a level playing field.

Henry David Thoreau, his words now unprivatized in the essays he wrote at *Walden Pond,* trumped Jefferson's minimalism. "I say that government is best which governs not at all, and that is the kind of government we will have when we're ready for it." Call him an anarchist subject to the autocracy of self-control, the kind of self-government we like to think makes for fewer committee meetings and fewer executive orders. If citizens have the habit of not killing each other, they don't need a Fourth Commandment to tell them not to kill. If the Israelites had been better behaved, Moses would not have had to lug those stone tablets down the mountainside. Good culture makes government controls superfluous.

Do we have commandments and commandants because we have too much government? I look in my dresser drawer and find twenty–two pairs of socks. I can only wear one pair at a time, and some are in mint condition, biding their time for possible release at the next garage sale. The same goes for shirts and pants, and shoes, and videos, and books, and tools, and cans of nails, and paper clips, and cell phones, TVs, weight-control machines, bicycles, and cars. I'm guilty as sin: Too much is enough. Enough becomes too much when it's time to have another garage sale, after which too much is still too much.

It doesn't occur to us to sell the garage.

And what we don't see as we idle in a swirl of exhaust fumes in another traffic jam are the 20,000,000 barrels of oil going up in smoke every single day, just here in the U.S. How many fill-ups equal a cubic mile?

Try seeing it.

Then try weighing that cubic mile in accord with surging prosperity in the developing world that has allowed China and India, for example, to increase their consumption of crude oil to 11% of the world's supply, up from 6% ten years ago. What, me worry? We're still far ahead in the race to crude: In the U.S. we use 25 barrels per person per year, compared to 2 barrels per person per year in China.

Try seeing two cubic miles of oil. Two huge black cubes looming above the white clouds drifting past Minneapolis and St. Paul.

Does the planet begin to wobble drunkenly during five p.m. traffic jams? Does the earth's tidy curveball spin turn into a knuckleball?

If an economic system's success story depends on Growth—call it "demand creation"—certain excesses seem inevitable: Population, production, pollution, and plague. If I—with my 22 pairs of socks, my shirts and pants and shoes and videos and books and tools and cans of nails and paper clips, etc.—am the benchmark, the human norm to which the world aspires, then demand creation aims to provide everyone in China (1,400,000,000 souls) and India (1,000,000,000 souls) with 22 pairs of socks. And eventually a family car or two.

Try seeing it. Try seeing all the threads that go into those socks.

Try seeing the parking problems. If every car in the U.S. now commands eight parking spaces for itself, Asians will have to turn the Gobi Desert into their parking lot.

Growth naturally grows government too. We can't have lions, oxen, and weasels parking just anywhere. So we'll need more meter maids, more cops, more taxes, more judges, more laws. As demand creation grows Growth, and as Growth breeds more population, production, pollution and plague, it's certain we'll have to make bigger parking lots for more government cars.

My hero Blake, always on alert for ways to marry Heaven and Hell, aims another consoling Parable of Hell at me. "The road of excess leads to the palace of wisdom." The headaches in the headlines that trouble us should encourage us to rethink our American Dreams. On a knuckleball planet wobbling off course and shrinking from us as we distance ourselves from its natural processes, there is too much for some of us to want and too many millions in real need. The Palace of Wisdom does not have a swimming pool next to a three-car garage, and it has enough space for a few pairs of socks. In that Palace essentials are properly valued, and they command the fair prices that are the basis of a balanced and sustainable economy. And because there would be less room in this Palace for useless socks, there would be fewer spaces and cars in government parking lots.

American Nightmare

I didn't want to pick the book up, but after I did I couldn't put it down. Written by Charlie LeDuff, it is called *Detroit: An American Autopsy.* Detroit, in my youth the fourth largest city in the U.S., currently is on life support, casualty of a cancer in the American Dream.

Charlie LeDuff and I grew up on the west side just a few blocks from the street, Joy Road, that marks one of the city limits of Detroit. He grew up on the Detroit side of Joy. I grew up on the suburban, Dearborn, side of Joy. There signs posted everywhere kept reminding me: "Help Keep Dearborn Clean," and our police officers did their best to keep people from the other side of Joy from crossing to our side of Joy.

I left Dearborn in my twenties. That was in the early 1960's, when I was too clueless to realize Detroit would never leave me.

I remember the city's elegance—the skyscrapers downtown, the vibrancy at the intersection of Michigan and Woodward avenues, the view of Windsor across the Detroit River, the J.L. Hudson (later Dayton-Hudson) store where we shopped as a family, the cold-hot ice cream waffle sandwiches we waited in line for at the Kresge five and dime across from Hudson's, the used bookstores I haunted at night after school, the old Briggs Stadium where the Tigers played, the green and expansive Rouge and Palmer Parks, the old Corktown slum where I routinely window-shopped for great deals, the elegant mansions on Cass and Grand Boulevard, the concerts played by Paul

Paray's Detroit Symphony Orchestra on Thursday evenings at the band shell on Belle Isle, free to anyone who wanted to listen, even from the river in a canoe. Detroit was vibrant and safe enough to wander freely in. It was a feast for a kid who was told to "Help Keep Dearborn Clean."

In August, 1967, I was a student in Paris, wide-eyed as I read the headlines: *"Detroit En Feu."* Detroit is on fire.

I returned a couple weeks later, arriving at the East Side bus terminal from New York City at 4 a.m. Detroit's streets are designed as grids overlain on wide avenues radiating from the downtown hub like the spokes of a wheel. The bus ride from the terminal to my Dearborn home was like a trip through Dante's circles of hell. The streets I knew— houses, mansions, storefronts, whole neighborhoods— were burned down, boarded up, abandoned, ghostly, scary, ruined.

"And it is awful here," writes Charlie LeDuff, "there is no other way to say it … Once the nation's richest big city, Detroit is now its poorest. It is the country's illiteracy and dropout capital, where children must leave their books at school and bring toilet paper from home…there are firemen with no boots, cops with no cars, teachers with no pencils, city council members with telephones tapped by the FBI, and too many grandmothers with no tears left to give."

And "Detroit" as a metaphor for unemployment, dysfunction, crime, corruption and hopelessness extends into parts of Los Angeles, Chicago, Cleveland, St. Louis, Baltimore and other American urban centers. Is "Detroit," like the blowback that keeps coming from Baghdad and Kabul, the future of America?

Charlie LeDuff is a gutsy and streetwise journalist who

knows his Detroit. He takes us to the arson sites, the broken and barren neighborhoods where hoods and the homeless squat in abandoned homes. He takes us to the victims of violence—mainly young black boys—and their broken-hearted mothers. He lets us eavesdrop on the deal-making that goes on in speakeasy joints, talk that ends up as corruption in City Hall. From up close he describes the individual losses, the fear, the grief, despair and hopelessness. He names names.

He describes the city I avoid after I left it decades ago. When I return to visit family and friends, I don't return to the old haunts. Detroit competes with Chicago's south side to be America's murder capital.

How do we account for the problems in Detroit, and who is to be held accountable? Who do we blame if the place is so dysfunctional that Britta McLean must leave her son piled up with other corpses in the morgue because she can't possibly find the money to bury her murdered teenaged son? "It would be easy," writes Charlie LeDuff, "to lay the blame on McLean for the circumstances in which she raised her sons. But is she responsible for police officers with broken computers in their squad cars, firefighters with holes in their boots, ambulances that arrive late, a city that can't keep its lights on and leaves its vacant buildings to the arsonist's match, a state government that allows corpses to stack up in the morgue, multinational corporations that move away and leave poisoned fields behind, judges who let violent criminals walk the streets, school stewards who steal the children's milk money, elected officials who loot the city, automobile executives who couldn't manage a grocery store, or Wall Street grifters who destroyed the economy and left the nation's children with a burden of debt while they partied it up in Southampton?

Can she be blamed for that?"

Can she be blamed for being so black and blue? While all the reasons LeDuff outlines as causes of Detroit's dysfunction are on the mark, there is one so obvious it's become hard to talk about: Race, especially now when so much progress on the issue is being made, especially among the young. Racism destroyed Detroit, and racism prevents its rebirth.

Adolph Mongo, longtime Detroit wheeler-dealer and insider wise-guy, understands the problem well: "In Detroit we all talk the race game. It's a way of life…Detroit's a code word for N…"

I don't use the N-word, though I was brought up with it where I was taught to believe that it was important to "Help Keep Dearborn Clean." If skin color is visible, the walls that locked blacks out are invisible along certain streets that represent apartheid boundaries and beliefs. The history of this apartheid is well documented and sits on library shelves for anyone who really wants to know. Black workers, many of whom were part of the Great Migration from southern states, were the descendents of liberated slaves stripped of property, education, and dignity. When they arrived alongside poor and resentful southern whites to work in the northern factories, the blacks were routinely locked into enclaves within city limits and into carefully designated suburban areas just outside. Hungarians, Russians, Poles, Italians, Irish, Germans—they also came to Detroit to participate in the feeding frenzy the auto industry offered. They too were poor outsiders, and disadvantaged, but they were "white" and therefore welcomed and not stripped of their dignity. Though I as a swarthy Italian/American never felt "white" enough, my skin color was never black enough for the city inspector to suddenly decide that there was so much fatally wrong with our house we'd immediately have to move to Detroit. In Dearborn our family benefited from very good public services, and I attended excellent public schools where I was taught, among other things, that black symbolizes evil and ignorance.

It's a simple and tragic fact that blacks were not routinely or graciously accepted by the southern white and European ethnic migrants, especially when Detroit was at the height of its prosperity. Real estate agents, politicians, bankers, and employers locked blacks out of the middle class, and white cops enforced unwritten laws. When massive job losses hit the blacks harder than anyone else, they were locked more tightly in. Whites fled the city limits for suburban sprawl, and left old problems behind. Detroit became one vast inner city walled in, and out, by a hard-core mindset and public policy best summarized by ex-Senator Daniel Patrick Moynihan, a Democrat who served as urban affairs advisor with the Nixon White House staff: Moynihan recommended "benign neglect." While Moynihan believed that ignoring race would benefit blacks, national policy solutions to racial inequality and inner city problems were largely neglected.

So how did Detroit go so wrong so fast? Why did entire neighborhoods collapse? Why did people trash and burn their own groceries, houses and neighborhoods? Why would a city commit suicide?

Hate—call it relentless rejection—has a way of getting under the skin. There it festers and eats away at itself, and there it turns its most powerful weapon, rage, against itself. "Benign neglect" makes no distinction between race as an

35

explanation and excuse for failure. Our Detroits are dying because loose talk and sullen silences about race—skin pigmentation—mask thoughtful consideration of how collective responses to the issues of education, economic development, unemployment, and social engineering of human decency create prosperity, safety and well-being. Loose racist talk in and around Detroit instead has given old prejudices new life. Sullen silences have given vague resentments depth.

What we talk about, the manners that come with our talk, and the stories we tell matter a lot. I'll risk being denounced as anti-American here by suggesting that the American Dream has a tragic flaw that has made a nightmare of Detroit. Central to this American Dream narrative we are routinely fed at school, at work, and through the media is that America is the land of boundless opportunity. We keep repeating the myth that everyone can succeed here if they work hard enough. That they can do it on their own. That losers are losers because they're little engines that didn't try hard enough.

Tell that silly tale to a single mother with three kids and no money to pay the rent or heat. Tell it to an unemployed father whose unemployed son wanders the streets, angry and depressed. Tell it to the teenaged girls who refuse to go to school because they're afraid of what might happen there. Tell it to the thousands of Detroiters who don't go to doctors because they have no health insurance, and often no doctor willing to spend ten minutes with them.

Tell them with a straight face that they'll succeed if they try harder, without asking for help. Convince them they won't be shamed by asking for help.

That we all should be hard-working little engines is a nice idea, necessary for teachers and parents to repeat as they try to inspire individuals to live up to their potential, and also useful to successful types who feel a need to congratulate themselves. But it is not a credible groundwork for public discourse or public policy. At the core of the American Dream narrative is its tragic flaw, a cancerous radical individualism that expresses itself politically on both the right and left, especially among libertarians. The cancer lurks in one of our favorite words––"freedom"—repeated like a meaningless mantra, drearily by preachers and politicians. The American Dream fiction claims that an individual alone is responsible for his or her fate, and that the individual is "free to choose" this fate. An individual's failure, a whole city's failure, is not to be explained in terms of a failing economy, or Wall Street addicted to greed, or mismanagement of major industries, or corrupt politicians, or drug dealers laundering big money outside Detroit's city limits who rely on those trapped inside to participate in the city's alternative and illegal economy. And certainly nobody wants to hear anyone explain Detroit's problems in terms of race. If black Detroiters fail, it's all their own fault, and they're just playing out their victim roles when they ask for help. If they can't succeed at the American Dream, they're not good enough. Why don't they leave us alone? Why don't they just go away?

The American Dream fiction, like the steady diet of melodramas we're routinely fed by Hollywood, has good guys and bad. The moral of this simplistic story is that those who make it are good, and those who don't are bad and deserve to lose. What's wrong with *them*?

It's this flawed narrative—widespread and profound in the many who live outside our Detroits, and invoked by those who do great damage from outside—that makes victims of so many Detroiters. What we as outsiders don't see is that we're victims too of the American Dream story we routinely tell ourselves. We have plenty of technical expertise, a lot of knowledge of systems, hoards of wealth, and, I think, a profound need for the gratification that comes from collective response tied to worthwhile purposes. Detroit, its many versions throughout the U.S., will require us to pay and pay and pay for our collective failure to respond.

Seed Thoughts

So what did I do on March 21, the first day of spring, in Minnesota's deep south, Winona? I planted a few tomato seeds directly into the dirt in my back yard. These were special tomato seeds, imported from Sicily. I probably did this because I can't rid myself of my Faustian urge to control nature's destiny. Natural curiosity lurks at the core of that devilish urge. I've always been dumbstruck by the sheer power of seeds—how, for example, an acorn can, in quiet good time, blossom into a giant oak. There lurks in me a certain jealousy of acorn power, and I resent acorns for keeping their secrets from me. My Arizona trip triggered in me an ancient form of curiosity that appears to lack respect in high-tech times: I want to know what a tomato seed from Sicily *knows*.

I figure it's a basic survival issue linked to tomato love.

Let me explain about the Arizona trip. It was inspired by two curiosities. One was to see the Grand Canyon before mining interests drill their holes in it. The other was to meet kinfolk I've never seen—notably descendents of a popular and well-known artist, a cousin named Ettore ("Ted") DeGrazia, who passed away in Tucson more than 30 years ago.

With my wife and two of my children, I left for Arizona on March 9. At noon, the temperature in the Minneapolis airport was 68 degrees (above). When we arrived in Phoenix a few hours later the temperature was about the same. Things seemed odd, but not upside-down.

The Grand Canyon struck me as spectacularly upside-down. The Canyon is a vast, long, and very deep fissure in the earth's crust that seems to peak way down deep where the Colorado River purls its way like a hairline crack around staggered rock formations. To stare into the Grand Canyon's depths is not unlike gazing upward at a purple and many-colored mountain majesty. In places it seems like an inverted pyramid, its steep cliffs rising like mountainsides as they descend into the gully below. To visit the Grand Canyon, a space filled with nothing but air and a solitary bird here and there, is to experience a wonderful Rocky Mountain vacation, of sorts.

The trip to Tucson was also wonderful. My blood-kin relatives, all strangers, were open-hearted, welcoming, generous, and obviously very intelligent and talented. Cousin Domingo, in particular, displayed his genius on a Spanish guitar while my budding musician son Dante took mental notes of what Domingo had to say about becoming a professional. The blood of strangers warmed into kinship bonds when the music made us want to dance. All strangers are also blood relatives so I suddenly was curious about another thing: Since it's easy to argue with but hard to wage war against blood relatives, can good music stimulate human genes to develop a resistance to violence and war? Would there be university funds for a research project on this topic? What do human genes know about music that might be useful to politicians and Pentagon analysts? Would waves of musicians be more successful and cost-effective than drones?

In my mind these questions are akin to my curiosity about what my Sicilian tomato seeds need to know in order to thrive. How smart are they? In a lot of ways they're smarter and more powerful than I am. I can't grow a tomato out of myself. I wouldn't know how to begin doing anything as profound, useful and tasteful as that. So much comes from such a dot-like thing. I stuck one of the seeds on a finger and tried to figure it out, but frankly, it was a rather homely sight, its coat dry and drab as an old man's skin. But in it, somehow, there was something resembling a tiny brain that magically would know what to do when the time and place were ripe. Some earthlings have always respected seed power. If one of those immigrant Sicilian stone masons who helped build New York's skyscrapers could plant a pebble that was also a seed, he'd probably get arrested for tapping into the city's water supply to grow an Empire State Building from it. If he's like me, he'd want to sprout Empire State Buildings on every vacant lot.

The Arizona desert was once a spacious expanse teeming with cacti and myriad plants and animals brilliant enough to make good homes for themselves on arid turf and in temperatures reaching 120 degrees (above). But huge tracks of that desert are beginning to look like vast parking lots. The cities of Phoenix and Tucson, which from the air look like square mile maps laid on desert dirt, also had small origins. In 1900 Tucson had 7,531 and Phoenix 5,544 residents; by the year 2000 Tucson had 486,699 and metropolitan Phoenix had swelled to 3,251,876; in 2011 Tucson had expanded to 520,116 and greater Phoenix to 4,192,887 residents. For centuries, Arizona had a wide variety and vast number of rattlesnakes. The variety allegedly remains, but in Tucson and Phoenix, they've gone into hiding now, either on strike or plotting their next moves. Heaven only knows what they know, or what's running through their minds when they hear the pickups tearing past. But one thing seems sure: They seem to have inhuman staying power.

My travels to the cities of Phoenix and Tucson also have triggered my curiosity about what water knows. I know my Sicilian tomato seeds know they need water to make tomatoes. For me. But does water know enough to flow where people live? Does it know how to make enough of itself to fill the toilet bowls and swimming pools of Phoenix and Tucson? Is water a wild-west free enterprise system that will do just fine without being regulated? Or can water be exploited and abused by outlaws? Does water know how to unpoison itself? Can water die?

My return to Minnesota, with its jet-lag confusion about what time of day it is, was compounded by uncertainty about what month I was living in. The seasons seemed turned around. It seemed unnatural to return to 75-degree warmth after spending a week in 75-degree Arizona heat. It was more odd to learn that just two days after returning to our Winona home major highways in Arizona were closed because a blizzard there had the right of way. North and south no longer seemed righted. A three-hour flight isn't supposed to cause extended jet-lag feelings that make everything seem vaguely upside-down, inside-out, and turned around. Was it still March? Buds were unfurling into blossoms on the pear, cherry, and apricot trees in my yard, and I shuddered at the prospect of unburying my fig tree a month and a half before May Day. What was my fig tree thinking way down deep? Robert Frost's worried line about frost keeps haunting me:

"There are roughly zones whose laws must be obeyed."

These thoughts trouble me when I visit the back yard dirt where I planted my tomato seeds. They haven't shown me anything yet, not one hint of green, and I wish they'd hurry up. I want those Sicilian seeds to have American Dreams—Faustian ambitions that make them proud and smart and big enough to supply me with Empire State Building explosions of tomatoes that could fill the Grand Canyon to the rim.

Is an April blizzard coming our mutual way, perhaps in mid-July? I like to think the little seeds know all about that too, and are smart enough to lie low.

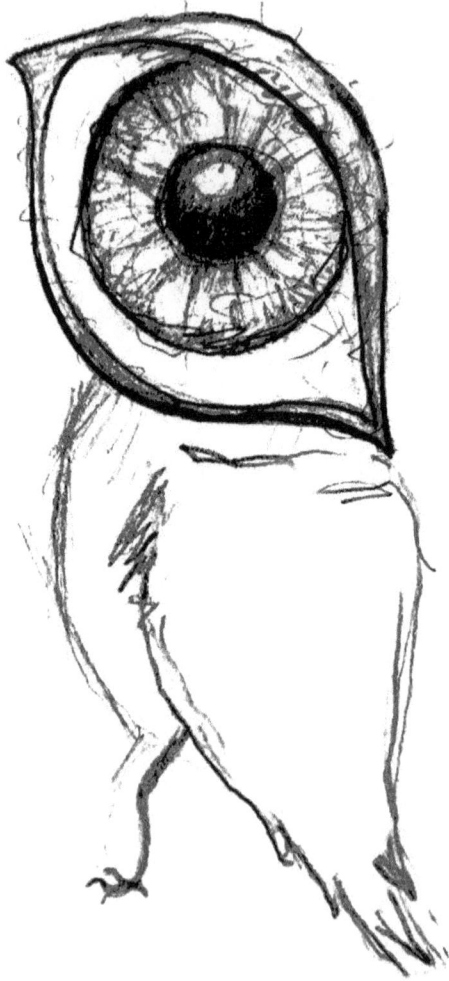

Endnote: Global Dreams

In his opinionated, terse, and well researched book
Sapiens: A Brief History of Humankind, Yuval Noah Harari
reminds us that "we are embarrassingly similar to
chimpanzees." But we begin to part company with our
early ancestors, he says, when we organize ourselves into
groups larger than 150, the maximal survival number for
humanoids operating freely in natural settings. When we
organize ourselves into villages, towns, cities, schools,
political parties, trade unions, nations, religions and
empires we need "glue" to hold us together. This glue is
secreted by the mind: It is made up of our imaginings, and
takes the form of myths we invent in order to confront the
threats inherent in nature. Unifying myths are necessary to
the proper functioning and survival of groups.

These unifying myths often are scripted by priestly
classes into sacred scriptures, into decrees monarchs
proclaim, and into constitutions and laws conceived by
founding fathers. They also lie hidden away in the truths
we take to be self-evident when we go to movies, churches,
or football games. Together our myths add up to define our
distinctive "culture."

"Globalization," the current unifying trend, is now
marrying into one lump many ethnic, national, and
religious groups that until recently had their own distinct
and unifying cultural myths. As diverse cultural myths
enter the global stew (spoken of as a "global village" by
some) they begin to dissolve, particularly under the
influence of firepower and global warming. A new global

myth capable of unifying the claims, aspirations, and dreams of groups losing their identities is perhaps in the making, but none seems visible as the global stew simmers and boils over here and there. Two options seem available: We can de-globalize—go back to the old myths and re-energize the sectarianism they represent, even as new science and technologies undermine their credibility. Going back puts old myths in conflict with each other as in the past, but also at odds with the global myth that may remain too inchoate to provide enough peace for the survival of the world.

The other option—also troubling—is to privatize. The poet William Blake argued for this option two hundred years ago: "I must create a system or be enslaved by another man's. I will not reason and compare: my business is to create."

Chimpanzees, the best of whom knew enough to avoid groups larger than 150, would nod and smile approval of this opportunity.

II.   True Stories

(from *The Oxymoronic Dictionary*)

Adjective with plural noun

1. Narrative entertainments on a joyride with imagined facts.
2. Tales told by tellers who never step twice into the same stream of consciousness.
3. In ancient and Biblical times hearsay recited for hundreds of years from memory, until written down by strangers who liked to go on joyrides with imagined facts.
4. Myths. In Greek *mythos* means "story." Myths were often about local heroes and their women troubles. When a myth's hero was said to win his battles against a monster or enemy—all of them terrible—his story became a true story. In that story she, the woman who troubled him, was usually the monster he had to slay.
5. History. Myths that never became her story.
6. Historical fictions, i.e. History.

Adjective: Fictional. Made up (never down). Make-believe. Fake. False.

Noun: Fiction. A fabrication. Fib. Lie.

Synonym: Yarns. Wayward threads hanging out, with their ends lost in the middle of a many-colored ball of strings attached to what might be important to think about.

Antonym: News story.

The Woman from Beijing

It probably doesn't matter that I've forgotten her name.
She was on loan from a university in Beijing, a soft-spoken
woman who had left a young child behind in order to take
learning wherever in the world it was going. She had
experiences unimaginable to me, had been victimized by
the Cultural Revolution, and had read widely and
thoughtfully. In her gaze I saw a hard but becalmed
stoicism that distanced her from sorrows, perhaps horrors,
that have to be abstracted in order to be endured. Her mind
turned smoothly and quietly, as if life had taught her that
holding back was both a useful tactic and way of keeping
in view the long view. She weighed words by the ounce.
She did not come off as brilliant. She glowed.

"Perhaps it is more important to forget," she said
quietly.

With the stroke of that simple sentence she brushed
over two hours' worth of my babblings about memory. The
importance of memory: How the Greeks had a goddess,
Mnemosyne, to honor memory, give it divine presence, and
how they assigned vital cultural functions to Mnemosyne's
nine daughters in the hope that these daughters' pregnant
powers would speak for important types of culture—
poetry (epic, hymnal, lyrical), history, music, dance, drama
(tragedy and comedy), astronomy—nurture them and
thereby make culture thrive and endure.

It is the quality of our memory, I recall myself saying in
preparation for a discussion of Elie Wiesel's *Night*, that
matters most. I'm aware of some of memory's thorns: The

tricks it plays on me, the way it reinvents itself, conflates fantasy and fact, is sensitive to pleasure and pain. I also take seriously collective consciousness: How nations recall, invent, mythologize, and institutionalize their histories, and how the construction of collectively shared narratives may affect the rise and fall of empires. I bore people complaining about general American indifference, even hostility, to history, to the stereotypical ways it is conceived as a series of conflicts defined by the dates of wars and names of generals. The quality of historical memory, I like to think, might be best served not by recall of actual events but by studying a culture's major and representative works of art.

Wiesel's *Night*, which depicts a Jewish boy's experiences as Nazis herd their victims to concentration camps, has gained stature as one such literary work. Secretly I've had misgivings about Wiesel's *Night*. While this powerful book provides a vivid account of an individual's harrowing experiences, it does little to provide an understanding of the complex causes, or *systems*, that made Nazi power and cruelty possible. While eliciting a wholesale emotional reaction against Nazi evil, it does not guide the understanding to an effective targeting of that evil, faces of which perhaps lurk in ourselves. In *Night* the Nazi world's evil is real if not well understood; the non-Nazi world includes the rest of us, presumably good. As such Wiesel's little book strikes a generic chord as melodrama rather than tragedy. The Greeks had no goddess celebrating melodrama.

"Why," asked the woman from Beijing, "should we read this book? Perhaps it is more important to forget."

Banishing books is unthinkable, but her simple comment suddenly made the thought of banishing thoughts thinkable. Why canonize, memorialize, Wiesel's book? She was too gracious to explain, confident that the silence that followed her question—like those Chinese paintings in which empty space seems the main subject—was large enough to contain unspoken answers to the objections certain to be voiced. Wiesel's book has brought the Holocaust to the attention of millions of readers, many of them young. But why remember the Holocaust? Maybe it is more important to forget.

I wondered if her view was both narrow and long. She had seen much—the busloads of families shipped off to re-education camps and collective farms. And she had read much—no doubt about the Long March and its pleasantries. And she came from a nation of 1.4 billion souls. Six million maybe seemed small in her view, both World Wars sideshows on a greater Asian screen. Was she saying that in the West we are self-absorbed? Should we pay more attention to her history and its enormities?

Eventually the obvious occurred to me: We are by nature calibrated toward forgetfulness, perhaps for survival purposes. As we age we forget where we put the keys, the eyeglasses, the book that was just in our lap, and if we live long enough we (most, not all) little by little seem to lose our minds, rather completely. If the opportunities for self-disgust also increase as we age—via the aches and pains, foul odors, incapacity, incontinence, etc.—memory loss may be nature's way of encouraging us to make a separate peace with death, one that makes it easier to leave our lives behind.

It's a dark view, perhaps realistic.

So how can we speak to the quality of memory? We know that even when we're old memory still serves us in pleasurably important ways. Nostalgic moments "relived," for example, bring an aching pleasure of sorts that evokes the sweet sorrow of loss. And we all recall the same old re-runs over and over again—those defining (call them seminal) moments: The home run we hit in the bottom of the ninth, or the pop-up we dropped, or our wedding night, or that time we told the boss where to go. These select moments are re-run more frequently as we age, digging calcifying grooves into our minds deeper than the furrows on our brows. They are one way we underline the episodes vital to the story of our lives we script in our minds. Yes, the past as memorized is mainly where we live, certainly at the end of our lives and also maybe starting on day one.

But where does this leave Wiesel's *Night*? Is it just another book to forget—indeed is it important to forget this book and the experiences it reflects?

I've been trying to fill in some of the blanks the woman from Beijing left in her silences. She did offer a frame. "In China," she said, "we have to forget. It is the only way we can continue to live." She knew aspects of her own history well, and would never be able to forget the painful episodes she had personally experienced. She had terrible ghosts haunting her, and she was conscious of her ghosts. So what she meant by "we have to forget" is not that we can or will forget—or that we ever will be able to forgive—but that we must move on, as if. She did not deny the existence of her ghosts, but found no use in passing her memories of suffering on to others moving on with their lives.

What ghosts of memory then should be heard? It's obvious that memory is selective. The millions of lives lost in World War I, in the USSR during World War II, and in various African nations do not equally have front and center seats in the theatre of the mind. And memory of what happened is always incomplete, sketchy at best and therefore a caricature, so why we remember is central to memory's usefulness. Do we read Wiesel's *Night* in order to remember the Holocaust and thereby justify a current politics? There is a moral dimension to memory. Reading *Night* to justify a current politics may be morally defensible if the current politics is morally defensible.

The jury is hung-up on that issue.

In such cases it is useful to pay attention to how memory is scripted. Do we become inclined to mis-remember our histories, public and private, when we script them as hero-tales rather than as dramas of the absurd, as melodramas rather than as tragedies? If hero-tales give us winners and losers, dramas of the absurd level the entire field of players and require a radical re-evaluation of where we fit on the stage. If in melodrama Good and Evil are morally unambiguous and justice is achieved via vengeance performed by heroic figures, it becomes easy to find someone to blame in black and white terms. Not so in tragedy. In tragedy a suffering hero is absurdly scapegoated, made to carry the weight of a historical burden many had a hand in shaping. We read tragedy to remember how we attach blame, misinterpret responsibility, and seek misplaced revenges. Tragedy gives us the scapegoat victims our bloodlust requires, then lets us move on beyond revenge by showing us that we resemble, at least dimly, those who brought the evils on. Such a view requires us to look at ourselves as if through a glass darkly, and to begin the healing at home.

The eyes behind that dark glass, the sense of tragedy inside a concentrated gaze, is what I remember best about the woman from Beijing.

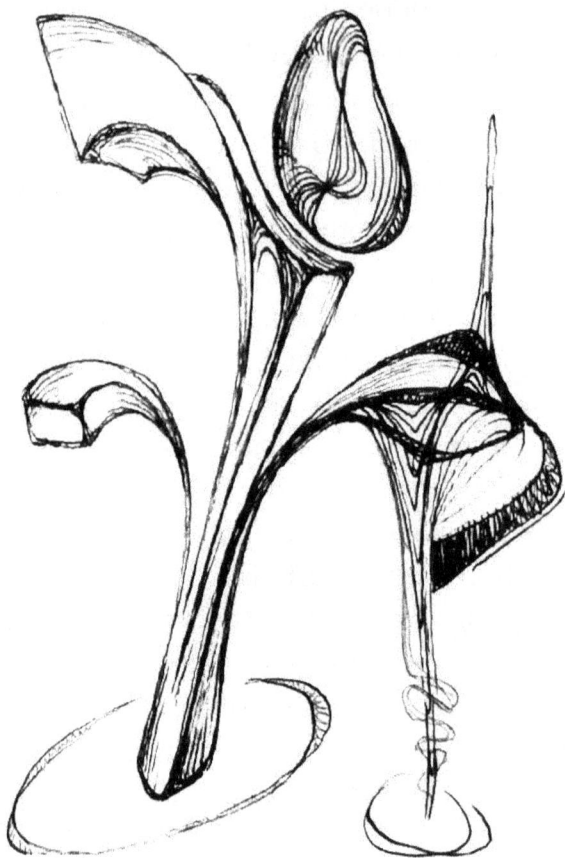

Eye Shadow

Whenever the Minnesota Twins play the Detroit Tigers I zip my lips. Detroit isn't really my home town. I was born in Dearborn just a few blocks from the limits of Detroit, but the boy in me still quivers when I see that gothic "D" on a white Tiger uniform. The quiver is for a Detroit I remember as a kid—the downtown skyscrapers, Belle Isle, the spacious parks, the Woodward and Michigan Avenue shops. When I visit Detroit now I imagine many of its desolate neighborhoods to be more devastated than war-torn Baghdad and maybe more dangerous. Detroit is a tragically dysfunctional city that does not inspire confidence in the American way of life.

Dearborn, the large suburban city that now makes a stranger of me, is someplace else. I find it hard to believe that Detroit's old elegance will be restored, but my recent trip to Dearborn suggested there might be an effective non-violent way of turning the other cheek to Islamic radicals.

By accident of birth, the few blocks that kept me on the Dearborn side of the Dearborn-Detroit divide, I escaped the decline and fall of Detroit. That divide was grounded on separatist beliefs that built invisible walls. "Help Keep Dearborn Clean" was the slogan I learned by heart as a kid. "Clean" was silently pronounced "White." Dearborn was kept "clean" by unwritten codes strictly enforced by goons who wore ties and rolled up the sleeves of their white shirts when they went to work to confront and intimidate anyone suspected of violating their segregationist codes. Real estate agents and city building inspectors ranked high in this army of goons. Of the tens of thousands of auto workers who routinely took buses from their homes in Detroit to work in Henry Ford's sprawling Rouge Plant in Dearborn, 80% were African-Americans. Not one black auto worker lived inside Dearborn's invisible walls. The goons made sure of that.

Nor did any Jews live in Dearborn.

While legendary Dearborn mayor Orville Hubbard kept Dearborn "clean" for decades, Henry Ford kept out the Jews. Ford's antagonism to Jews pre-dated World War I, when he concluded they were not good for business. He mounted a visible campaign that lasted into the World War II years, with allegations of his cozy relations with Hitler often surfacing. Ford's local solution to the "Jewish problem" was to encourage the development of an Arab-American enclave in Dearborn's Salina district near the Ford Rouge factory. Arab-Americans settled in the Salina neighborhood, worked in the Ford Rouge, and began to prosper and expand beyond Salina. Dearborn now has the nation's highest concentration of Arab-Americans. In my day Salina Junior High was one of four junior high schools that fed into my old high school, Fordson. Today the student body of Fordson High is more than 90% Arab-American. If the smokestacks of the huge Rouge factory now look sullen and defunct as they loom over the east side of Dearborn, many Dearborn streets are alive with small markets, restaurants, and shops owned by Arab-Americans.

Meanwhile, just a few blocks away on the other side of invisible walls, Detroit continues to decline. The billions we've spent in Baghdad and Kabul have not trickled down inside those walls.

I return now and then to visit family, aware not only of the long-term and ongoing conflicts between blacks and whites but of the anti-Arab suspicions and fears exacerbated by the so-called war on terror associated mainly with Muslims in the Middle East. When I drive past Fordson High what troubles me are the schoolgirls wearing headscarves and, in a few cases, face veils, symbols in my mind of a vast divide between secular modernists and Muslim immigrants. Anti-Muslim feelings, periodically enflamed by a faraway terrorist act, run high in places where Muslims have not been visibly assimilated. Europe also knows the issue well. As people of European stock see their populations level off or actually decline, they see swelling numbers of Muslims in their midst. Most visible are Muslim women and girls distinguishable by the traditional garb that clearly is intended to keep them covered and backgrounded, if not invisible, to many who turn to stare at them on sidewalks and streets. Keeping them inferior also comes to mind. Traditional Muslim garb casts a shadow over the more fashionable and revealing styles conspicuously advertised and now standard to the Westernized eye. How can conservative Muslim attitudes toward women co-exist with the open if conflicted sexual attitudes of modernists? Traditionalist and modernist views of women collide. The gap between the two ways of life seem so deep and wide that we're reminded of the epigraph to E.M. Forster's timeless novel *Passage to India*: "Only connect." So does the pessimism of the novel's final page come to mind, where the best intentions of the novel's main characters have gone so awry that they leave West and East five hundred years apart.

It's easy to be pessimistic about Detroit. The solution there would require the equivalent of a new urban

Marshall Plan, one that addresses neighborhoods one by one while putting in place the systems needed to turn around individual lives. Such a plan is conceivable and would work, but what's lacking is political will to put it in motion. The "war on terror" not only distracts us from such a plan but is ongoing, exhausting, and virtual, having no clear boundary lines. In that war the walls are also mainly invisible, if semi-permeable. To win is to make small but steady inroads into hearts and minds.

Dearborn, with its majority of Arab-Americans, seems like a good place to start. My Italian-American relatives still living there are decent hard-working people who have endured their share of the troubles most immigrants face for a generation or two, at least. But it didn't take long for me to understand that many of these good folk harbor a resentment of the Muslim "takeover" of their neighborhoods and schools. Did I know that a few years ago a Muslim father shot his Fordson High daughter because she, without asking for her father's consent, was dating a boy? My relatives ask, How can we live with people like that? And now they, these Muslim outsiders, own more and more of the local businesses, so in a few years we'll be nobodies again. All women will have to wear headscarves and veils if we let them have their way.

My standard response is to heap praise on good old American separation of church and state, and thank God we don't have prayer in the schools, laws against it some of my bitter Christian relatives would like to see reversed. "Can you imagine how fast test scores would drop," I said, "if students were bowing toward Mecca five times a day."

I persuaded my sister to accept the obvious: The Arabic-American restaurants in her neighborhood are fabulous. Could I treat her to dinner in one of my favorites?

The offer was almost as hard for her to accept as it was to reject. She loves to eat, but she shops in Italian markets, not Arab ones. What's wrong with Italian restaurants? she asks. But I knew of one Arabic restaurant, just a few blocks away, she would not be able to resist. I reminded her of the fragrances she knew well—cinnamon, cumin, cloves. Food. Fresh food in dishes well prepared. And beautifully served.

The profound desire for good food—it got to her as true love got to her when she was a teenage girl. The allure of it, the attraction she had to work at so hard to suppress.

If we—Italians and Arabs and fascists and communists and blacks and whites and pinks—could routinely feast together on the very best dishes of beautiful food, some good peace might come of it.

I saw the young woman right after my sister and I entered the Arabic-American restaurant. She was about eighteen, dark-skinned and slender, one of *them*, with all but a few strands of her black hair hidden from view. Her head scarf, tightly wrapped, draped down over her blouse, framing her face in an oval that sharpened the fine features of her face and the depth of her eyes. And there, on her eyelids, I saw the hint that inspired my hope that terrorist wars, like old warriors, someday might just fade away.

Eye shadow.

A thin layer carefully applied, as if to obscure against the darkness of her skin the thoughts behind her lovely dark eyes: Eye shadow at once veil and mask, behind which a young woman lurks with intent to defy conservative Islamic patriarchs.

Her father stood to one side of her, staring at me with an expression that warned me to keep my eyes off her, as if they were hands. He is not pleased with me, or with her.

59

I keep my eyes to myself, though I'm certain her father suspects she has eyes for someone else, a boyfriend, or a young man she is yet to meet, the lover in her mind. Her eye shadow advertises her desire to be seen.

Where is the hope for an end to terrorist wars in the two smears that adorn her eyes? Hope shows its perverse ways in her angry father's face. Her eye shadow is her mark of defiance of her father's ways, his need to control her destiny. He is losing her; he can't prevent her from painting her face. The headscarf will have to do, and she is willing enough to hide her lovely hair in it, perhaps for now or for a much longer time. Father and daughter walk an unsteady Islamic line on American streets where women enjoy walking alone in open view. The father loathes the ideas these bold American women represent, but he can't keep himself from now and then secreting a glance toward them. He could love what he hates.

This drama repeats itself daily worldwide.

Because his daughter, like all daughters, is ready to love. Love is natural food for her young soul. If her headscarf honors her origins and signals her willingness to respect her traditions and family, the eye shadow advertises her attraction to *the other*, even, perhaps someday, a Christian boy. Her eye shadow reveals that she has the courage to negotiate her way into the modernist world while requiring that world to honor the modesty of her traditional ways. She is an ordinary Muslim adjusting to a modernist world.

But much of modernist culture seems vulgar, greedy and violent to her. Its Methodist Sunday School picnics and genuine pieties and charities do not appear on the reality shows or movie screens. The young Muslim woman sees garish American decadence as she looks for the right person to love. She is modest, decent, perhaps confused. She will have to negotiate her way through two worlds seriously at odds with each other, find a middle way that will allow her love to thrive and endure. She will have to find good reason to become the moderate Arab-American-Muslim she prefers to be. This means that one day, perhaps, the headscarf will go and she will let down her beautiful black hair for the world to see.

Her father will not want to let go of her. Like fathers everywhere he resists losing control of her, and no boy not of his choosing will be worthy of her. Father and daughter will rage against each other, perhaps not quietly. Her eye shadow is an act of rebellion against him. When she is sixteen he will make her wash it off, but she will put it on at night when he's asleep and look at her face in the mirror. When she is nineteen she will say no to him again, and he again will rage against her. Her little sister shrinks from their war, but she's on her big sister's side. The father will lose.

The worry is what she will have to gain. A lover, perhaps a decent Arab-American-Muslim youth. But what will American decadence make of them, or make them do when they have their own teenage girls? Will American culture have anything better than its reality shows, Hollywood movies, video games, greedy capitalism, and vulgar ads targeted at girls nurtured on modesty and decency? Will it be time for headscarves and veils again?

The Arabic restaurant was no McDonald's or Burger King. The dishes were beautiful and fragrant with nameless spices from the East. The eye-shadowed girl did not know I existed, but I watched her eyes dart around the room as she and her father got up to leave. I felt sorry for him, for the battle he would lose while letting go of her, and I wondered how he would negotiate his way past big differences. I regretted not being able to talk to him, explain to him that I thought of Dearborn as my home town and once felt an ownership of the place. And that I had to give up my old sense of ownership, because now it is more his than mine. Over good food we easily could have agreed to be agreeable.

Where are the voices of the moderates, those able and willing to balance conflicting claims? Are they lost in the vengeful prayers of Muslim radicals, in the noise of American vulgarities, and in the purring pieties of self-righteous crusaders? In good time maybe all three types will simply ignore the eye-shadowed girl when she leaves her father's house. Maybe she'll seem enough like them that they'll just let her be.

When I leave a Detroit perhaps more hopeless and off the radar than Baghdad or Kabul, I will take her eye-shadowed hope with me to my Minnesota home.

Two footnotes:

In the summer of 2010, the year after my visit to Dearborn, the French assembly voted 490-0 to ban the face veil in public places.

Rima Fakir, of Dearborn, Michigan, was selected as Miss USA for the year 2010. She's Arab-American-Muslim.

How I Became a Real Man

I suppose most boys have to overcome something terrifying in order to have the conversion experience that makes real men of them. Though Achilles dressed up as a girl and Odysseus pretended to be blind in an effort to stay out of the Trojan war, both these classic draft dodgers became feckless killers on their way to achieving hero status. If medieval knights have to slay dragons to qualify for saving damsels in distress, and if young soldiers everywhere have to persuade their legs it's wrong to run away from bullets flying their way, even Hemingway's anti-heroes have to confront the terrifying bulls horning in on their minds. After years of meditating on how swiftly my maturity makes me shrink from most forms of heroism, I too recently passed a major manhood test. I drove a car in Naples, Italy, and survived to tell the tale.

Imagine a different kind of basketball game in a local gym. There's one smallish court, and three hundred bodies crowd in to play, most of them testosterone-engorged males. Everyone brings a ball. There are ten backboards and hoops—call them goals, or maybe home, where mamas are waiting to serve boys very large dishes of pasta after having done the boys' laundry and made their beds. Every score inspires a salivation response; make one and you want more. Naturally everyone wants to score first and move on to another score. No one sounds a horn or buzzer for the game to begin—or end. There are no lines or lanes and nothing is out of bounds. There are no rules, no timekeeper, no scorekeeper, and no referees, and everyone is calling fouls on everyone else—and you have a picture of a normal traffic day in Naples, Italy.

I had seen Naples a few times before, but always from the safe distance of a train going to and from a quiet village in the deep south where, just after the invention of cars, my parents were born. That small village, San Pietro, has one main street called the Via del Popolo (the Way of the People), with a couple arteries branching off from it. A grandmother or grandfather is normally seen taking a stroll along the Via del Popolo, and now and then an auto twists and turns its way past them toward the road leading down to the Mediterranean. From a train window Naples seems like a bigger version of this village on a mountainside— static, charming, tanned by a romantic sun.

But to venture into Naples takes manly resolve. I had just read a disturbing book about the Camorra, the city's Mafia, that inspired me to shy away from the place. My memories of the mean streets of Detroit had something to do with that. But my adventurous daughter Emily had set the agenda: We were to dine at the historic pizzeria made famous in the movie *Eat, Pray, Love*, then continue our journey on the Autostrada to a village in the south. When she handed me the keys to a slick BMW rental car I decided to gird my loins for the great trial ahead. The years have been drying out my bones, but with manly resolve I decided I was crustier because of it. If all those pint-sized Italian boys could drive in Naples and survive, why couldn't I? Besides, it wasn't death I had to fear most. With traffic going almost nowhere one small leap at a time, I might be maimed but not murdered by another car. My secret challenge was to return the slick BMW without a nick on it.

I entered traffic in Naples without really knowing where my daughter's pizza joint was, and I hadn't driven a stick-shift car in over thirty years. Feet suddenly had to remember what my mind had left behind. The only thing I knew well about Italians is what I said to my wife years earlier about my mother. "She says ten things, but she only means one and a half of the ten things she says. She's Italian. You have to figure out the one and a half things she really means, so subtract everything said by eight and a half before you take offense." Italians, in short, incline toward overstatement. Ask an Italian how many times he makes love in one week, then subtract the answer by eight and a half. Ask a lecherous Englishman the same question and he'll say, "Yes, I play a little tennis now and then."

It's understandable that the English have a hard time driving on the wrong side of their streets in Italy, and one also must pity them for their confusion on discovering that in Naples there is no wrong side of the street. There are only very small opportunities, some merely crevices, instantly filled by a fender, bumper, or grille, with riders on scooters and motorbikes deftly maneuvering their way into leftover square inches. Car horns scream at each other, but their noise falls on deaf ears more than eight and a half times per honk. In a city where no birds sing many birds are flipped in a hand-language for which no dictionary exists. Add to this *panicata* (a useful southern word, not found in any Italian dictionary, that—clearly, in dialect—means "panic" and "mess" and is most often applied to ill-prepared food) crowds of pedestrians playing chicken with the metallic mouths threatening them if they make a wrong move, and throw in too the arrogance of those on sidewalks who refuse to make way for cars that hop the curbs to gun them down—and you get a picture of a normal traffic scene in Naples.

I only saw one police officer in the whole *panicata*, and he seemed to be in a deep meditative trance as he gazed toward the sea.

One has to admire the skill and athleticism of these drivers, their ability to secrete themselves into the small spaces getting them ahead. Though most of them would be jailed for driving that way in American streets, car owners in Naples have created a standard of behavior gaining currency in many parts of the world. Some would call the process anarchy, but I think of it as individualistic entrepreneurship on wheels, a free enterprise system minus eight and a half parts of system. In Naples driving is both taxing and deregulated. The old charm and elegance is still visible on the city's monuments and avenues. The streets are teeming with people, businesses, and peddlers hawking mostly illegal merchandise. Also in clear view are heaps of trash, the outward and visible sign of the deep corruption driving the city's economy. The Camorra, the Mafia clans of the Naples region, have capitalized on the national government's failure (and perhaps cooperation) to govern and regulate. Naples, an Italian city, is also a de facto Camorra fiefdom run by brutal and wily businessmen (and now women too), bosses who have infiltrated the port, manufacturing facilities, and distribution outlets for a wide range of enterprises. Waste management is just one of them.

It's an old trick really, the use of garbage to extort cooperation from individuals who don't want to play ball with gangsters. In my home town, Dearborn, Michigan, the mayor who ruled there for forty years, Orville Hubbard, used garbage as a way to enforce his racism. Those who were suspected of renting or trying to sell a house to blacks would suddenly find their garbage piling up, and then the city inspector would show up to discover several expensive code violations. In Naples non-cooperation with the Camorra leads to trash being heaped on the uncooperative, much of it brutally toxic.

Italy and its enchanting monuments are ancient, but Italy as an experiment in self-government is young. Only by 1861 did Italy's national heroes Garibaldi and Cavour manage to make a "nation" called "Italy" from the diverse regions, ways of life and dialects that are to be found on the length of the long peninsular boot. Profound differences still exist, and the people of Naples, those who drive their cars recklessly and those who drive significant parts of its illegal economy, seem to have chosen—and are stuck with– –disorder reeling out of control of anyone except the criminal class. The chaotic incivility of traffic in Naples is a disturbing sign of the times, especially as the planet's bulging population is streaming into urban sprawls.

Dysfunction and eventual collapse are becoming the general rule as millions of vehicles fuel the economies of urban growth, often in cities ill-designed for traffic flow and lorded over by entrepreneurs, criminal or not, eager to deregulate in order to liberate their greed. Will street crime and criminal syndicates become the norm when the state, and the common wealth it is supposed to represent and regulate, surrenders its responsibility to govern the few who make *laissez-faire* a religious right? My manhood survived not only Naples traffic but a wild 130 kilometers per hour road race over the Autostrada on our return joyride to Rome. On the Autostrada those caught in congested city traffic break free, as if to make up for lost time in vehicles that seem to be saying, "Nothing can stop me now. I can fly!"

One couple no longer on their motorcycle, whose bodies I glimpsed in the glare of flashing lights, came crashing down, perhaps because the young cyclists, feeling the rush that comes with breaking free of congestion unworthy of their machines, slightly miscalculated the skill that had worked so well for them in log-jammed city traffic. The tangled mass of metal that once was their vehicle looked like a newfangled piece of postmodern art. And as the streams of traffic passing the wreck slowed, I felt as if I were part of a funeral procession paying its last respects to the two bodies laid out on the concrete, victims that seemed like human sacrifices to some alien faceless gods.

Some Italians still credit the fascist Mussolini for getting the trains to run on time. When out-of-control disorder is called freedom, and when criminal syndicates justify their business success as a function of free enterprise, I suspect we're not far from the collapse that will allow the next Mussolini to turn the national state into a criminal enterprise. When I was stuck in the middle of the Naples traffic jams I felt powerless to do anything but barge recklessly ahead with whatever clogged flow there was. If a dictator were busy taking my basic rights away I would not have the time, energy or parking space that would allow me to register a complaint.

It was comforting to return to North American soil, where the streets are rationally laid out in straight-line grids, where most drivers (even in New Jersey and Chicago) stay in their lanes and obey the traffic signs—here where traffic signs and some regulations are still in place, intended to make travel and business as usual safe, productive, legal, and possible. I find beauty in the vast empty spaces of the Great Plains and western states, all that lush emptiness I like to imagine as immune to the congestion creeping up on it from suburban sprawls.

But the "Wild West" that seems so important to our "American Dream" scares me too. Many of the frontier freedom fighters who oppose all government restraint and who say they oppose government *per se* also believe that if you outlaw guns only outlaws will have guns. The Western-hero type, made popular in so many films, takes the initiative to take the law into his own hands. He usually has a six-shooter in each of them. His city-slicker counterpart comes in two unsavory brands: Either as romantic urban gangster, or as "urban cowboy" who routinely deems himself above the law as he fights against lawbreakers. Both shoot their way into our living rooms after the troubling evening news. The behaviors of both are so common they seem socially acceptable as norms. Given the popularity of these types, and their presence as realities rather than as imaginary models, I'm not sure what fate would be worse for me, the streets of Naples or the sidewalks of Chicago's south side.

I stay clear of certain city streets and look forward to trips I can take without a car. Whenever there is one available I prefer taking trains, even though they're state subsidized. I'm glad to know somebody in the democratic government I still believe in is wise enough to see the efficiency and cost-effectiveness of trains over the long haul. I look forward to meeting strangers on trains and engaging in civil conversation with them. I'm amazed by the speeds trains are capable of achieving, and I'm consoled by the opportunity for leisure they provide. Like a worthwhile nation-state not engaged in corruption, graft, and crimes against humanity, the train seems like a good enough community free enterprise system.

My manhood? Now that I've achieved it by conquering the chaos of Naples traffic, I'm prepared to send my manhood back. I'm hoping I'll have no further use for it here.

Baronics

Imagine how surprised—and confused—I was to learn that I had extraordinary blood coursing through my body parts. From my father I learned that the original "DeGrazia" probably came from some backsliding nun who delivered (no doubt in swaddling clothes) the very first DeGrazia to the Mother Superior of some nunnery in the south of Italy. "Where did this infant come from?" asked the Mother Superior. "De Grazia," replied the pious-sinner nun. From the Grace of God. God only knows how everything comes from God.

Imagine how high-minded my feelings became when I later learned that my heart also might be pumping noble blood. To descend from an aristocratic line seems more classy than to be a mere child of God. If I were entitled to a noble title, what else would I be entitled to? The question is especially important in a political climate where some use the word "entitlement" as a cuss word.

Because I minored in French as an undergrad I knew that the prefix "de" introduces individuals to an aristocratic family name that confers special perks on it. As "DeGrazia" am I, therefore, a bastard child of God, or a noble man, or both? If the backsliding nun was no more than a low-down sinner and I'm just the offspring of her rather unoriginal sin, it would tarnish my claim to being God's gift to the world. But if I'm the scion of nobility then what does the world owe me?

The answer to that question became more complicated when news arrived that I was (indeed?) one more great-

great-great-great-etc. ordinary grandchild of a long established noble line. On receiving this news I started drinking imported beer. My first cousin Louis, a born genius, discovered through a grapevine that my grandfather's sister Maria had been banished from her village for giving non-virginal birth to a bastard son. In her exile she mothered into being a sizeable (and wonderful) alternative DeGrazia clan that kept her maiden name, DeGrazia. This exiled part of the generic DeGrazia clan did some genealogical research that fleshed out my father's legend about our family origins. From my newly discovered cousin Rick (in Toronto) I learned that, "We are in fact descended from the famous Baron DeGrazia family." The family palace, I'm told, still exists somewhere in Italy, with an engraved family emblem dating back to before 1600. Someday when my ship comes in, I tell myself, I'll go searching for the palace with my name on it.

Now that my nobility issues are well-enough resolved, I've turned to worrying about my Social Security. This is, I'm told, an "entitlement," as if I don't deserve it. If I'm supposed to feel good about my aristocratic "blood," I'm supposed to feel guilty as a thief for expecting a Social Security check every month. Some politicians are also suggesting that I'm like a common thief for taking Medicare payments. These, I'm told, are like "welfare" payments I don't deserve. They say, without using proper nouns, that it's their money I'm spending. So while genealogical research makes a child of God and nobleman of me, I'm a real bastard for believing I'm entitled to Social Security and Medicare.

Because I'm still entitled to my own opinions I began thinking about how people in the past went about the business of entitling themselves. Though the ancients had no noble titles such as "duke," "baron," or "earl," and only a few called themselves "kings," the heroes of Homer's Greece entitled themselves to honor, respect, gold, slaves, and the sexual services of women, men and boys. How did the heroes become heroes? Mainly by invading cities and villages where they killed rival heroes, old men and ugly boys who might grow up to be heroes like them. Not many classics professors call them mass murderers, even when mentioning that they routinely put whole populations to the sword to secure their hero-rights.

These heroes fathered many bastard children, with some of the descendents inheriting the bloodlust of their hero-fathers. Because these hero-fathers eventually got tired of doing the dirty work themselves, they devised ways to force peasants and village youths into armies that did it for them. They made names for themselves this way, and entitled themselves to the honor, respect, gold, slaves and the sexual services of women and handsome boys that came with the glorious victories of their armies. At the peaks of their ladders of success they built fortresses and palaces, hired high priests to explain their laws and divine mysteries, and passed their plunder, with interest, on to family members, all male, as if by blood transfusion. They also were fortunate to have Disney reinvent their history for us.

Was Baron DeGrazia a nobleman and a Robber Baron? If traces of his blood course through my body parts, what am I to do? Am I entitled to a portion of the Baron DeGrazia's lost treasure, or do I owe his victims a share of my Social Security and Medicare?

The morality of nobility is a tricky business.

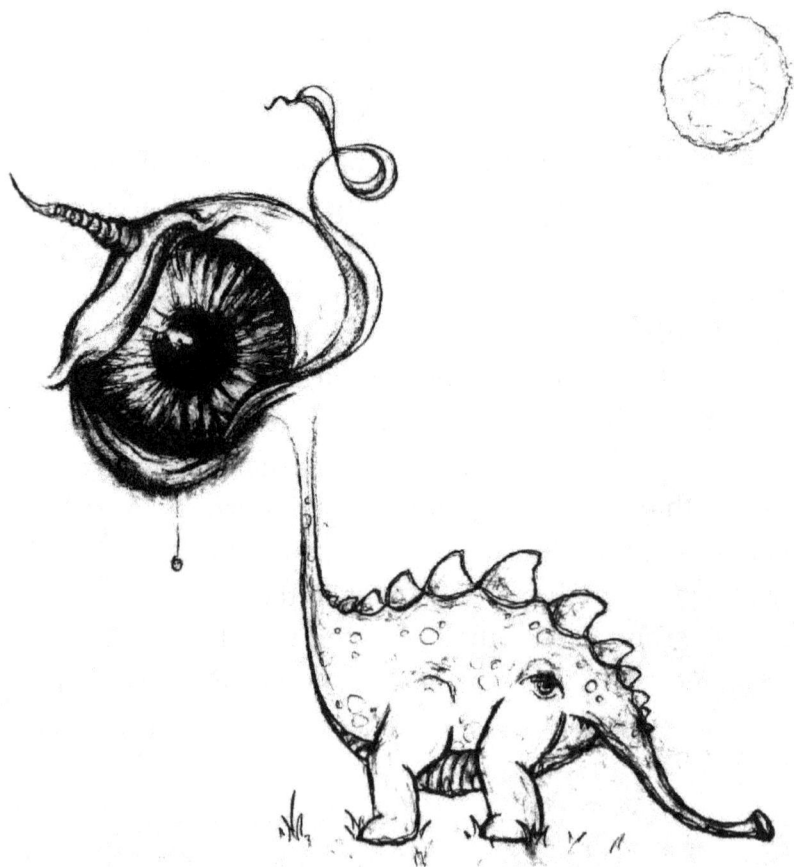

Story Junkie

Now and then I take my old copy of Charles Dickens'
David Copperfield off the shelf. All story junkies love its
opening line: "Whether I shall turn out to be the hero of my
own life, or whether that station will be held by anyone
else, these pages must show." I confess: Because I'm a story
junkie and because news stories are what we get as news,
I'm a news junkie too. If the Dickens opening line hooks me
every time, so does TV news: It tells me I need to figure out
my role in the story I'm telling myself about the stories
being told about what's happening in the world. While that
opening sentence from *David Copperfield* reminds me I have
to find a good story to live in before I slip away into one of
history's black holes, the TV news offers me a chance to
make a hero of myself.

During the hours I spend watching the TV news it's
easy for me to get nostalgic for the story O.J. Simpson had
us living in for over a year. His story had everything: Sex
and violence. It starred a handsome black NFL star and his
blonde beautiful wife in a bloody who-done-it murder
mystery plot that included a car chase, big name lawyers,
and a tense courtroom drama that went on day after day
until the breathtaking verdict came in that opened the door
to sequels yet to come. Nobody in real life Hollywood
could have fed me a better junk food story-line. I was
hooked. The nation was hooked, like a gaggle of big-eyed
fish.

The political stories coming out of the TV from now
until the next election day can't compete with the gripping

power and dazzle of the O.J. serial. But between now and election day TV politics will provide me with story lines I'll be weaving into some sort of tale. If the networks hooked me into a plot with a rising action featuring O.J. in an uphill race to outrun his murder rap, this season's 24-7 political episodes will be running everyone down to the climax on election day. I'm a sucker and I'm weak, like a few normal people I know: I take the hooks, if not all the lines, so I forget to think long and hard about whether I'm wasting precious time on bad stories, whether the hot-air spewed out by political talking heads poisons the TV air, or what will befall when the falling action brings on boredom too dull to interest me in big-time board meetings happening off-screen.

Political stories have to compete for my attention against formidable same-old action fixes—a burning hut or rocket fire in somebody's war, a riot in somebody's neighborhood, a flood, a storm or forest fire on somebody's turf, a juicy red murder in somebody's basement. As I swallow gobs of fast-food news I seldom feel a thing.

Fortunately I have a rapid-fire barrage of commercials to keep me from being sickened by fast-food thrills and chills. For every half-hour of TV news I'm also offered at least twelve minutes of TV ads, most of them devoted to pills certain to make the general public's arthritis and sexual impotence improve. The pricey pills, of course, have another use: They're good for paying the fees for making more TV ads designed to comfort us, while warning us about the side effects of the pricey pills—the rashes, headaches, blindness, diarrhea, heart attacks, nausea, lawsuits, and humiliations caused by four-hour-long erections that require medical but never psychiatric help. These side effects have their own side effect: When we get medical and psychiatric treatments our insurance rates go up. It's news to me that so many things can go wrong from taking a pill, and I'm so grateful for useful information I get from pill disclaimers that I think they should be subtracted from the twelve minutes of ads.

Since almost all news stories are downers and I can't always depend on pills to cheer me up, I can always find myself in the heart-warming human interest episode that comes at the very end of newscasts. In the heart warmer someone normal does a good deed, survives a terrible disease with dignity and grace, or saves a cat from certain death in a sewer. From now until election day the heart warmer will restore my faith in humanity and make me feel good again until the next station break occurs and political ads return to make the gravy trains work on time.

It's not hard keeping score of the news stories I love. My mother always used to tell me she didn't want to ask me twice to do this or that, so I know that hers is not the voice on the telephone that so far this month has called me twice to ask my opinion about this or that. Opinion polls are like scoreboards at sporting events. They not only tell us whether we're winning or losing the game, they tell us what's really happening on the field so we don't have to pay attention to the game. On a daily basis I have polls telling me what peoples' opinions are, mainly about questions I wouldn't bother to ask. At any moment I can learn from polls whether I'm a winner or loser, who to blame for everything going wrong, and whether I should change teams or find some other country to live in. Some seers swear that the poll numbers on graphs make for better viewing than the talkative pols, perhaps because polls have more character. It's also exciting to enter a news broadcast wondering whether the numbers, like Wall Street tics, are going up or down. The day is coming when pollsters in Las Vegas will track—with scientific accuracy plus or minus a point or two—the public mood swings that occur from the beginning to the end of each half-hour TV news programs we watch. I'm betting on it.

Campaign managers—whose coffers are a royal flush bloated with funds—are dedicated, with religious commitment, to those who have too much money to spend. They should get credit for providing us with political ads we pay for but don't buy. One problem with political ads is that we're never warned about the ad's dangerous side effects. Though the biology lessons we learned in high school should raise some red flags, I never see any warnings on even the most unreadable print on the TV monitor about one very troubling side effect: The unseemly consequences of incest. Those who run TV news are in love with political campaign managers, and their love affair is conducted behind closed doors in the wide open marketplace. Because election time is our nation's off-holiday shopping spree season, it's easy to turn a blind eye to the invisible ways politicians and newsmakers share the same beds, off and on, with a few nods and winks. Together they create the news, from an unholy union of fact, fancy, and flesh that spawns cacophonous bodies with talking heads.

Because talk about incest is taboo, a code of honor must be upheld: The incestuous partners are held to a vow of silence, especially when the very noisiest ads disturb the peace. When they make enough noise they then move over into the eighteen-minute slot: They become the news. If on occasion it is acceptable to air complaints about the media being too liberal or conservative, it is impolite for the media to inform us that politicians often say things that are absurd and false. Best to be polite when journalist-politician bedfellows need each other so deeply and therefore need to honor and obey each other.

Where does the bulk of the money come from to make TV political ads, and where does it go? Most of it comes from millionaires and billionaires with a few million to dispose of as chump change to enhance their private purposes. And a healthy part of it comes from sponsors who sell us pain and impotence cures with their disclaimers about life-threatening side effects. A lot of other ads come from oil and coal companies that want to lubricate our downer trends by solving our energy problems without mentioning any side effects at all.

What is obvious is that long political seasons—no matter how ugly or negative—are good for the economy of those who can afford to play the game. Though political coffers are overflowing with enough money to start new businesses in thousands of hurting communities, we keep depending on polls and the pols to know who to blame for failing to satisfy our desires and needs. Those in the business of news will have something to brag about to their bosses as they rake the ad money in. We can't blame them for doing their jobs so well. We know that political TV works because we know that negative ads, in particular, work. Polls tell us that negative ads do a lot to shape the opinions people express in the voting booths. Because the TV industry depends on popularity ratings to pad its bottom line, it has little incentive to hire staff qualified to fact-check the ads or debunk them entirely. Those in the news business work hard, and effectively, to sell more ad time, a lot harder than those of us who spend time hooked on their story-lines.

I'm a story junkie because I take my David Copperfield seriously: I love a good story line that will make a hero of me while giving me a place in society that validates what's humane, fair, reasonable and responsible. But in my election season story, the one I enter when I turn on the TV, I wait for the fool in me to make a hero of me. That hero will do nothing politically useful with all the time he wasted watching the talking-head cheaters smile at him on TV, the way O.J. did when most of us were pretty sure he got away with murder, with that smile on his face.

Why Humpty Dumpty Fell

Did he fall by accident, or was he pushed? Did he opt to end his life or did he leap for life? Were hidden hands behind his fall, or did he let himself go over some terrible edge? Perhaps he was a Lost Boy who sensed that something was going terribly wrong, and who suddenly resorted to the ultimate avoidance response.

The nursery rhyme plot-line of Humpty Dumpty's story is American enough by now. So his true story has national implications.

Jerome Bruner, renowned psychologist noted for his "outside-in" approach to human development, would take Humpty's story seriously. Bruner focuses on "the kind of world needed to make it possible to use mind (or heart!) effectively." "What kind of symbol systems," he asks, "what kinds of accounts of the past, what arts and sciences" have a deep influence on our lives? After a lifetime of research in the various branches of psychology––experimental, clinical, developmental—Bruner, in his book *The Culture of Education*, concludes that stories, the ones we tell about others and about ourselves, are "the most natural and the earliest way in which we organize our experience." We live and die by stories; they are not mere "entertainments" but organic to our self-definition and well-being. "It is not surprising," Bruner says, "that psychoanalysts now recognize that personhood implicates narrative," and that what we call "neurosis" is a reflection of an "insufficient, incomplete, or inappropriate story about oneself."

And it's not just the "content" of stories that matters; it's how the stories are told. When Peter Pan asks Wendy to return to Never Never Land with him, he wants to teach the Lost Boys there how to tell stories. "If they knew how to tell them," says Bruner, "the Lost Boys might be able to grow up."

"We live in a sea of stories," Bruner says, and we find ourselves treading water as thousands of stories make their claims on us. Unless there's a tidy moral or dogma attached, we seem ill-prepared to make sense of the many narratives streaming past us from year to year. Most come and go so swiftly we seldom pause to ask if they collectively "add up," but now and again a few make the news. Take, for example, Daniel Goldin, head of NASA under President Bill Clinton, who provided a bottom line to his own narrative when he made his pitch to Congress for increased funding for space exploration, and for its Star Wars ballistic missile offspring: "When a nation turns inward," he claimed, "its empire is in decline."

Others have chimed in with variations on Goldin's theme. "The decline of the Roman Empire began like that," warned former French Prime Minister Michel Rocard, after the economic collapse of 2008. "The national turn inward assures decline, assures recession." Was he echoing a theme stated earlier by a fellow Frenchman, Denys Arcaud, who was concerned about another downside to our inward-turning trend. Arcaud, in his award-winning 1986 film called *The Decline of American Empire*, compared the U.S. to the Roman Empire. The decline of both empires is attributed to excessive focus on self-centered gratification. And Justin Raimondo, writing for Global Research's Center for Research in Globalization [January 31, 2013], agrees: "...modernity is characterized by a turning inward on the part of individuals and nations…. At its worst it is simply narcissism, an unhealthy and debilitating obsession that can only end in a kind of cultural madness. Think of Nero fiddling while Rome burned."

This inward-turning trend: Is it terrible for us? Don't we value inwardness as the path to the quiet self where our spirituality lives? If we lack this inwardness are we fiddling while Rome burns? Are there different types of inwardness? Are there narratives that can save us from ourselves?

There certainly is a lot of bad music, call it noise, in the airwaves these days, much of it attached to narratives. Are we in "decline" because the "sea of stories" we're living in also may be drowning us? Hollywood, TV, the Internet, and yes, even book publishers bless/curse us with literally millions of narratives. Since we, Americans, generate roughly 250 million tons of garbage per year, or about 1.35 billion pounds of garbage every day, we wonder what weight the lightweight best sellers we consume contribute to that gargantuan tonnage of waste. Forests no doubt are felled to feed the paper industries from which the pulp of our worst bestselling novels are made. Thousands of stories line the shelves in book and video stores or in the Netflix queue. The available choices between the good, the bad, and the ugly bewilder us. Does such a glut of options give us good reason to celebrate the power of American imagination and economic energy, while leaving us confused about how to spend our dollars and the remaining hours of our only life? Does such excess distract the Lost Boy or Girl in us from constructing a story worth living in? Are you, Lost Boy or Girl reader, wasting your time on my words right now?

The story tidal wave is swelled by the advertisements that incessantly intrude on our consciousness. Researchers tell us that the average American experiences 600-625 "exposures" to ads every day, or about 1500 per day for a family of four. If there are 1440 minutes in one twenty-four hour (sleepless) day and night, and if each ad we see is on average one-minute-long, each individual would be spending almost three-quarters of each 24-hour day (and night) exposed to ads. If ads were one-minute-long, and if spouses, children, friends and God are said to be presences in our lives, these presences would have precious little leftover undivided attention given to them.

Most ads are much shorter than one-minute-long, and many have thin, almost invisible story lines. Their magic— routinely an entertaining stew of distortion, deception, disconnection, and distraction—is usually concentrated into short bursts of high energy images that point to one bottom line: Buy It. Most ads function as carefully designed mood-altering moments, like short poems. As a kid I grew up with this jingle, and ironically it's still part of my personal narrative:

Made you look,
Made you look.
Made you buy
A penny book.

Obviously, ads trigger desire for consumables. They're designed to make us want—and to leave us ongoingly unsatisfied. And they work, as the word "work" goes these days, at getting us to spend the money we earn at work. But the ad culture, however effective it is at stirring us emotionally, provides us no definitive personal narrative. Should Mr. Goldin of the Space Agency be pleased that ads deny us the "inwardness" his NASA friends find dangerous to the future of empire?

So what stories, familiar enough to most of us, do we live by? It is arguable that the narratives we are routinely exposed to today are so numerous, diverse, disconnected and "noisy" that nobody can make sense of them. Also plausible is that in those "slower" times when books, newspapers and the spoken word were the vehicles for story-making a more coherent public discourse was possible. Today it is difficult to agree that Americans share an "official" national myth that is generally understood and claimed by the majority, but certain dominant recurrent types were popular before the age of the radio, TV and computer.

That America might be in decline has seldom been part of the typical story we used to tell ourselves about ourselves, and today that theme is still one we don't easily tolerate. We traditionally have preferred the type of tale that proclaims America to be "exceptional," the land where the Judeo-Christian God intends to make heroes and successes of us. This type of tale comes in many versions, but that narrative, call it our unofficial national myth, has celebrated territorial domination and prosperity as the God-given right of a God-chosen people. Soon after the Pilgrims landed at Plymouth Rock American writers began scripting the story-line, at once imperial and religious, that kept American eyes looking westward toward "the promised land." As settlers grabbed more land, and as armies pushed Native American tribes into obscurity and poverty and expropriated Mexican territories on their way to the Pacific, American authors wrote popular novels, poems and histories that blessed the conquests and became the staples of children's school texts.

Historian Frederick Jackson Turner's "Turner Thesis" explained the thrust of American history in terms of the westward movement and its expansive terms. The Turner Thesis also imagined the future as perpetually in front of us while promising us better and more. California, with its gold rush, became a symbol of an American destiny to be concluded in a heaven where the streets are paved with gold.

This type of narrative called for heroic saga rather than folk tale. America, as poet Walt Whitman argued, was destined to be "large," and to "contain multitudes." In his epic *Leaves of Grass* he took the American expansionist narrative further than any other writer. In his view "America," synonym for democratic empire at its greatest and spiritual best, would make a "Passage to India," expand its glories beyond the American West and Europe to the Far East. New technologies—in Whitman's time the Transcontinental Railroad, Transatlantic Cable, and Suez Canal—would be the silver bullet enablers, binding the planet together into a globalism defined and dominated by American democratic values and a tolerant and generous spirituality.

Whitman was born too soon to envision the automobile, hydrogen bomb, and computer as technologies, or globalism as we now experience it, but currently we are busy putting into practice a less generous version of his grand American Dream. We still send our ads, entertainments, missionaries—and troops—to foreign lands to give the people there Americanized versions of how to live their lives.

This saga about America's "exceptionalist" right to expand its spheres of influence focuses on going out rather than in. As such it is the type of tale the Greek epic poets knew by heart when they recited Homer's *Odyssey*. In this manly tale a clever and often odious man (the word "odious" is at the root of Odysseus' name) successfully endures three stages of life: Separation, Initiation, and Return. The Separation-Initiation-Return pattern repeats itself in countless variations. A young man leaves home, endures a series of trials on the road imposed by a succession of rivals, monsters, natural obstacles, temptations, seductive females, and wars—and returns triumphantly home as a conquering hero, allegedly hardened into a wisdom young men setting forth should strive for.

The pattern also appears in John Bunyan's *Pilgrim's Progress*, published in seventeenth century England but required reading for most Protestant Americans before 1900. In this tale Mr. Christian also leaves home and faces temptations and trials on the road. But there is a significant variation on Homer's pattern: The "home" returned to by our Christian hero is not a place of birth; it is a heavenly city visible on the other side of the River of Death. There is no home for our redeemed hero on earth. He is an alien enduring his own presence in a sinfully fallen and despicable world.

Though there is a profound contradiction between America as "promised land" and the "fallen world" our Everyman Christian desires to leave behind, both types of narratives promote the purposes of a popular hybrid, the American self-help story. In the late nineteenth and early twentieth century the self-help narrative was the staple of streams of novels written by the likes of Horatio Alger and

General Charles King, whose works were mass produced for adolescent males. If General King's frontiers are conquered by heroic explorers, pioneers and warriors, Horatio Alger recast the saga as a narrative in which heroic tests are suffered on Main Streets by out-of-luck but plucky teenage boys. In these stories the young hero, typically a wandering lost soul or orphan, is taken in by an adult entrepreneur, and the youth fulfills the American Dream by lifting himself up a ladder of success to respectability.

It is one of the ironies of history that Horatio Alger, a closet gay, died poor. His inspiring story had no place for him in it.

The analogous self-help story for young women was the romance. In some respects the Separation-Initiation-Return pattern still holds, with domestic variations. In the romance a young woman is separated not from home but from girlhood, and her initiation experience is a series of mating trials she must endure on her way to making the right marriage. Her "Return" stage takes her to a home ruled by a husband who loves her romantically while earning enough to support her comfortably. Her home is what she abandons in order to achieve success as wife in her husband's house.

While these "classic" narrative types were part of the normal canon for educated Americans, no such body of required reading exists today. That maybe is a good thing: A standardized canon and dominant national myth may straightjacket minds rather than liberate and guide them. But the sea of stories our young people are drifting in is a violent one, many of them derived from Hollywood and TV. On TV we can't escape images of people pointing guns, blowing something up, or beating each other bloody. The typical PG and R-rated Hollywood movies turn mayhem, violence and the destruction of whole worlds into spectacular entertainments, with each generation of movie goers exposed to escalating violence. Research indicates that by age eighteen the average American child sees 200,000 acts of violence and 16,000 murders on TV alone. What are Lost Boys and Girls to make of them?

It seems clear that the popularity and profitability of thrill-seeking action narratives have expanded our range of the permissible. They provide a strange "pleasure" as we approve and are thrilled to see armies and gladiator-heroes destroy each other, while worlds collide and cities are destroyed and women become killers too as they flee from monsters and machines destroying huge bug-like creatures that leave blood and destruction everywhere behind. If such narratives harden us, give us the insensitivity we need to deal with the terrible and real violence we get hints of on the news every day, do they also give us permission to enjoy and normalize destruction and death? Their entertainment value seems oxymoronic in a society living in fear of terrorist threats.

Do such narratives foster a terrorist culture, abandon us to the paranoia of dark streets where it becomes difficult to believe that mainly good people reside? Is the world's factory of dreams, Hollywood, manufacturing ongoing episodes of fear-based blockbuster narratives that take us out and away from who we really are? It's perhaps not entirely accidental that so many Hollywood action movies are set in space. Does Mr. Goldin of the Space Agency see these extra-terrestrial places as possible new American frontiers worthy of conquering?

We have a more important question to ask: Do our more deeply held individual narratives add up to a tale very different from those seen on wide screens, and if so what common denominators would they—those we live by but don't call our own—collectively express?

*

The invisibility of more benign alternatives becomes troubling when we face the facts: Traditional heroic narratives are not true to some current basic facts of American life. Most frontiers, except space, have been conquered, and now we build walls on our borders to keep others out. Space adventures are popular in the movies, but rather impossible for all but a very few. Our ongoing wars provide adventure opportunities—on several continents—but our wars have gone sour, only thinly connected to God-justified exceptionalist purposes. Heroes still return from our wars but not to joyous victory parades. Meanwhile, "home" as a place to return is elusive in a society as mobile as ours. Americans happily leave home towns to chase jobs somewhere else, even as the diaspora of families and the problems that go with alienation often go unresolved. The traditional romance narrative for young women is increasingly sex rather than marriage-oriented, complicating the complex options contemporary women face, one of which allows them to become warriors too.

The old-fashioned American hero and heroine myths are largely irrelevant, and stories that reflect a truer sense of things are lost in the sea of stories available to us. In the absence of a single shared narrative that tells the truth about who we are as a nation, are we doomed to a poisonous self-centered inwardness—national narcissism—certain to lead to national decline? Or is there a non-narcissistic inwardness that we associate with mindful purpose, one also capable of preventing national decline? What kind of story should we tell our Lost Boys and Girls in the schools, and is this a story we would want to live in too? What stories do we best tell ourselves about ourselves?

*

Poor Humpty. So many children grew up not knowing what this egg-head was suffering from. What in the world did he have going on in that huge neuron-packed head of his?

It's unlikely we'll have a new national myth worthy of belief any time soon. The creation of a national cultural myth depends on its having a place in major institutions—churches, schools, art centers, production studios and sports arenas. If such a myth is to be vital it also must have a place in popular rituals deemed, in some sense, communal if not sacred. In their yearly Dionysian drama festivals the ancient Greeks expressed their sense of how life was ordered and how that order could be cursed and healed. The boldest Greek dramatists publicly exposed the problems plaguing their societies. Tragedies, with all their inwardness, had institutional standing in holy-day festivals, and its authors were given prizes and the blessing of the gods. The open celebration of tragedy gave discussions of inwardness public standing.

In America today the story-making process is largely controlled by the demands for profit. The profitability of stories and movies on best-seller lists is often the main feature of the news stories they generate. We lack sacred, unifocal, and ritually regular venues where the best stories may live on.

Only one story has prominent standing—the story of Jesus Christ. But how that narrative is interpreted profoundly divides our nation. In its very earliest versions––those that drifted from speaker to speaker in the first three centuries following the death of Jesus—that story had some common but also many strange features that were told in fascinatingly diverse variations that eventually were congealed into an "apostolic" version by the Romanized church. That congealed version we still find in most churches today, even Protestant ones, and we ritually perform scenes from it on Sundays and holidays. Though not all Americans are Christians, and though not all Christians take their primary myth seriously, the Christ story and its implications provide Americans their most visible and communal story line. Divisive, if seldom discussed, offshoots of it appear frequently on the evening news and they profoundly affect domestic politics and foreign policy. Certainly the Christ narrative, with all its variations, has some sort of influence on most Lost Boys and Girls.

It seems odd that the Christ story, invented by mainly oral cultures in faraway desert lands allegedly to give presence to a God of love and sacrifice, would so easily lend itself to the mission of making an empire of America. What the Puritans brought to Plymouth Rock was a vision of a City on a Hill, a New Jerusalem destined to prove itself exceptional because directed by an exceptional race of God-chosen people. From the beginning the New American Jerusalem's eyes turned westward, toward the lands and peoples who had to be conquered there in order to be saved. The Christ story found the American frontier story useful as the wagons moved west, and their marriage of convenience is still invoked as "American" by citizens of a so-called "superpower" trying to expand its influence through military adventures still justified, by a silent majority, in the name of God. If the sacred Christ story and secular American frontier myth seem contradictory, they have been twisted together to serve each other's purposes.

How we collectively interpret the Christ story, therefore, has an important influence on our history. We might begin by rethinking how we conclude the story. Do we more properly end it in heaven or on earth? Is resurrection of the individual body this story's happy ending done deal—Christ's as he emerged from the tomb, and ours as we ascend to a heavenly mansion? If so, the sacred Christian and secular American myths take on a common theme: God rewards those who seek a paradise in a heavenly mansion. What takes root from this mix is what sociologist Max Weber called "The Protestant Ethic," the basis of the capitalism and much of the brutal partisanship that divides Americans today. Making money is a sign God wants us in a city where the streets are paved with gold.

From the Protestant Ethic to empire-building wars is a short step. Since 1846 the U.S. military has intervened 79 times in neighboring Latin American countries alone. Our defense spending is 25 times greater than the combined defense budgets of seven countries we consider "rogue" nations. We have troops in 150 foreign countries. Meanwhile, I'm sure the director of NASA believes that his space ships are also taking Americans "Nearer, my God, to Thee."

When stripped of its heavenly promises, however, the Christ story resembles a Greek tragedy, with Christ the redeeming scapegoat victim who suffers unfairly to disentangle a long history of sin and resurrect the potential for new life. In this version the redemptive power of love and sacrifice are not sent to a static rest home in a kingdom in the sky. Redemptive love and sacrifice hang on and live on in the real world, resurrected by the suffering heroism of the unjustly condemned Christ. And resurrection, a living earthly process rather than a heavenly stasis, is the story's daily bread, an ongoing necessity for ongoing life, atonement and healing.

Because we wait and watch in our own confusion, we are like all the king's horses and all the king's men, deeply interested in the hidden hands behind Humpty's fall. And we, as the Lost Boys and Girls, are also looking on, desperately trying to find ourselves. How the Humpty Dumpty story is retold may lead to discovery of those hidden hands. I'd begin my version with the horses and men examining Humpty's entrails for a clue, and conclude the tale with Humpty in mid-flight. So in my Humpty Dumpty version the Lost Boy doesn't die. He's still alive at the end, alert enough in mid-flight—as we all are—to be wondering with us about those hidden hands. And in the end we don't really care if he ends up in heaven or hell. What matters most is whether he is living a meaningful life.

Much in our personal and national life turns on the twists and turns given to the Christ story. It's clear that the frontier myths of an earlier America are becoming irrelevant and even defunct. It's also clear that no other single national myth has taken its place, or that any current one can or should. Our national turn "inward" has released a pervasive narcissism that makes a few rich while leaving many spiritually bankrupt. Meanwhile, good Americans everywhere look for a different kind of inwardness in the hope of discovering their authentic spirituality. Individually their stories get lost in the national noise. Collectively their common denominators could add up to have real if quiet power that dims the noise.

Today we again return to a home to wash the dishes and make the beds. Those simple and redundant actions give us plenty of good life from which to create new narratives. Because we believe in creativity we read stories to our children, encourage them to do art, and try to keep kindness and cooperation at the center of what we teach in the schools. New stories are born when we sit in a chair and stare at a blank page on our way to making a journal entry. Some of us will write only to ourselves, not on a page but in our own minds. This too is a good way to begin a story worth living in, a form of writing that has the staying power of invisible ink.

Endnote: *In Medias Res*

Milton begins *Paradise Lost* in hell—*in medias res*—"in the middle of things." My life story was dated by the time I was born on that cold as hell night of February 16, 1941. How was I to know then that bombs had no choice but to fall on Pearl Harbor later that same year, and that World War I had set the stage for Hitler's theatre of the unthinkably absurd. If those events post-dated me, they also pre-existed in me. Incomprehensible events had entered and were already happening to me, not only in the nine womb months I spent hidden away from this confusion, but also in the years, even centuries, before I first saw the light coming from the bulb above my mother's bed. My life story also began *in medias res* on my birth day, a night. Now, decades later, as my story concludes I'm still *in medias res*, with little promise that any rising action will bring a wholly satisfying climax with it.

So here I am, living the stories my mind has invented for me, based on an incomplete understanding of the plots, characters, and settings my consciousness provides. I conceive my life stories as if they are entertainments, like novels and movies, each with a rising action that surges toward a climax before a happily-ever-after falling action sends me searching for the rising action of a better tale. The shape of the tales by which I frame my life seldom fits the facts. In my case my real-life climax occurred on day one, the night I was born, and the second occurred when I first had sex. After that the facts of my life have come as fits and starts, all of them happening *in medias res*. There have been ever-widening circles full of the facts of life. What I don't like to tell is that everything went downhill from those two high points—suddenly past the fits and starts toward the aches and pains that are petering me out.

Too seldom have I allowed death to be the co-author of the story of my life.

What makes my life-story so worth living is the belief, even toward the end, that a climax is still coming my way——as the high point of that prurient desire that nags me to know while I'm wondering how the story will turn out.

What's most troubling is that I'll never know how the larger history concludes—the big one with wars, pollution, music and nature's beauty in it. I'd love to be around to see how its loose ends resolve themselves, even though I know full well that both the stories—my personal tale and the historical one I'm a minor extra in—begin and end *in medias res.*

III. Human Nature

(from *The Oxymoronic Dictionary*)

Adjective with singular noun

1. Two words certain to cause short-circuiting flare-ups in the glob of neuroplastics encased in anthropod skull-shells lording it over tender flesh. Archaeological evidence discovered at the bed sites of *homo erectus* in central Asia strongly suggests that human nature evolved from the love trysts of mammals and reptiles.

   By coloration human nature is deemed *noir* or garden green, with some eighteenth century scribes finding it as white as a blackboard waiting for impressions to make their marks on it.

2. For teachers preoccupied with the test scores of their pupils' human nature registers as a blank blackboard to be written on.

3. In ancient times human nature was routinely depicted as pagan gods. Godly people today routinely deem it mankind's enemy number one, the underlying cause of crimes, wars and children.

   Most people decline to credit human nature when they confer blessings on their enemies.

Synonym: Jumbo Shrimp.

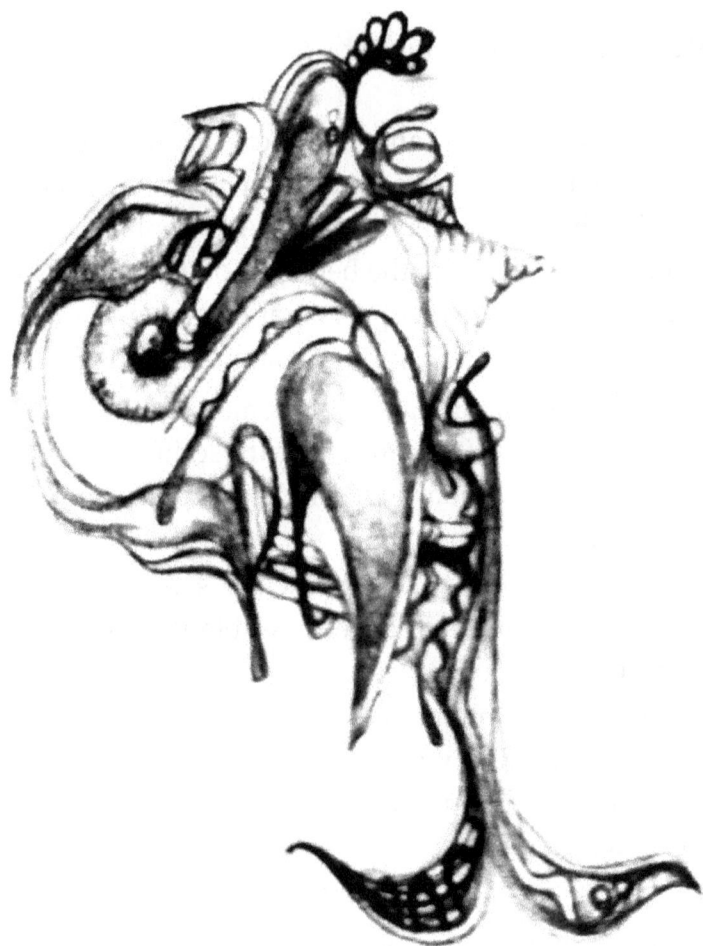

Body-Parts

Because I've always been interested in what people believe, I've spent a lot of time looking at pictures of their gods. For many years the ancient gods—Egyptian, Mesopotamian, Greek—seemed very bizarre to me. The people in those old lands had so many strange looking gods I wondered how they knew what to believe. And so many of these gods had hybrid body-parts—human and animal on the same frame—I wondered if the diets or drugs of those primitives made people delusional. What did their weird hybrid gods have to do with anything real? Why didn't those early civilizers have just one God, or a plain and ordinary Holy Trinity, like a lot of us?

The Mesopotamians, who allegedly helped cradle our civilization into its later adulterated forms, had a favorite hybrid god: A beast with the head of a human and the body of a bull, winged. This creation seemed, as we say today, comfortable with itself. While Mesopotamians also had a fearsome array of other hybrid gods, their Egyptian neighbors made them seem boorish and unimaginative. The great Egyptian Sphinx, familiar to us as a heap carved out of stone to resemble a lion body adorned by a human head, is not as interesting or complex as their other gods, routinely pictured as upright human bodies topped by the head of a monkey, jackal, crocodile, falcon, cow, snake, hippo, or you-name-it head. The classical Greeks, who inclined to personify their gods as powerful forces resembling us, or to abstract them into the stuff of naked Thought, backed away from the Egyptian trend toward god-complexity. The Greek Medusa, for example, a terrifying female force, has a snaky head of hair we can easily imagine belonging to somebody's unhappy wife, and Pan, with his cloven hoof, is also a lesser god who could pass for some old goat we see lurking in a public park. Centaurs and satyrs, crude mixes of human horse and goat, respectively, clearly suggest that the ingenious Greeks cared so little about genetics that it never influenced the conception of their gods.

As a rule the early Christians were unfriendly to the popular pagan hybrid deities, though church fathers had a hard time figuring out whether their God was One or Three-in-One, or both. But visions of Satan excited Christians to do their cut-and-paste best. Satan became a mix of the pagan gods, and other frightful creatures. So over the centuries Satan has come in many complex hybrid forms featuring reptile, bat, dragon, and human body parts, all of which Hollywood geniuses today routinely retool into the metallic monsters that star in a lot of our popular, and monstrous, action films.

Satan's future as a hybrid reptile was sealed when he/she? made the mistake of appearing in serpent form at the Garden of Eden scene. When he/she? ends up getting his (her?) head crushed underfoot it marks the beginning of a centuries long campaign to destroy all alien gods, most of them of the hybrid variety. Most of these alien gods lost their original names and roles, and assumed generic names: "demons," "devils," "idols," and "false gods" are a few. Once they had generic names it became easier to kill people who grew up being fond of them. To have so many gods, especially strange hybrid ones, complicates life. It's easier for those who pride themselves on law, order, and organizational efficiency to make religion, like big businesses, lean. As a result a lot of these hybrid human-animal gods, like so many animals in the wild, are all but virtually extinct, except in Hollywood.

Because I have a strong yen for law and order tidiness I spent frustrated years trying to make heads or tails of Sophocles' play called *Oedipus the King*. The Sphinx in that drama makes the Egyptian one seem like an overgrown cat-body. Her genetic history would stump Nobel Prize-winning geneticists. Daughter of Typhon (a titanic monster) and Echidna, a serpent-nymph, sister to Cerberus (three-headed dog who guards the gates to the Underworld), Hydra (a many-headed creature), and Chimera (a terrifying beast-"specter"), the Sphinx in Sophocles' tragedy has a forepart made of the head of a maiden, a hindpart made from the haunches of a lion, and wings. This riddled mix of ancestry and body-parts has a favorite riddle she doesn't want anyone to answer: "What is at once four-legged, two-legged, and three-legged?" Oedipus solves the problem with one simple word, "Man," and because he got the answer right Oedipus begins thinking he's smarter than the Sphinx. But as the drama unfolds he learns, mainly from the blind man/woman hybrid named Tiresias, to see what he didn't see about himself until, of course, it is, tragically, too late. What does he learn when he finally "Knows Himself?" That though he still sees himself as an ordinary man (though he's also blind by now) his inner nature is sphinx-like too, a hybrid mix of the human and animal, with clipped wings.

The play makes more sense to me because I have animals in the house—ants, spiders, and an occasional bat, mouse, sparrow, or squirrel, a dog named Bella, a girl-cat named Margeaux, and Milo the boy cat-brat. In my way I love all animals, preferring not to maim or kill uninvited creatures, even the ugliest insects. I worry that my wife will get to them first. When a bat shows up I play a game of catch with it, tricking it into the cave-mouth opening of my shopping bag net. Then I deliver it to the great outdoors. I love Bella dearly, despite her nosiness, but I'm especially fond of Margeaux and Milo, their living style, their fur, their purr. I can't keep my hands off them, as if with my hands I can somehow make them more "mine." I have a keen nose for my dog's fragrances, and when one of the cats falls asleep on my chest I think it's my own purring I hear. Somewhere there's a cat in me, and the nosiness of a dog. If I were a god I wonder how weird I'd look sculpted in stone.

So I wonder if those old Egyptians, Mesopotamians, and Greeks were at least as realistic as some of the modern artwork I see in museums. Was their strange god-art—so foreign to our rational minds and high-tech eyes—their way of depicting the world as they thought it really is? It took Milo's purring for my mind to develop a nose for the obvious. Animal nature and human nature cannot be separated, they are a unity, and this unity comes in a variety of often bizarre hybrid forms. Who doesn't know a jackal-head or two, and who doesn't have a cousin who is half-horse or half-goat or a complete horse's ass?

So how are we, because we're all human-animal hybrids, going to get along without going wholly wild or turning society into a prison-zoo? Individual instances of bad manners are easily dealt with in common sense ways: We serve a half-horse cousin who can't be reasoned with another beer to keep him from trampling us as he stumbles toward the refrigerator. It would be painful, immoral, illegal and untidy to cut him off below the waist in order to have him better resemble whatever it is we are below our own belts. But body politic behaviors, when expressed on behalf of ideals held by self-interest groups, seem divisive on a grand scale. Democrats and Republicans are at each other's throats, just as some Muslims, Hindus, Christians and Jews can't seem to agree with each other or with themselves. As a body politic we seem polarized in disturbing ways, with those lurking to commit purity and holiness wielding the sharpest knives to whack away at anything human that has an animal scent not resembling theirs. Our passion to divide and conquer has the stench of suicide and noise of civil war in it. Civil society ends when the state shrinks to exclude one or more of its civil parts. Then the shooting aimed at body parts begins.

Our hybrid roots run deep: From way back in time we're all black and white, rational and irrational, believers and skeptics, smart and stupid, superstitious and scientific, flesh and spirit, zany and sane, good and evil, female and male, human and animal. And these opposites all live in each of us in some proportion, more and less. These bi-polarities, some of them outspoken and exaggerated, don't always show themselves as outward and visible signs on our body parts. If we're bird-brained we don't grow bird heads. We look a lot like each other, even though we all know a scientifically trained engineer who also believes God made the world in six twenty-four hour days so Noah one day could float his overcrowded zoo in it. But if he's a bird-brain, so am I bird-brained enough to believe in something as empirically unproven as string theory or that nothing happened before the Big Bang. Bird-brained as we all are, we're likely to be worse off with our brains removed. There's a fair chance that if we don't whack each other's heads off we can live next door to each other and get on with life just fine. The burning of heretics who didn't

105

share priestly beliefs did not make saints of pyromaniac priests, and no beheading has ever been proven to improve a mind.

I'm consoled by the repose expressed by the Mesopotamian human-bull pictured in one of my mythology books, and by the dignified and upright bearing of the Egyptian god-humans with animal heads. Not all the ancient hybrid gods are so at ease with themselves. Many are as scary as the insanities that possess us. Nor are we at ease in a society that approves of legalized killing and surgical strikes. Perhaps if we re-compose ourselves, achieve the balance and dignity of one of those Egyptian gods with falcon-heads, we may picture ourselves accordingly and make a better nation of our fertile diversities. "Unity," says Ruth Anshen in her book *Biography of an Idea*, "whispers in some remote region of our consciousness that everything exists at the courtesy of everything else."

Jackal-Heads and Holidays

It's been my fortune and fate to live next to a university campus, where bar closing time allows little gangs of scholars to air the noise and other fluid substances that drunk undergrads discharge on their way to crashing on somebody's bed. My dog Bella has marked the campus turf as her own back yard. Her hungry sniffer is always on high alert for rich rotten smells, and she's something of a celebrity, the Little Dog on Campus who can attract a small crowd with a few wags of her tail.

I don't clue the students in on Bella's attraction to strong underwear. I was once a student myself. But when they stop by twos and threes to give my pooch a belly scratch I have a question for them: "Who do you miss more, your parents or your dog?" So far the answer has been unanimous, except for the sad co-ed who told me her father died just last year.

I'm not ready to conclude that the student preference for dogs is one more sign of the decline of the family. If family has anything to do with people putting their money where their hearts are, some leading indicators suggest the family is becoming extended in an original way. A recent Associated Press poll tells us that 52% of U.S. pet owners plan to buy their creatures a holiday gift, with six of ten dogs assured of having not only presence but presents near the tree on Christmas eve. The pooch belonging to the poor girl who lost her father last year might turn out to be a very lucky dog.

I have two close friends currently experiencing profound grief over the death of their dog. When their first dog died some fifteen years ago I was unprepared for the deep funk that possessed them for months. I've often looked to them for friendship and advice, for I respect their practical good sense and the perspectives they've gained through long study and experience. Now it's happened to them again, and the loss of the first has not made this second death easier. They've gone into hiding with their grief, telling me that when they're ready they'll get in touch again. It's been weeks since I've heard from them.

My friend Ray Howe does keep in touch. Maybe because he has a nose for the faintest—and often most revealing—hints. He routinely sends me news of the unheard of ways wildlife is losing both its wilderness and life. Though he's something of a loner who seems to keep solitary vigil at nature's deathbed, he now and then picks me up with a bit of good news. Recently he sent me a clip of a young bobcat and fawn—huddled together, cuddling, perfectly comfortable with each other's company. They had been rescued from a California wildfire, and the rescuers, lacking proper cages and facilities, herded the unlikely young pair together, only to find that they behaved like the Biblical lion and lamb.

After I feast on pork tenderloin and hit the sack for a nap I sometimes wonder why I don't kick my cat Milo off my bed. Am I more animal for eating the pork tenderloin, or has the pork tamed my savage hunger and made a civilized human being of me? If I'm a civilized human what's that cat doing on my bed? My Christian upbringing requires me, a soul duty-bound to subdue the earth and separate myself from the savage in nature and my own beastly self, to think of myself as above the animals. In short, the civilized good Christian human being in me would kick that cat off the bed while I coddle my salvation dream and snore the tenderloin away.

I once asked my dental hygienist what the white teeth inside wide smiles say about the meaning of life. I reminded her that teeth are there for eating other living things, a lot of them already dead.

I'm usually the one who looks the other way when a Sunday drive takes me anywhere near one of those pig confinement factory farms you can smell across state lines. The unseemly things that happen to the pigs in those sheds happen off my watch, I suppose, because my pork tenderloin comes from supermarkets rather than pigs. To enjoy pork I need to convince myself that what happens to pigs is their fault because of their hostility to human rights, particularly the one pork tenderloin eaters enjoy. Pigs would agree that pigs and people do not have the same rights.

But I'm like other civilized human beings, so I have a weakness for Wilbur in *Charlotte's Web*. Wilbur is too human to die so some stranger can eat Wilbur's tenderloin, and our affection for the condemned hog goes beyond words when Wilbur leaps off the page and is realized for us on the silver screen. There Wilbur takes his place with the other Animal Kingdom celebrities—from Mickey Mouse and Bugs Bunny to Bambi, Nemo, Antz, and the Lion King. If stuffed animals and robotic hamsters are crowding sleepers out of bedrooms these days, on Hollywood screens cartoon animals are no longer mere appetizer preludes to the feature film; these days the animation is the main course.

What's the attraction? Hollywood loves the sound of the cash register, so as it picks our pockets it dulls our grave concerns. Do we want our animal life sanitized and sentimentalized into cartoons on the screen because we don't want real Mickeys in our kitchen cabinets and Wilburs in our yards? Are animated films our way of memorializing the decline and fall of animal life on planet earth? Or do we mainly watch these films because Bambi, Nemo, the Lion King and even Antz are versions of ourselves, useful as models by which we may reinvent ourselves? Name one red-blooded boy who after watching the Bambi movie doesn't want to be a stag.

We have the Book of Genesis to thank for blessing us with one of the major ways we reinvent ourselves. There all creatures great and small are invented in turn, and all, even those that creep, are declared "good" by God. Then comes the Apple Episode—the temptations offered (variously) by the Tree of Life and Tree of Knowledge (of Good and Evil.) We take the bait, "fall" into Life and Knowledge, and Eden, a garden in which lion and lamb shared the same bed of grass with things that creep, becomes a jungle red in tooth and claw. From then on our challenge as humans is to tranquilize the teeth and claws we're told are necessary to our fitness to survive in the current market economy, and to seek tenure in a Heavenly Kingdom where we are free of the desire for tender loins.

In these high tech times it seems that money rather than teeth and claws is advertised as the way the fittest survive. As tasty brands of animal life are industrially multiplied before their leftovers are industrially dumped, zoos follow unnaturally enough. With animal turf shrinking and entire species giving up the ghost, it's getting harder to find a patch of wilderness where we can exercise our teeth and claws. Hunters know the problem best, some of them going ballistic as the season opener draws near. Guns, their power and precision carefully engineered, are the enablers of man's back-to-nature schemes. Next to the animal blood stir that occurs when Bambi cluelessly wanders by just in time to be blown away, zoos are boring. And when eyes staring at the antlered heads mounted on den walls begin to glaze over, the wide-screen TV lights the way into the wilds, with all those documentaries of creatures running free shrink-wrapped for posterity as CDs in our memory banks.

We have to wonder if we'll be next. If we, as cellular globs, rose from the swampland of DNA to become (like some of the male undergrads who pet my pooch) *homo erectus*, if our Edenic apple bite then made us *homo sapiens*, and if then we learned to farm and then invent huge and now tiny machines, are we on our way to reinventing ourselves as digitized technological wonders wonderful for us to behold as ourselves on wide-screen TVs? Will the opposable thumb that did so much to get us out of jungle swamps become disposable as it goes digital?

We find consolation in our pets from such thoughts. There we reconnect ourselves to fur and flesh, to the slow and regular rising of breasts, to purring that makes affection audible, to adoring eyes that make it obvious. We speak to Milo the cat and Bella the dog as if they were human beings, and we deem them almost civilized. We wish that Milo the cat and Bella the dog were not in the least interested in the tenderloin on our dinner plates, and that pet food came from supermarkets rather than factories that grind and concoct bite-sized pellets out of unmentionable animal parts and chemicals. We prefer Milo and Bella to lions in our streets lurking with intent to make tenderloin feasts of us. And while some members of our species insist it's only natural to mine uranium on the million acres surrounding the Grand Canyon, we want Milo and Bella to console us as we become participants in the feeding frenzies of Wall Street sharks.

I prefer to do without uranium, and I feel safer knowing what's eating me than I do reminding myself I am what I eat.

It's easy to get cynical about what's eating us. When students stoop to scratch Bella's belly, I carefully avoid mention of Cerberus, the three-headed dog of Greek myth poised to make a meal of anyone getting out of hand on the way to the underworld. Nor do I give them a lesson on the etymology of the word cynic, which derives from the Greek word *kyon*, meaning "dog," or on cynicism as a moral philosophy inspired by the dog-eat-dog habits of nasty Greeks not nearly as starved as the strays they routinely abused. In a dog-eat-dog culture corporate greed comes to mind, though I'm sure even the nastiest profiteer now and then stoops, out of a vague nostalgic yen, to pet a pooch when the market is bullish again.

Greedy or not we wonder if we pet ourselves when we pet our pets. Is the cat or dog a version of ourselves we're trying to love? When the family dog but not the sullen teenager speaks to us, when we clean up the stains on our rugs but not in our lives, when we stroke the cat but not the woman in the bed next to us, it's easy to conclude our pets exist mainly in our minds. What is it our minds say to us then: That this stroking of fur is good, and the creature we're stroking is good, and the life we're living right then is good, and there is good in life.

Yes, we're capable of making little gods of them. And there's one question I don't have the courage to ask the students who pet my pooch: Who do you miss more, your dog or God? Dyslexics who just say yes perhaps understand the question best, and no doubt are the least inclined to roast me as a heretic. To mention an animal and God in the same breath seems...primitive. But it's been standard practice for thousands of years. Take, for example, the ancient Egyptian civilization that began cradling us toward the "end of nature" that appears to be the end-game of our current self-improvement schemes. We've all seen the jackal-headed figures—dog-men— pictured on Egyptian walls thousands of years ago, often alongside hybrid humans who have the heads or body parts of falcons, crocodiles, lions, baboons, bulls, cows, and cats. Henri Frankfort, Egyptologist of renown, assures us that the artists of these sphinx forms drew the world as they saw it. What did they see? That these hybrids authentically represented the identity of human and animal life, an identity at once sacred and real; that animals, even jackals, were divine because as such they possessed a "static reality," a permanence more vital than individual human warts that come and go. For these inventors of civilization animals reflect the *anima*, or soul, of the universe.

Think about that when you're stroking your cat or dog. Does your stroking smooth over the differences that make enemies of Nature, Man and God? As we destroy what's left of wilderness areas is the permanence of animal life— and of God's identity with planet earth—an endangered species?

I'm reminded of one of my favorite poems by an almost forgotten poet named Hilda Doolittle, also known as H.D.

Scribe

Wildly dissimilar
yet actuated by the same fear,
the hippopotamus and the wild deer
hide by the same river.

Strangely disparate
yet compelled by the same hunger,
the cobra and the turtle-dove
meet in the palm-grove.

It's probably no longer possible for humans and
animals to be actuated by the "same fear." Animals are
perhaps blessed to be free of the fear of global warming
and nuclear war. But we do share the same hunger—for
food, shelter, warmth, affection—and are capable, when
these needs are met or when we face terrible emergencies,
of hiding by the same river or meeting in a pine-grove.
When the wildfires arrive a small bobcat and fawn know
enough to give each other the space required to just be.

Whenever Milo the cat sidles up to her my jackal-
headed Bella knows enough to let him be. Because I've
never yet seen them fight like cats and dogs, I will have a
little holiday gift for each of them this year.

Horn Lore

Lore, like music, honors the lures of poetry over the nets of reason. If the geneticist can provide a wholly credible scientific explanation for how the leopard got its spots, Kipling's story has its own charming, if too innocent, rationale. If poetry's genome, language, clusters metaphors, and if metaphor's bias is to establish associative connections that eddy and swirl in cultural streams, we're most likely to find the clues to the origins of our lore in the headwaters of those murky streams.

The horn, celebrated as a musical instrument, is also known in its natural configurations as a thorny protuberance emanating from an animal's head. As antlers, particularly of well-endowed stags, for example, they look down on us when conspicuously displayed as trophies in the dens where humans hibernate. If we ask the trophy hunter what the antlers symbolize the answer might dispirit us: The hunt, conquest of a wild beast, a great accomplishment achieved through skilled use of a gun, proof of the kill. Ask (French) horn players what the horn means to them and not one is likely to make a connection between those dead antlers hanging over a fireplace and the horn that brings music into them while sending it forth into the air.

If biblical lore is to be trusted we would say that in the beginning was the word, in this case "horn." But Shipley's *Dictionary of Word Origins* does not bother with the word horn, sending us directly to the word "bugle," where we learn that a bugle (Old French, from the Latin *buculus* and diminutive of *bos*, bovis, or ox) originally referred to a buffalo, and that the English word "buff" (think also beef or in French *boeuf*) made superficial work of its subject by identifying the ox by its hide rather than its horns. As tribes crossed paths and exchanged words the bugle's bovine associations were grafted onto the Teutonic word "horn". From northern Europe the word traveled south again to become a cognate of the Latin *cornu*, the basis for the English word for grains (notably the specific version that covers Iowa), for several scientific words (e.g. cornicle, cornify, etc.), for the unicorn as a mythical beast, for the region of Capricorn in the zodiac, for the cornucopia, an object Americans associated with the Thanksgiving celebration, and for the musical bugle, akin to the cornet.

If the horn's marriage to the word *cornu* widened bovine associations to include grains, ancient myths deepen the symbolic meaning of the connection. These clues are best understood in the context of basic geographic facts of life, notably the general aridity of the landscapes of Mesopotamia and Egypt, the twin cradles of Western civilization that developed in the Tigris-Euphrates and Nile River valleys. Because life is hard to sustain in desert landscapes, water is especially revered as the stuff of life, a seminal fluid for the growth of grains and the survival of herds. Also especially revered (sometimes as "sacred cows") are the animals themselves—the cow and goat for their milk (mainly) and meat, the ox for its strength, and the ram and bull for their power to inseminate. When life is hard and survival is at issue value is measurable by the size of the herd. And when life itself is a bizarre mystery linked to the seasons, rainfall, fertility, sexuality, blood, and the mysterious role of death it is easy to see why life-sustaining beasts would be revered as representatives of the gods.

Mesopotamian myths show that the bull had a prominent role as personification of dark but powerful life forces. In the Mesopotamian *Epic of Creation* the absolute ruler, Marduk, slays the bull man (*kusarikku*, or "bison") so that he—Marduk, powerful male— may become the "bestower of ploughland who fixes [its] boundaries, creator of grain and linseed, producer of vegetation" (Tablet VII). This usurpation of power is deemed, especially by male tyrants, a natural sign of progress, with the shedding of the bull's blood a ritual sacrifice necessary to lubricate the creation process. Many other horned creatures adorn the Mesopotamian myths—rams, goats, serpents—all of them suggesting that the horn is the outward and visible sign of nature's powerful life-force.

The suggestion is given more sophisticated expression in the iconography of the ancient Egyptians. Here horned creatures are conspicuous as sacred symbols, often in hybrid combination of the human and animal, with the animal nature deemed (as Henri Frankfort suggests in his book *Ancient Egyptian Religion*) more powerful because more pervasive and enduring than individual human identity. Amon, king of the gods, has the head and horns of a ram that symbolically legitimize his rulership. The goddess Hathor, depicted as a cow with the sun between her horns, is a nourisher and protector of both the living and the dead. Isis, major goddess associated with the fertility of the Nile plains, is often depicted sitting on her queen's throne, with a disk suggestive of the moon (a marker of the months and of a woman's fertility cycles) set between cow's horns. Nut, a sky goddess and mate of Geb, an earth god, is personified as a cow that nourishes mankind. Again the link of associations is clear: The powers of the bovine and the bull, the fertility of the earth, the cycles of sun and moon, of seasons and woman's fecundity are represented by horns.

The Canaanites no doubt did not have the horn as a brass instrument in mind when they worshipped their golden calf, but their god as a type was representative of the worldwide reverence accorded the power and prosperity offered by bovine and other horned beasts. In Leviticus of the Old Testament we are told that the sacrificial burning of the bull on an altar creates a pleasing odor for the Lord (Lev. 1:9). J.F. Cirlot in his *Dictionary of Symbols* itemizes many other instances that link the horn with nature's fertility and gods—the Cilician horned god of agriculture holding handfuls of corn, the African rhino's horn prized as an aphrodisiac, the horn as decorative motif on Asian temples, the cycle of the Zodiac initiated by Aries and Taurus, both of them horned. In Greek mythology the infant god Zeus is fed goat milk through a cornucopia, and in the heyday of the Minoan culture young girls ritually entered womanhood by literally taking a bull by the horns and gymnastically vaulting themselves onto the bull's back, a feat requiring what every good horn player must achieve, the balance of power and grace.

Many of these fertility associations—suggesting the terrible beauty of the enigmatic mystery of life and death and the need to revere the harmony and balance implied in nature's seasonal rounds—are inverted with the historic triumph of Christianity and its disdain for the world, flesh and devil. The horn—and the powerful sexuality it represents—is demonized, notably when the old horned pagan gods are demoted into devils. By God-fearing minds these devils are assembled out of pagan body parts through a highly fanciful process of cut-and-paste that gives the new demons the scales and tails of reptiles, the cloven hooves and beards of goats, as well as various configurations of horns that once adorned the fertility gods of pagan lands. In the ritual arena the Minoan bull dance featuring young woman and bull becomes a wholly masculine affair, the Spanish bullfight, its outcome not the balance of male power with feminine grace but the death of the bull. The bull and his horns represent terrifying death rather than awe-filled life, and Nature, the bull, is to be conquered rather than revered. The word "horny" enters our vocabulary as a vulgarity in high tech times, when astonishing discoveries begin to empower scientists to engineer unnatural fertility processes and robots. "Virtue," in ancient times descriptive of the worth and excellence of life-forces in humans, things, and animals, is narrowed to focus on moralistic suppression of the powers of the horn.

The horn as a musical instrument was conceived in a Christianized culture when industrial processes were still primitive. Its inventors probably saw the natural horns of beasts as idealized forms by which to conceive a variety of music-making devices. From the fiery ashes of new alchemies the horn was hammered into various shapes. The spirit of experimentation drove inventors to improvise on the forms offered by bugle, oboe, bull-horn, and perhaps conch shell. The craftsmen stirred new metal recipes in their smelting pots, fine-tuned the thickness of the metal's gauge, twisted and turned the tubing into strange new shapes, and eventually added valves. The prototype of what we now call the French horn emerged as the hunting horn, with its simple coiled tubes and narrowly flared bell. Then unnatural alchemies gave us the natural horn, also valveless but including a mouthpiece, longer coiled tubes, and wider flared bell. Then came the horn as we know it in its present incarnations, with valves and complex coils, in single, double and even triple versions. Whether golden or silvery they, as objects, seem strangely alien outside the chambers where music is performed. But now it is the horn's natural original that is more alienated. Contemporary horn players, going cross-country to a concert or music camp, see a solitary bull in an open field and probably think nothing of it.

The horn's ancient fertility associations were not lost on its early users. Long before it established its place in elegant chambers as part of the orchestra the horn participated in the hunt, sounding, in the excitement of the chase, chords recalling ancient animal sacrifice as a token of the bounty of nature at harvest time. Several composers conjure these chords in renditions both simple and sophisticated, but lost to most of us today is the often subtle and deep symbolism once represented by the horns on an animal's head.

No doubt we still have some questions to ask about the horn whose sounds so often haunt and thrill us in ways no other instruments can. If it is true that form is function, what is it about the horn's form that provides its capacity to so deeply, and comprehensively, move the listener? It seems silly to ask: Is the horn male or female? Allow me a few poetic liberties here. The bugle, cornet, and trumpet stand out as conspicuously "male"—often used as instruments of the hunt and warfare too, their clarion power not often softened into the quiet tones we associate with peaceful domestic life. This phallic quality is at odds with the French horn's circularity, suggestive of the body and belly of the well-rounded woman. The cornucopia is perhaps a fitting analogue, its curved form androgynous, phallic on one end and open-wombed on the other, its bell shape pouring out the fruits of the earth. Is the French horn music's cornucopia, its form also androgynous, capable of including and balancing the male power and female grace that recall us to ancient mysteries and rituals?

As an object the horn is simply an instrument for circulating air. No literal fruits pour forth from its bell. The horn player is the vehicle, like the horn itself, of the horn's raw material. Through the agency of the player air undergoes a conversion experience, with music emerging as a refinement of air's raw power. For the Greeks and in the Gospels the word *pneuma* refers to both "breath" and "spirit." Like earth and its growth processes air too is a life-giving power. If the horn on the beast's head once symbolized the power of the earth to bring forth new life, the horn takes a finer, more invisible vital substance in, circulates it in its guts, and alchemically transforms it into beautiful art. This music, like sound knowledge, is also the fruit of nature's womb, often available as a gift in the marketplace where few come to buy.

Whalehead Therapy

Whenever I play Rock-Paper-Scissors I have an urge to change the rules by adding Water to the game. If my hand could turn up Water rather than any of the other three, I'd never lose. Scissors rust as water easily slices through them, and paper dissolves in water, and water erodes rocks into sand. Water's the joker and ace. I'm like everyone else: I don't like to lose. If I had Water in my arsenal I'd settle all arguments by washing them away.

In my college days we sorted profs into two camps— Steel Woolies and Warm Woolies. Warm Woolie professors encouraged us to talk and helped us find our way. Steel Woolies rubbed us wrong and were Never Wrong. Capital N.W.—nothing in between—Period.

My Warm Woolie sister is a Steel Woolie Christian who predictably shoots out Rock fist beliefs even though she's smart enough to know I'll Paper her Rocks. And when my mouth shoots out a quip that nips at the edges of her hard-core beliefs, she lets out a demonic little laugh as she smashes my Scissors to bits with her Rock.

It's tempting to go head-to-head with true believers whose authority is based on complex and sometimes incomprehensible texts such as Bibles, Korans, and antique legal documents whose ambiguities and silences on matters of contemporary importance have calcified in some minds into simple Truth. I try to resist arguing with them by meditating on how Melville's great whale sees the world. A whale is a huge creation with one eye on each side of a monstrously bald head. "In a word," says Melville in his whale bible called *Moby-Dick*, "the position of the whale's eyes corresponds to that of a man's ears," a physiology well designed for listening. Therefore, is it not probable, as Melville suggests, that the whale "can at the same moment of time attentively examine two distinct prospects, one on each side of him, and the other in an exactly opposite direction?"

A different temptation arises from this bi-polarity: The habit of calling everyone either a Rockhead or a Waterhead. Rockheads are like Steel Woolies whose beliefs, as if carved on tablets of stone, are recast in printed form as laws, sacred texts, and nasty letters to the editor. Rockheads, especially their talking head representatives, call people unlike themselves—especially other Rockheads who don't hold the same beliefs—infidels, fanatics, terrorists, and Dead Wrong. Waterheads are like Warm Woolied evolutionists, certain only that beliefs change and that survival depends on the ability to muddle along in untidy fluid environments. Waterheads, sometimes at a loss for words, tend to turn the other cheek to avoid getting their heads cracked.

Since whale bibles are written in languages difficult to understand, and since I believe exegesis saves, I keep trying to make sense of Melville's turgid prose. My view is that Melville's whale is simultaneously a Rockhead and a Waterhead. If a human were like a whale its mind would be a symphony of opposing views. The performance in the whale's head would be attended by realists and idealists, extremists and moderates, Creationists and Darwinists, capitalists and socialists, pro-lifers and pro-choicers, Republicans and Democrats, and, simultaneously, those trying to advance the claims of black and white, prose and poetry, reason and intuition, fact and myth, shore and sea, permanence and process. We'd all be members of congress in that head, listening to more than simple-minded tunes.

While whales loll in the seven seas I live on shore in a house full of clocks, none of which tells precisely the same time. I find it easy to panic when the shifty quicksands of time move along without either my approval or any particular approval of me. I too feel the need for at least a soft core of belief, something substantial enough on which to stay afloat. My Rockhead religious friends tell me I need to believe that the universe was created in six days, that Eve was made from Adam's rib, that Jesus walked on water, and that inexhaustible martyrs in heaven get to enjoy 28 young virgins as thanks for blowing themselves up in a crowded marketplace. Rockhead patriots tell me that the U.S. Constitution makes it as clear as window glass that U.S. citizens have a perfect right to carry AK-47s into grocery stores.

But I see through a glass darkly. Even though the Rockhead in me wants to draw lines in the sand, the Waterhead in me wipes them away. Through my dark glass I see that throughout the ages codes, hard-headed truths and Rock of Ages creeds tend to have conversion experiences. And the slippery truth Heraclitis established centuries ago still stands unmoved in the stream of history: We never step into the same stream twice.

I try to balance the solid and liquid in me into what I prefer to call common sense. Because I live downstream with everyone else in the world I have good reason to believe that all the lines drawn in upstream sand one day will, in some shape or formlessness, end up in my yard. I do my best to fight off my urge to change the rules of the Rock-Paper-Scissors game, mainly because I remember from my Sunday School days the old story about how God (unfairly, I firmly believe) sent a flood holocaust to wipe out the world, mothers and babies too. Does that make God guilty of genocide? I could make a hard-headed case for that. But whenever that urge comes on to win at all costs I know it's time to find a cozy ark-like bed where I can roll gently back and forth until a good nap takes hold.

Naps are a good enough way to tread water or muddle through the craziness of troubled times. Naps are known to cause civility, and they're famous for cleansing the brain of madness, cruelty, and noise. More than a few honored saints have described the floating sensation naps provide, the blessed calm that grounds their souls in deep water sounds resembling the songs of whales.

Hair Roots

For those who require real proof I have photos and an actual clipping to verify my claim. Yes, until I was four my head was adorned by golden curly locks. I don't know what happened to those locks when I entered my kindergarten year. My hair turned dark brown like that of my mom and dad, my sisters, and all my cousins, uncles and aunts. My hair began living up to my Italian-sounding name.

That dark brown hair, what's left of it on my head, is now wholly gray. And now I call myself a blond. It's my way of establishing that I'm an all-American guy who belongs among the Viking hoards of Lake Woebegone land.

I fit in and don't fit in wherever I am these days. When I visited Rome a few months ago I expected to be lost in enough crowds to look Roman enough. There a wide diversity of faces, hues, sizes, shapes, designer labels and languages manage to make room for each other—refugees from Albania, wanderers from Romania, the homeless from North Africa, Pakistan, the Middle East, and tourists like me from everywhere sharing the sidewalks with natives. All roads lead to Rome. Why expect anything but a stew of hybrid variations in a city whose legendary founders, Romulus and Remus, were, without prejudice, famously suckled by a wolf.

But I did a double-take outside the Vatican Museum. There a pert and very pretty Asian-looking woman had gathered about herself a group of tourists, a couple of them sporting New York Yankee caps. She was their tour guide. As I eavesdropped I heard her deliver extraordinarily learned comments on Michelangelo, Leonardo da Vinci, and Raphael, with asides that featured a few of the more corrupt popes. I heard her address the Yankee fans in seamless Italian, the Tuscan dialect that is now the official "high" language of the whole peninsula. I knew some Italian too, but it's the southern Calabrese dialect that makes northerners wince as they dismiss southerners as "terroni"—peasant "earthlings." "Terroni" is the Italian "N-word." As full-blown hybrid American I can afford to make light of such slights, but listening to the Asian woman gave me pause. This woman—whose ancestors might have come from China or some other exotic land—was crowding in on my cultural roots and making me feel like a weed.

When I feel like a weed I begin thinking more deeply about whether there's room for me someplace in the world. I worry, for example, that China's population is swelling toward the one billion four hundred million mark. I imagine that the tour guide (or her parents or ancestors) is one of several millions who leave their homeland to find a better life. Boundary lines appear especially imaginary when hunger and desperation are real, and when multi-national corporations, willing enough to enhance their bottom lines by debasing the wages and working conditions of host countries, make it easier for border guards to look the other way. The multi-nationals know how cheap labor, uprooted like weeds for a harvest of profits, belongs to a classless society easily had.

Since my own parents were working class immigrants to the U.S. I should know better than to be hard on Asian-looking refugees trying to make a place for themselves in the world. Their diligence, resilience, thrift, intelligence, and practical good sense rewards many of them, as do the brutal lessons learned from long marches, totalitarian rule, cultural revolutions, and starvation diets. We offshore not only factory but engineering jobs to Asians now, and we're told they work harder for less, and they produce a lot of what we buy, and we borrow billions from them so we can buy their stuff from them.

My wife Monica, impressed by the diligence, resilience, thrift, intelligence, and practical good sense of several Chinese women we've encountered over the years, says it's a good thing they're getting out and about. "Chinese women," she keeps reminding me, "one day will rule the world, and we'll be better off for it."

It's hard not to agree, especially if it comes down to a choice between Chinese women and a gaggle of American politicians calling the shots.

But it's not easy to visualize Chinese immigrants in the farm fields of Madagascar or oil fields of Libya, mainly because we don't see much of anything going on in most parts of the world unless it has entertainment value. But when I looked twice at that tour guide outside the Vatican Museum I saw a class act. And the troubling questions didn't go away: What was she doing in Rome, and what was she doing representing my culture to Yankee fans who probably also have Italian-sounding names? Is she the avant-garde ripple of a human tsunami coming our way? And it's not just Asians coming our way. The French, nervous that the storming of the Bastille will come to naught because women in Paris suburbs prefer to hide their faces behind veils, are passing laws that make legal taboos of the preferences of some Muslims. In Germany the immigrant labor force is stirring up old talk about racial purity, and that angry conversation's echoes have crossed the Alps down into Italy. My hair stands on end as I recall the ominous words of the eminent racist Dr. Frank Lydston, who in his 1908 book *Diseases of Society and Degeneracy* reminds us that, "A hair divides the 'soul' of man from the brain attributes of the lower animals." Should I alert the U.S. Coast Guard to the specter of boatloads of Asians sneaking across the Pacific to invade San Francisco's Chinatown so we can keep "lower animals" from sneaking into our souls?

My thoughts get less lowdown as I pause to wonder if Eros is properly influencing my thoughts about the tour guide outside the Vatican Museum. One thing is certain: Eros, nature's lubricant, is the leading cause of global warming. But unlike oil it offers itself to us as an endlessly renewable energy source, one experienced daily and worldwide by millions of normal teenagers and young adults as nagging volcanic tremors in the private parts. But alas, alack, Eros is also single-mindedly stupid about its role in creating the dangers posed by the human tsunami gathering strength in overpopulated hotbeds of the world. Eros knows no geography, biology, psychology or languages. And it seldom knows how to count past one, especially if it has a Ph.D.

What do my long-gone golden curly locks have to do with stupid Eros? A little historical research leaves me with a better informed ignorance of the roots of my blond hair. Long before Romulus and Remus were fattening up on wolf's milk, Germanic tribes were invading southern Sweden, the Danish peninsula and northern Germany, while the Celts were venturing into northern Spain and the Alpine regions. Six Germanic tribes—Visigoths, Ostrogoths, Vandals, Burgundians, Lombards, and Franks–

–took turns raping and pillaging their way south into the Italian peninsula, with Rome suffering blowback from its empire ambitions by being sacked by the Gauls in 390 B.C., the Visigoths in 410 A.D., the Vandals in 455 A.D., the Visigoths again in 476 A.D. and the Normans (of hybrid Viking stock) in 1084 A.D. The Greeks, of course, were already there in ancient times as colonists, and Helen of Troy was said to be a gorgeous blonde. And the invaders who came from North Africa and the Middle East were already lost in the crowds when Charles of Spain sacked Rome again in 1527 A.D., making a bloodbath from the gene pool bouillabaisse out of which new "Italians" were conceived. My golden curly locks no doubt had their origin as a DNA tendril learning to swim in that murky soup.

So how does she, the bright Asian tour guide with silken black hair, fit into the current stream of Italian history? Does she "belong"? Is she perhaps child of one of "your tired, your poor, your huddled masses yearning to breathe free," committing a subversive act of culture war as she presumptuously speaks on behalf of masterwork icons generated and located in a place called "Italy"? Even if she were able to hustle her way to citizenship and a job, and in spite of her command of the major Italian dialect, will she ever be Italian enough?

If she's like me she does in Rome as the Romans do. When I'm in Rome the golden curly locks I had as a little boy that were transfigured into old man gray are no longer Viking strands. I tell everyone who asks (they don't, since this conversation, like most unspeakable ones, goes on in my mind) that my hair was once like a dark Italian red wine. In Rome my hair is Italian hair. I also remain mum about the swarthy and grizzled Greeks, North Africans and Middle Easterners who colonized southern Italy centuries ago. Though it lacks the silken noir luster that perfects the Asian tour guide's face, I don't want to leave the impression that my "terroni" hair is impure.

What claim do I have on Italian culture, my "roots"? In what sense are Michelangelo's "Moses" or "David" mine, or Leonardo's "Mona Lisa," or Dante's *Divine Comedy*? My son, also named Dante, recently informed me, in no uncertain terms, "I'm not you, Dad!" as he escaped me (again) to do his own thing. Moses and David were from a land called Israel or Palestine, and I'm not. Mona Lisa does not resemble my Irish/German/American wife-with-Italian children, though I see hints of my eldest daughter's face (she's a gorgeous blonde) in the portrait. My second daughter is dark-haired, her name Leah taken from the Old Testament. Dante's *Divine Comedy* is about Heaven, Purgatory and Hell, but no one in our family believes Dante's heaven and hell are actual places. So how "Italian" am I, and how Italian are the artists who created these masterworks? As with sinners and saints, is it also true of artists: We know them by their works, really good, or not.

While globalism is making homeless tourists of more and more hapless laborers, the world's population tsunami is swelled by the refugee lines. Religious objections to birth control persist, with Christian, Jewish, and Muslim leaders aware of the importance of market share as population growth strains existing national boundary lines. Eros, meanwhile, pushes its own interests, and prefers exogamy. As our bodies tell us to have babies our genes tell us to go out, not in toward the familiar. Biology suggests it's a very bad thing to mate with our mothers, brothers, sisters and first cousins. It inclines us to leave home to mate with *The Other*, strangers who live in villages we've never visited, people with faces, body types and hues different from our own. In this way babies sporting blond curly locks may be born from parents with very dark brown hair, and biology's good intentions for the future of the human race will be well-served.

Biological facts of life have always troubled me. They're never cut and dried and they do not obediently respect the laws of culture and nation-states. As we keep spawning an unprecedented population mass that keeps shrinking the planet and its resources, biology challenges us in unprecedented ways. How do we control its urges? How do we adjust to the tide of refugees coming our way? How do we convert the creative force of Eros into the politics, arts and sciences that make life efficient and worthwhile? How do we maintain rule of law when refugees get out of line to get to a slice of bread? How do we in good conscience deny them that slice of bread?

It's a problem that makes saints and sinners of us.

When I stand at attention while the "Star-Spangled Banner" is being played I try to remind myself that all my names—attached to the identities by which I'm said to be known ("American," "Minnesotan," "white," "male," etc. etc. etc.)—are also just noise. It helps me confront my prejudices, including the one that reared its ugly head to convince me that the Asian-looking tour guide in Rome was not Italian enough to be Italian at all. But if biology is absurd enough to encourage us to fall in love with perfect strangers, why not let the Asian/Italian tour guide fall in love with Michelangelo's "David" too? Who knows what stranger perhaps already has fallen in love with her, and what lovely girl with blond curly locks ("like gold to airy thinness beat") may come of their love, and how this girl-child one day may govern, and improve, our world?

...so...

On the Inside We're kinda Mushy

Endnote: Memory Loss

I'm curiously involved in watching myself lose my mind, its inevitable disappearance into the labyrinth of old age. With the hardening of arteries many of us endure the hardening of beliefs, even as we glance at their truths in the shifty rear-view mirrors of memory. I'm perhaps exceptional. My beliefs dissolve as I age, mainly because memory plays hide and seek with me. I can spend half a day staring into memory's mirrors with nothing I'm looking for coming back to me, especially when I'm hunting for the names of actual people I knew or still know. Many are still present, including the dead, but what are their names? Duh? I draw a lot of blanks.

I prefer to think that flight into thin air is vital to their disappearing act. When we lose the names in our minds is it a foreshadowing of the fateful fact that every one of us will be nameless one day? Sooner or later anonymity comes to us, certainly in the end as the peace that passeth understanding. Even the names of those mentioned on monuments and in books are destined, one long day from now, to disappear into the debris from which strange new cities and jungles are made. Even if our name appears in some Book of the Dead it is inscribed there by a felt-tipped quill in disappearing ink.

Yet no nameless one of us will be entirely gone. The force that was our life—be it for good or ill and usually both—multiplies as it divides and disappears from view, turning into new fragrances, new musical tones, new noise, new tendril turns of mind, new love and hate. We have no names for the spirits winding their ghostly way through winds. In their airs we live bodilessly, and namelessly, on.

Every name forgotten reminds me of that.

IV.   College Education
(from *The Oxymoronic Dictionary*)

Adjective with singular noun

1. For a few a thoughtful pause in the journey toward the school of hard knocks.
2. For many a commitment to forms of recreation enjoyed as a right to a well-subsidized lifestyle. For them "hitting the books" is a form of revenge.

Antonym: MBA.

Big Bird Goes to School

I was afraid they'd call and I was afraid of saying no. They called and I said no.

They offered an honorarium, but my saying no had nothing to do with money. Some things are too hard for me to do.

It seems easy enough. Show up for a writers' workshop for children in grades 4-8. Meet three classes for two days in a row, teach them how to write, then smile, answer questions, and behave like a writer.

I had done it off and on for several years, and then one morning, months before the next conference was scheduled to take place, the dread set in. Anything, almost anything, but those three hours again for two whole days. Please, thank you, no thanks this time.

If the children's evaluations can be trusted (they can't) they liked me enough. And there wasn't one kid I knew well enough to dislike. I'm well credentialed as a classroom pro. Decades ago I was certified to teach in the public schools, but I went on to spend 39 years teaching in college classrooms instead. I never dreaded my college work the way I dreaded kids in grades 4-8.

After spending three hours in a row in a classroom full of fourth and fifth graders I always felt an enormous mix of fatigue and relief. I tried consoling myself by saying I wouldn't have to do it again for another year. I could return to discussing the types of classical rhetoric Thomas Jefferson used in *The Declaration of Independence*, the metaphors lurking in the poetry of Wallace Stevens, and the mythological structure of *The Epic of Gilgamesh*. Easy stuff.

What did I find so hard about the kids? I like squirrels, and they are squirrels, as naturally they should be, primed to hop up and around whenever anything just slightly nuts pops up. The youngest ones are full of good life—fresh-faced eager-beaver squirrels hungry to see what a full-bodied out-of-school experience can offer them that an ordinary school day does not. They have the energy of dervishes and attention span of fireflies. And hardest of all on me is that they expect to be entertained.

In the last decade of my college teaching career I routinely asked my students if they learned the alphabet from *Sesame Street*. Almost all hands went up.

I was not about to teach classes in a Big Bird suit. But I was worried I'd bore them. Their response to my Big Bird question was revealing: They were convinced they learned a lot from TV. For them TV, a technology now deemed quasi-primitive, was "educational" in a way classrooms are not.

How could I, no Big Bird, compete?

Entering schools as teachers now are the children suckled on TV, cell phones and computerized devices. And there's a lot of noise in the air waves accusing these teachers and their schools of failing our kids, our economy, our moral values, and all those standardized tests. The Asians, we're warned, are beating us in science and math, and our companies are hiring not only their peasant factory hands but their sly engineers adept at plagiarizing our latest inventions. Critics keep saying our schools are going to pot because teachers, the very ones who learned the alphabet from Big Bird, are not good enough for our economy, moral values, and test scores. Talking heads remind us daily that our schools are causing the decline and fall of the American dream.

Until recently the war on public schools was waged by indifference and snide. We know the new mantra: Get rid of tenure. Too much vacation time and too many benefits. Get rid of unions. Get rid of student bad behavior, bad test scores, bad teachers. Get rid of buildings in neighborhoods. Get everyone in line and put a lot more on-line. And a few say it out loud: Get rid of public schools. Privatize them all—all, that is, except those we need for the warehousing of kids the private schools don't want.

I prefer to point the finger of blame at Big Bird. Though most kids would have learned their alphabet in good time in a good kindergarten class, Big Bird no doubt hustled them along. But he also confused millions of little tykes about the difference between the exhilaration that comes from the mind's discoveries and the fun entertainment provides. Put rather simply: Learning spikes the pleasure that comes from knowing the world with our minds; entertainment makes it socially acceptable to lose our minds.

It's hard not to take a dim view of all the glitter and glitz generated mainly by two powerful poles, Madison Avenue and Hollywood, with the wheelers and dealers in the shark infested casinos of Wall Street and Las Vegas rolling the dice to see which of them will become our cultural capital. By the time kids walk into their elementary schools they already have been defined—and already are defining themselves—as consumers. The relentless flickers of the commercials they see fill them with fantasy, stereotypes, and the soft sells (like soft porn) that are too attractive to ignore. All the ads tell us that something is missing from their lives and they therefore are unfulfilled.

What they lack is alluring, funny and fun, and they need to be more like what they lack. They'll find what they need not in a school but in a shopping mall.

How many kids are not hooked on this mainstream American culture by the age of twelve?

The kids have two favorite words for whatever vague thing is demoralizing or discouraging them: It sucks.

It sucks the curiosity, creativity, and respect for honest clear thinking out of them. School, its tests and science and math and worksheets and reading and writing are a hard sell. And what's the reward? A job after they put in their time? A job they don't really want to do because they don't know what they really, passionately, want to do, or because they have no sense of ownership of the company they're working for. The Big Bird in them promised them something more fun. Maybe a stint in the army will turn out to be like a video game.

I suspect that more than a few parents are enormously relieved when their kids are safely off to school. Let the teachers figure out what to do with them.

I used to wonder about the faces in front of me in my college classrooms—thirty normally, forty or even sixty at times. I tried linking their faces with names on a seating chart, and I'd remember a few when I saw them on the sidewalk. I wondered too: How many came from dysfunctional families—drugs, alcohol, verbal or sexual abuse? How many had been to war and back, or had a friend or uncle shot dead in a street gang brawl? How many had guns in their cars? How many came from a home where the TV is always on, where not one thoughtful book is on a shelf? How many were fatherless, friendless, angry, raging inside, embarrassed by their looks, afraid of something they couldn't explain, feeling deeply inadequate? How many were depressed? In my last semester of teaching I knew of seven in my classes who were clinically diagnosed as depressed. How many of the others were on drugs, prescribed or proscribed?

In general I see confusion and need. A lot of the kids are someplace else, plugged into the latest devices at home, in a car, and walking down the street. Apparently where they actually are moment by moment isn't good enough. They want to be someplace else.

So all you teachers out there—would you hurry up and save the world for a change. Our workforce is suffering and the Chinese are beating us at our game and our economy's feeling down and we need to sell more stuff. And nobody in the world loves us the way they once did, so what's the matter with them? And it's the teachers' fault because even with tenure, benefits, summer vacations, and unions our kids aren't passing their standardized tests. And if teachers don't change the world we'll put Smartboards in charge.

Meanwhile, teachers, don't get cynical, demoralized.

I'm not cynical, but I'm convinced I can't handle three hours in a row with kids in grades 4-8. It's too hard. I don't know how anybody can, five days a week for nine whole months. But they do. And many do it well.

Subs

Years ago when we were sixth graders Virgil Davis and
I had a saying we loved to repeat: "Flannery will get you
nowhere."

Mrs. Flannery was the substitute teacher we'd see a few
times a year when Mr. Spinelli, our regular, took a day off
to see to his sniffles and mental health. I haven't seen Mrs.
Flannery for decades, and I owe her a profound apology.
When I imagine her at the front of the class trying to herd
all of us squirrels back to our seats I keep seeing Edvard
Munch's *The Scream*.

Mrs. Flannery came to mind the other day as I strolled
through the Winona State University campus near my
home. I struck up a conversation with two middle-aged
women who were there to take a class designed to teach
them how to teach. "What is the class about?" I asked. I
saw their faces begin to contort themselves into versions of
The Scream. "It's supposed to teach us how to be better
substitute teachers," one of them replied, her eyes looking
at the ground.

While my sixth grade crimes came into view so did the
enormity of the task they were taking on.

Let's pity ourselves. An early morning phone call blasts
away the poor sub's sleep, and off the sub goes, cup of
coffee spilling in hand, to some classroom full of children
full of energy, creativity, and fun, most of them strangers to
the teacher making a house call on them. The sub flips
through the absent teacher's lesson plan for the day, trying
to make sense of somebody else's agenda for the smiling

faces lying in wait to act up, as Virgil Davis and I more than once did, just for the fun of it. Math, science, social studies, grammar, reading—who really cares? And why care? Mrs. Flannery doesn't know what math or reading level each one of us has achieved so far, or what we could achieve if we tried. She doesn't know our names, and probably nothing about our home lives—whether our parents ever read to us, or if there was one book in the house, or if we had breakfast today, or if our dad lives with our mom, or if he drinks too much or takes drugs and pounds on her, or if mom pounds on us. Math, science, social studies, grammar, reading—why did we forget to do our homework again last night? Again. Do we hate school? Are we present but absent? Is there something we are trying to forget? Don't we know there's a test coming up? Do we want to fail? Why should we learn this stuff? What's the sub's name? She doesn't want us to call her that other name. Her name's on the Smartboard. Her name's not Mrs. Flannery. She doesn't know our names and she'll soon enough be gone again, so later today let's just watch her scream. Maybe that would make us laugh.

As I walked away from the two practice teachers trying to learn their trade, I thought maybe I should enroll for the class. Though I'd spent thirty-nine years in classrooms and have three children, the eldest now 40, it occurred to me I'd been a substitute both as teacher and parent the whole time.

Recent surveys about parent-kid time do not console me about my parental influence. In a study done for the Brookings Institute two economists, Garey and Valerie Ramey, conclude that college-educated parents spend on average 9.6 (waking) hours per week with their kids, up from 4.5 in pre-1995 years, while non-college parents spend

6.8 hours per week, up from 3. Good news? Less than an hour and a half per day, at best. Time spent how? Discussing Plato and Aristotle or algebra or the latest crisis in the Mideast? Sitting in front of the TV with the kid in the same room, or in a car on its way to some soccer tournament? How much parent-kid time is good time, and how much "good" time is educational time? If absent fathers are reliable indicators of family dysfunction, how much of that hour or so do kids spend with mom, rather than with dad?

When I look realistically at how few hours I, a wonderful father in my own mind, actually spend with my kids, I conjure *The Scream*. I'm even less cheered by another survey, this one by Betty Stevenson and Dan Sacks, also economists, done for the Wharton School of Business. Only 41% of parents today, they conclude, deem children "very important" to marriage.

As Yogi Berra might say, "Marriage, like the future, ain't what it used to be." What a lot of people call "family values" are also not what they seem and also are not what they used to be. Like a past perpetually reinvented to serve special interest groups with political agendas and products to sell, "family values" probably never were, or are, how we imagine them.

If some of our kids are dropouts and a majority are absent from school even while sitting in their seats, they're like most of us, the adults charged with showing them the way to live. Like substitute teachers we're seldom there, and when we're there in the same room with the kids we're often somewhere else, like them. Mrs. Flannery got us nowhere because she had little chance to know who we were and what was irking us, and because there was little coherence, continuity, or credible meaning attached to the fragmented learning tasks schools require. Try inspiring a twelve year-old by saying, "Learn your math for the test or else you won't get a job when you grow up." Spitballs, figurative of course, are the proper response.

Should we be surprised that so many teachers and parents duck out whenever they can? Raising kids is hard, and educating them is harder. It's a complex, time-consuming, and often maddening process that requires the patience and perseverance of tortoises not interested in winning somebody else's race to the top. It also requires presence—physical, mental, emotional and moral. Our economy's improvement now seems inextricably tied to uplifting our children's test scores by providing them the technologies that encourage our kids to duck out on us. Show me a teenager who doesn't text at the dinner table or on the way to the soccer tournament a hundred miles away. What kid, or parent, isn't cell phoning, i-Podding, or video game playing while I-Padding (or driving) down the street? We leave them to their owned devices.

It's telling that the parent/kid surveys were done by economists, whose professional interest in consumers and the stuff they buy is likely to result in children (somebody else's, of course) being targeted as "engines of economic activity." From studies like theirs, advertisers learn how to flatter kids into purchasing products, many of which will provide parents time-outs from them. In this way the values of business, also known as busy-ness, become family values.

The family values we reap are those we sow. The lifestyles we require for ourselves and our children often depend on double incomes that make absent parents of fathers and mothers alike, and these lifestyles place a high value on the time needed to accumulate wealth and debt.

How many kids can spell the word "conservation," let alone have parents who personify and explain its best practices? How many parents have the courage to tell their children they can do without some gadget or thing, and convincingly explain why? How many parents structure into the daily lives of their business weeks actual educational experiences calculated to develop their children's curiosity, creativity, critical thinking and mindfulness of the needs of others?

Our current family values, confused with political noise about job growth and deficits, do not address the real deficits our kids have to deal with on a daily basis. Family value deficits make substitute teachers of us all while making us unable to compete with the powerful influences cleverly constructed by commercial interests unashamed to bring horrific violence and demoralizing vulgarity into the video screens in our living rooms. Full time teachers are substitute teachers too, except when we need someone to blame for bad test scores. Then we point a finger and speak the only piece of mind we have going for us: Our schools are failing us.

When I recall Mrs. Flannery it's now easier for me to see why she failed Virgil Davis and me, and how I failed her. But I rarely scream, except quietly to myself.

Reading between the Lines

I remember the moment the lights went on for me in Mr. Meeker's tenth grade English class. Vickey D., class genius, raised her hand and said that the whitewashed walls in Rolvaag's novel *Giants in the Earth* had something to do with Beret's sex life. And Mr. Meeker said yes, that's perhaps true. Explain.

Vickey D. didn't really use the words "sex life." In those good old moral days sex lives carried on as usual but never at home, in churches or schools. A few of us caught Vickey D.'s drift. Whitewashed walls were not just white walls. They had something to do with purity and a need to cope with a sense that sex was unclean. In our silences we read between the lines.

Books became a lot more interesting from that moment on.

If literature is like life—that is, if the world's best (not always "classic") books provide models of experience—then there is something to be gained from studying these models carefully. Though I never saw myself as priest probing the entrails of texts for life's sacred clues, I entered the teaching profession, I suspect, in part because I wanted to initiate students into the practice of reading between the lines. I wanted them to learn the art for themselves so they could respond—consciously and critically—to what's so often being said without being said. Teachers of literature, the contemporary version of temple priests, accumulate a certain power and pleasure, if not prestige, from reading between the lines.

For many years I derived quiet pleasure as teacher-priest by coaxing my students toward the clues lurking in the smallest details of one of my favorite, because most teachable, books, Joseph Conrad's "classic" *Heart of Darkness*. It's a "dark" book about the brutal underside of European colonialism. In it a sea captain named Marlow goes to Brussels to sign a contract for a trip by riverboat into the Belgian Congo. In Brussels he finds a city so defined by buildings made of stone that it makes Marlow think of the city as "a whited sepulcher." There, among other things, he notices "grass sprouting between stones."

When teacher-priests and priestesses stumble across a conspicuous image they raise a hand and ask their students to stop, look, listen. What does this image say to them? How are the book's large themes suggested by small details? What can we discover about the whole from a tiny part? Pay attention. Think. Connect the dots. Evaluate. Respond.

From between the lines we create food for thought from grass sprouting between stones. Nature, we conclude from other clues too, is alive beneath the facades of the "whited sepulcher" city we call "civilized," and like a jungle its growth is irrepressible and wild. Civilization is "white" and the jungle is "dark," dangerously lurking to do us harm. Beneath the white veneer of civilization lurks a subversive "heart of darkness" that is persistent and perhaps more enduring than stones, bricks and mortar. Present in modern Brussels is Conrad's view of "Africa" and Belgium's Congo, an evil wilderness inhabited by "black" people. "The horror, the horror!"

Think. Explain. Is this true wholesale, in part, or not at all? Respond thoughtfully.

One bad habit I very much regret having developed

over a lifetime is the tendency to miss out on what's in front of my nose. When I take a walk I seldom see birds in trees or trees in bloom. I stare at sidewalks a lot, lost in the turns of thought or nonsense I'm trying to untwist. I have a recurrent nightmare: I'm alone on a city sidewalk and I look up to see a massive garbage truck bearing down on me.

My bad habit kicks into overdrive on sleepless nights during those long weeks of midsummer rain and oppressive heat. That's when I notice weeds sprouting between the slabs of concrete on my driveway and sidewalks. These weeds explode from their underground lairs in the middle of the night or when I chance to look the other way, and inevitably a certain mad desire for perfect order kicks in. The weeds have to go. They have no right to exist in gardens and lawns, or in the cracks between concrete slabs surrounding a civilized home. So I stoop, grab them by the hair as if they were juvenile delinquents, and begin tearing them out by the roots until nothing remains but the beauty of barren concrete.

I'm not one to use weed killer on the little beasts, for I'm nervous the killer might secrete itself into the actual house where I sleep. But after rounding up a handful or two of weeds I begin experiencing the peace that surpasses understanding that must enter the soul of every industrious farmer when he returns at sunset from another Roundup day for a good night of sleep: Perfect rows of nothing but soybeans and corn, straight as the yard marker lines on a football field, all the soybeans and corn standing at attention, saluting in unison as they pass in review before the setting sun. Not one weed rearing its delinquent head between all those tidy lines. No jungle in those purified perfect fields. Meanwhile, the weeds that survive stand outside barbed-wire fences looking in, big-eyed with curiosity.

By chance one day I nibbled on the leaf of a weed I was yanking from between the driveway concrete slabs. Weed-killing is sweaty work so when I wiped my face with my sleeve a bit of weed leaf slipped between my lips. In revenge I nipped at it. To my surprise its bitterness went down well with me. When my loco-biologist friend Bruno happened by on his bike I asked him about my tasty weed.

"Arugula," Bruno said. "You pay big-time for it in the store."

When I was a kid my father ate weeds—dandelion greens—that my mother picked tender and young right out of our front lawn. But I was too sweet a boy then to tolerate the taste of dandelions. I also had developed the conviction that real food comes from supermarkets, not dirt. Dandelions were embarrassingly homemade. Why couldn't we eat iceberg lettuce like my Norwegian friends, and Wonderbread instead of that crusty stuff my mom made in the oven at home even when it was 90 degrees outside?

After I slipped a few arugula leaves into my salad my mouth watered for more. I spent that night in a long dream that featured me, panting as I salivated over endless rows of arugula disappearing into the sunset like fields of soybeans and corn. I awoke to a more prosaic prospect: Why not farm arugula at home, just leave the plants alone in the cracks between a few well-chosen concrete slabs? I would have fewer weeds to pull. And to keep my car from crushing my crop I would get out my old bike. My heart, suddenly exercising my mind, said Yes!

Bruno happened by again as I was attacking a different gang of weeds hanging out behind the garage. He looked at me as if I were half-crazed as I was clubbing them to death. "Weeds!" I said as I stepped on their necks and chopped off their heads with my hoe.

"*Urtica Dioica*," he announced. "Great for treating arthritis. You just rub fresh leaves against the skin."

I yanked out a different weed.

"*Atropa Belladonna*," he said. "This is where the extract comes from for the drops your eye doctor uses for dilating the eye pupil." He pointed at a delinquent in what looked like a patch of grass. "*Rumex Crispus*. Beautiful. They taste like spinach when boiled. And there—*Taraxacum Officinalis*. You can eat the tender leaves and brew a delicious coffee from its roots."

Taraxacum Officinalis. Also known as dandelions.

"But I don't eat them," Bruno said, "because I love the yellow flowers they make."

Suddenly the weeds had names. And they could be beautiful. Why not allow the best and useful ones to fulfill their destinies? So my thinking about food for thought that comes from reading between the lines was turning toward thoughts about food made from greens sprouting between stones. Weeds, when they had names, became vegetables, herbs, medicinals. In tight small spaces a vast new world loomed, enlarging a New World already blessed with wide freeways and streets, hillsides, Great Lakes and smaller ones, purple mountain majesties, and amber waves of grain on the vast fields of the Great Plains. So much space had fallen into the cracks of my small consciousness: The two feet of dirt next to the garage; the vast expanses of lawn waiting to be reconfigured into gardens blooming with flowers and vegetables; the dull slabs of concrete repressing the witchery from which an apple, apricot, pear and cherry tree might blossom; the crawl spaces waiting for pole beans, cucumbers, zucchini, and grapes to climb

their walls; the ledge of a balcony overhang ripe for a pot
of basil or savory. As I began thinking small a vast new
world was growing in front of my nose.

Robert Engleman of Worldwatch tries to tell us what we
already suspect: "Half of the world's original forests have
been cleared for human land use, and UNEP (United
Nations Environmental Program) warns that the world's
fisheries will be effectively depleted by mid-century. The
world's area of cultivated land has expanded by about 13
percent since its measurement began in 1961, but the
doubling of world population since then means that each
of us can count on just half as much land as in 1961 to
produce the food we eat."

These warnings fall mainly on deaf ears. India's
population has passed the billion mark, China's closes in
on 1.4 billion, and even in the U.S., where wide open spaces
are still available for exploitation and use, population
grows even if its rate of increase slows. As we approach the
7 billion mark in a few more years the planet continues to
heat up, species become extinct, and increasingly toxic
oceans are being fished out. High-rises are the order of the
day in China, towering precipitously over landscapes.
When the earth's balance begins to wobble will these
towers tilt and come crashing down? Do we need wider
freeway lanes or more bike paths? Are we better off
chasing jobs hundreds of miles from home than we would
be creating work we can do within walking distance of our
front doors? Could we have a happy wonderland vacation
exploring the exotic spaces in our own back yards?

How we answer these vital questions depends
importantly on the names we use. If the grass growing
between stones is a "weed," the word makes a killer of us.
If it's a "jungle" down there with a "heart of darkness,"

then African and other rain forest regions are ripe for the rapacious exploitation visited on them by forces we misname "civilization." This misnomer makes it easier to make racists and killers of us.

In crazed moments I see myself as a Johnny Weedseeder weaving vast armies of soybeans and corn into a rich fabric of Edenic garden plots. Imagine how many cracks there are between all those rows of soybeans and corn—how *Taraxacum Officinalis, Rumex Crispus, Urtica Dioica,* and *Atropa Belladonna* could flourish there next to well-kept orchards and patches of tomato, pepper, eggplant and potato plants. All those straight lines would have to go, but I wouldn't really mind. My eye gravitates naturally toward beautiful curves.

As a child I was warned that if I stepped on a crack I'd break my mother's back. My effort to avoid those cracks probably helped spoil my view of whatever was going on all around, and even now as an adult I keep stepping over them. I'm not sure why. Maybe it's because it's not some evil heart of darkness lurking inside those cracks, some dark jungle we have to eradicate. Maybe it's one more expression of the miraculous creative force we still call Mother Earth.

Just Because

It seemed odd to be sitting on Nellie Dreiss' front porch, with nothing better on my mind than the massive maple across the street that, fifty years ago, probably was no taller than I was. My tree-gazing had me wondering: What moist rich loam was hidden deep inside the ground where the tree's roots spent decades quietly digging in and down? That tree had achieved a blossoming glory that had outlived Mrs. Dreiss and no doubt would leave me in the dust.

It's odd too that my sister Aurora had bought the house from Mrs. Dreiss. My sister, now retired, had been a school teacher for the better part of her life, so the old house, modest and well-kept, had a lineage of educators that went back almost a century.

I'm not sure I really liked Mrs. Dreiss. She was my English teacher for my senior year at Fordson High (in Dearborn, Michigan), and there were times when she rubbed me wrong. I somehow became aware of a controversy stirred by one of the papers I wrote for her class. Because I was a pitcher for the Fordson High varsity baseball team I resented the fact that our field didn't have a raised pitcher's mound. So I wrote a paper and made my pitch for raising the mound. At the time the English faculty at Fordson High apparently was having a debate about what subjects were worth writing about. Mr. Cardone, who the year before had required us to know the "arguments" for all the books of Milton's *Paradise Lost* (we were tested on them), thought it acceptable for me to write about raising a pitcher's mound. Mrs. Dreiss did not, because she did not find the topic sufficiently challenging.

The A-minus she gave me on the paper irked me, but I had to admit I liked her class. Everything we talked about was interesting, and everything seemed important and serious. We were never bored and usually left the class talking about what we had been talking about. I never knew what I was supposed to know or what would be on a test, and I can't remember what I learned.

What I remember most about her class are the words "ethical injustice" and "just because." The subject this time was Dostoyevsky's *Crime and Punishment*. In my review of the book I wrote that Raskolnikov, the book's main character, committed an "ethical injustice" when he split the old pawnbroker's head open with an axe. Mrs. Dreiss circled in red the words "ethical injustice" and covered them with a big question mark. What did they mean, these words?

My teacher and I had words in front of the whole class, in a conversation that went something like this:

"What those two words mean is obvious," I said.

"No, it's not," she replied. "Think about those two words, the way you put them together."

"What I mean is obvious," I said again. "Those words mean what I said."

"Are you sure they're saying what you think?" she came back at me.

We both raised our voices.

"It's obvious."

"How do you know it's obvious?"

"Because…"

"Because why?"

Her question floated in the air for the longest time, and I think I can still see everyone in the class looking up at it as if it were circling their minds too.

"Just…because," I said to put a stop to her silliness.

And everyone laughed.

Our little battle ended right there. She just smiled and nodded as she let go of me, allowing my self-esteem to have its little victory. I had the last word,

For years those words kept haunting me. "Ethical injustice." What Raskolnikov did to that poor woman was really wrong. How could I have been wrong about that?

I got a B-minus on the paper but had no complaints about the grade. *Crime and Punishment* had really grabbed me, but I also knew I had not given my paper enough time. She irked me, but somehow she just knew I hadn't given it my best.

Eventually I became an English teacher too. There I was, in front of all those eyes watching me the way I had eyed Mrs. Dreiss years ago. And one day, when I was well into my teaching career, I found myself drifting off into a deaf silence while I waited for a student to quit jabbering so I could enlighten him. The words "ethical injustice" crept into that deaf silence, and suddenly the lights went on.

Ethical injustice: An injustice that is ethical? Can injustices be ethical? Can ethics be unjust? What was I thinking when I wrote those words? I had said both more and less than I meant. I had not made sense.

Mrs. Dreiss already had retired by then, and my sister Aurora had bought her house without my knowing Mrs. Dreiss had spent the better part of her life in it. As I sat on the porch gazing at that massive maple tree across the street I began believing in ghosts.

I pay a lot of attention to words these days—not so much to spelling but to what words mean and how meaningless they so often are. I like breaking words open to see what's inside. The word "influence," for example, suggests "in-flowing," a concept so simple we seldom conjure it when we use the word. How do influences work? How do powers flow in—and out?

These days teachers are under intense pressure to make their influence obvious. They have to itemize their goals and objectives, dot every "i" on their lesson plans. Their worthiness is made dependent on their students passing standardized tests, and their teaching performance evaluation is tied to measurable results. I'd like to see a test that measures the curiosity, creativity, critical thinking, and no-nonsense seriousness Mrs. Dreiss generated in her talk-filled classroom years ago.

I see now that the untidy controversies that swirled in Mrs. Driess' classroom were part of her well-conceived plan to allow for the realistic free flow of important attitudes stirred by challenging subject matter. She became important to me because she was patient about outcomes, willing to wait years for the lights to go on, without being thanked. There is no test for what I eventually learned from her. Today she'd probably be sent off to summer school with orders to improve her lesson plans.

When I'm out and about with my sister she sometimes happens upon a student she had in one of her classes years ago. They always seem so pleased I'm sure some good in-flowing between them has occurred. I want Mrs. Dreiss to be more than a ghost in my sister's house. I'd like to thank her, yes, and tell her I became a teacher too—I'm not entirely sure why, one with a red pen in my mind poised to strike out at words that make no sense. And if she still has her red pen handy I'd like to put her to work improving some writing I've done that did not come about just because.

Diminishing Dots

The unveiling of the bronze statue of Minnesota Twins star slugger Kent Hrbek seems star-crossed to coincide roughly with the hundred-year anniversary of the sinking of the Titanic. Hrbek, no lightweight, was a titanic presence on the baseball field. Who can forget the home run he hit in 1987 (or was it 1991?) that won the World Series final game for the Twins? And who hasn't forgotten (or never known) that the Titans were a race of gods doomed to be overwhelmed by the Olympians, a coalition of younger gods?

I had the bronze statue of Hrbek on my mind when a friend of mine, a very bright pastor of a local church, confessed that he was afflicted by a bout of sermon block, a condition I routinely experience when I face the blank page with pen in hand. He was stressed about what message to deliver at the Easter Sunday morning service, a renewal celebration that also coincided with the sinking of the Titanic. What were my thoughts about that?

In my mind baseball's opening day is a renewal ritual too, a sign of spring that happily coincides with the rebirth Easter represents. Happily coinciding with pagan rituals that celebrate nature's cycles, Easter chimes Christian promises with ancient notions of natural recurrence and renewal. Though spring now and then can have a premature February birth that can start us fretting about whether we're doomed to experience the re-seasoning of our months into a long globally warmed summer of our discontent, we love to bask in the early blossomings that melt winter's frozen heart. Baseball, with its outfield and infield grasses, with its wind-ups and walks toward nine inning yawns, has all the excitement of a normal pregnancy. When baseball air is fragrant and warm it seems reassuring to be safe at home enjoying what's on our plate.

While the recent unveiling of the graven image of Hrbek shows him frozen in bronze, it also renews the Clark Kent stature that cooled when he became a TV salesman for air conditioners. As statue he hardens our memory of the slugger who hit that fateful home run in 1987 (or was it 1991?). If princes and popes once employed great artists to memorialize their kingdoms and Church, Hrbek's bronzed form puts a new shine on American glory. Children born after Twins World Series glory days can now learn history lessons by way of the teachable moments their parents offer them from Hrbek's bronzed form and games mainly watched on TV.

I've been fortunate enough to stand in European capital cities. I've spent hours there gawking at statues, many of them of gods and saints but also of heroes, kings, and generals. Most of their names I never knew or had forgotten, and often their victories seemed more hollow than the solid artwork of the nameless men (why always men?) who worked hours, even years, to carve the stones or cast the bronze. As I get older all the history I've learned seems to fail me in some way, because memory fails and because many of the history lessons I learned in younger years fail to pass the tests provided by time's shifty perspectives. Still, haunting questions keep resurrecting themselves. Who, really, were these men shaped in stone or bronze? Is their memory worth keeping alive in statues and history books? In some dim way their lives live on, famously, infamously, or, like most of us, anonymously. Are the famous worthy of their fame? What has fame to do with "the life of the spirit"? The philosopher in me also can't shut up: Does spirit have ongoing life?

I'm enough of a realist to believe what scientists say about energy: Except for the infinitesimal amounts lost through nuclear explosions, energy can change its forms but cannot be "destroyed." If life is an energy, it therefore lives on and on, even while human artifacts keep disappearing and we as individual identities bite the dust. My simple logic, therefore, concludes that everything achieved by Moses, Caligula, Napoleon, or John and Mary Doe, for good or ill, lives on in some form as a force in history. Everything ever caused has an ongoing effect, usually unfelt, invisible, not measurable, unnamed, and often unknowable. When tiny (or large) forces add up to push in the same direction, be it for good or ill, historians write books about "trends." They rarely use terms like "the life of the spirit" but don't shy away from referring to "the spirit of the times" or "the spirit of the age."

Some newer historians, perhaps tired of thinking of history as a succession of wars won and lost on dates students are required to memorize, have begun studying the impact of everyday people like you and me. What they study are small routine acts of ordinary folk, hoping to account, by their accumulated force, for the outcome of famous or infamous historical events. What is difficult to calculate and often overlooked as "alive" in "the spirit of the times" are routine failures to perform certain acts. What did German preachers and priests *not* say when Hitler was coming to power? How did "the life of the spirit" in thousands of German pulpits worm its silences into the "spirit of the times," and from there into the death chambers of Auschwitz and Dachau? That which doesn't appear to count often counts terribly, and wonderfully too. But it is difficult to cast in bronze those powerful words and deeds not said or done.

I'm finding it easier and harder to remember things. With a few clicks of my mouse I can access endless tidbits of recorded human history, trivial or not. I'm also so overwhelmed by the sheer mass of what's available to both know and believe that I'm rather paralyzed by most of it. A lot of my research now turns inward toward my own ignorance. How do I prioritize what's worth remembering, resurrecting and keeping alive as my own "life of the spirit"? It's tempting to gravitate with prejudice toward the merely cheerful. Cheerful optimism helps me feel good, especially when it's spring and another baseball season is coming around. But the confidence cheerfulness inspires dims when I wonder whether billions of people who refuse to recycle their waste can imagine a time when the seasons will discontinue their recycling on our behalf.

Fame and what we remember and value by it is, I suspect, mainly non-seasonal. Fame seems linear, its impact diminishing over time like a line of shrinking and disappearing dots. Who remembers the writers John Skelton or John Clare these days, for example, or reads their works or books about them? They are disappearing dots. And though Shakespeare and the Bible continue to have celebrity status and star power, they, their complex originals, also become diminishing dots when the big splashes made in their names read our minds rather than theirs. Like John Skelton's or John Clare's, the texts of these celebrity authors live mainly incognito, mainly—like the Bible— unread by millions of believers in Hebrew or Greek. Or English.

There's something to be said for losing our minds, as we inevitably will. If memory loss is one terrible way nature has of spring cleaning us, it's probably a natural and good thing that kids, most of them originally creative and curious, resist memorizing answers for standardized tests. They know enough to get even with tests by spitting lots of wrong answers out on them. Standardized fame in particular poses disposal problems. It's easy enough to diminish the once famous to small dots by forgetting them, but what do we do with statues cast in bronze? Memorabilia piles up over time and gets stuck on Ebay until luckily it's picked off by someone anonymous in cyberspace. Many memorable artifacts lose their place in history this way. Most don't lend themselves to composting, though they, like everything and everyone else, will turn into something else and have an ongoing existence, for good or ill.

This gives us good reason for profound cheer. Things become invisible, they lose their names and identities, and we all die. But "the life of the spirit," also invisible, lives on. New life becomes possible even as, and perhaps because, the old goes somewhere away into deep dark memory holes. Loss usually opens up new spaces and provides the opportunity to build something new, for good or ill.

So Easter rose again this year on the fragrant breath of new blossoming, even as the Titanic sank out of sight for the hundredth time. What suggestion could I make to my preacher friend with sermon block?

There's a book I can't forget and love to reread. It's called *Moby-Dick*, one of the most famous of all time. Though millions know the words "Moby-Dick," mainly from picture books and cartoons, only the rarest child will grow up to actually read the book beyond page two. So

Herman Melville's "classic" *Moby-Dick* is also a diminishing dot.

On the last page of that memorable book Ishmael, its main character, is saved from a sinking ship by his best friend's coffin. Ishmael then reappears on page one to tell his tale.

How Smart Is Dumb?

I recall how stupid I felt when I first learned about Howard Gardner's "Theory of Multiple Intelligences." Gardner, in his 1985 book *Frames of Mind*, tells us that "I.Q." should not be narrowly defined by intellectual capacity, or, in other words, the ability to "think." Rather, he says, there are diverse "intelligences"—Spatial, Linguistic, Logical-Mathematical, Musical, Interpersonal, Intrapersonal, Naturalistic, and Existential—each with a measurable I.Q. I'm convinced that there are a few others that never crossed his mind, especially when I look around and see how popular and shrewd some politicians are.

Gardner's theory has some appeal to me. In my vaguest moments I'm always sure my Existential I.Q. is operating in high gear. But most of the other intelligences on Gardner's list leave me feeling dumb, especially when I'm on the basketball and tennis courts and my Spatial I.Q. fails to figure out whether the ball should go in or over the net.

I wish I'd been savvy enough to think up Gardner's theory before it dawned on him. A fat book contract would help, given the big bucks we pay for my children to get a few college smarts. If I had a variety of smarts, I'd be less uptight about whether I'm making a smart-aleck of myself. What I don't know makes a big enough fool of me. During those brilliant moments when my Existential I.Q. kicks in I tend to stare wide-eyed at the black hole of the unknown, and that hole is so bottomless I get a profound view of how deep and wide my ignorance is. The insights I get down there, however, provide me some pleasures too. Because my lack is so low-down visible in that hole some of the guilt that attaches itself to the moral responsibility for overcoming my cluelessness gets lost in it. If my free-fall into the dark gets me off the hook, it gives me little shivers too: They're like the kicks we enjoyed as kids when we closed our eyes and chanted, "Ashes, ashes, we all fall down."

But these pleasures don't compensate for other reasons I have for feeling ignorant these days. For one thing, my mind shrinks at the thought of being globalized. When I contemplate how many multiple intelligences there must be in the whole world, most of them not speaking English, I get confused about what I'm supposed to know, and in what language. I'm told that China and India are full of geniuses. Is it too late to learn Chinese, and whatever it is they speak in India? The internet loses me too, makes me nostalgic for a plain and simple 24 volume set of *Encyclopedia Britannica.* I could get through one volume per month of that set and in two years end up feeling as if I had a Ph.D. in something. But the internet makes me an Alice in Wonderlander. A few clicks drop me into cyberspace's rabbit hole, where I drift in an endless swirl of unalphabetized infobit debris while I wonder which of the multiple intelligences I should invoke to give me grounding again. With so much infobit debris available it's no wonder standardized tests fail reality tests.

I'm also dizzied by the multiple intelligences that have no names. How do my two eyes know enough to get their acts together so I can see straight? How do flowers know enough about dirt to decide whether or not to blossom in it? How do butterflies know how to make themselves so beautiful before they fly to Mexico every fall? And how do some politicians know enough to make themselves successful and popular, especially those we enjoy calling stupid and dumb?

I don't think it's smart to call them stupid and dumb. Nobody would accuse two flowers or butterflies of being stupid and dumb. But we hear it said about certain politicians every day who have made it part of their mission to make non-credible, extremist, or those obviously false statements we used to call lies. As we laugh at and reject these politicians what we often forget is that they've learned how to make all sorts of multiple intelligences kick in lots of money to get them where they are. So they're maybe not as stupid and dumb as we think. I suspect it's very smart of them to get us calling them stupid and dumb.

I dimly remember the days when Ronald Reagan was running for president. I was one of the liberals sitting in my easy chair agreeing with other liberals that he was too stupid and dumb to be elected. While we sat around agreeing about how stupid and dumb he was an army of conservatives was busy organizing, creating think tanks and media outlets, and developing the vital strategies, alliances, and fund-raising schemes that have given liberals the politics they today think are stupid and dumb. We were oh so smart, while they were oh so busy getting political hard work done. They kicked our intellectual buttheads.

If I were a smart politician I'd play dumb now and then, and I'd want my rivals to call me dumb every time I agreed out loud with the crazy things a lot of people maybe believe. There's a lot to be ignorant about these days, but people as a rule don't enjoy being dumb. I'm one of them, except in my clueless Existential I.Q. moments. So if I'm feeling dumb and people call me dumb rather immediately I develop an urge to dislike them for accusing me of being what I don't enjoy being. I'm also likely to try to work harder to prove, at least to myself, that what I believe is not unbelievable. I gain strength for even my most unbelievable beliefs by identifying with those in high office who agree with me, those smart enough to use their multiple intelligences to become prominent by not calling me dumb. I make them more prominent when we agree to agree, and together we enjoy disliking people who accuse us of being what we don't enjoy being.

We win a lot of elections this way.

For good reason we should be suspicious of the high intelligence we associate with intellectuals. The best and the brightest Harvard minds coolly reasoned us into Vietnam and other wars, the geniuses at MIT have provided the fancy weaponry, and the think tanks "head-quartered" in Washington D.C. that help spread some of our current messes all over the planet are crowded with Ivy League success stories. It's useful to imagine that Dr. Kissinger's absent father was Dr. Frankenstein, and (I'm told by a liberal who really really knows) Dr. Strangelove is Dick Cheney's real dad. Would the world be better off if the great I.Q. of all these powerful men had been channeled into playing the violin, or hockey, instead?

What good does the wisdom of serpents do if doves fail to coo? What good is any intelligence if it fails to express the practical value of compassion and community? More good is likely to come from open ears than from open mouths. And minds often have less to say than hearts. A host of politicians endowed with all of Gardner's multiple intelligences would be fine, and several no doubt exist, but the nasty mouth of a genius gives off a nasty stench when it airs its nastiness out loud.

Intellectual Honesty

A lecture delivered at Winona State University, April 2008.

In his novel *Light in August*, that profound exploration of how one man, Joe Christmas, is violently victimized by his lack of knowledge and his murderer's perverted knowledge, William Faulkner begins Christmas' narrative with these enigmatic words: "Memory believes before knowing remembers, longer than knowing even wonders. Knows remembers believes a corridor in a big long garbled building of dark red brick." These suggestive words take us into the psychic corridor of the school where the conspiracy of circumstances that doom Christmas as an adult are set in motion. The passage at once distinguishes the mental powers—belief, knowledge, memory, and wonder—we so ineptly confuse as we try to find our way in our own schools and life journeys. More importantly, Faulkner prioritizes the mental powers and suggests how they work in combination as driving forces. "Memory believes *before* knowing remembers. Believes longer than recollects, longer than knowing even wonders." What we call the human mind works in complex but predictable ways. Belief, for better or worse, is the main force driving us, and memory (or recollection) follows belief, is prejudiced by it. Knowing comes in last.

If what Faulkner implies about human nature is true— that our hybrid psychic processes, and our actual lives, are driven most forcefully by belief—it would seem wise and practical, in institutions of higher learning, to explore with deep seriousness the relationship between knowledge and belief. I'll try to be intellectually honest with you. I'm not wholly equal to the task and suspect that my conclusions would be driven by my beliefs, colored by my memories, and clouded by my wondering.

What I offer here is much less than a new profound theory about how we can balance conflicting claims and arrive at truth: I present instead a few impressions, something of a sermon actually, about "intellectual honesty," a phrase I first heard in college many years ago.

Frankly, I haven't heard those two words very often recently. I seldom used the phrase in my own classrooms, assuming perhaps that it was unnecessary in a climate of opinion where the concept was supposed to be well understood, just everywhere out there in that classroom air. But the words were not in that rare air, and rarely used by faculty or administration colleagues. So I've begun (what Faulkner perhaps would call) wondering: Has my memory been failing me? Does the concept still have currency, perhaps in other terms? If so, what real viability does it have? What do I believe and know about intellectual honesty? What is intellectual honesty? Is it something I just made up? Is the concept, and the reality it is supposed to represent, terminally ill, maybe dead?

If so, I'll venture a revival by defining it into being, first by negation. In my mind, intellectual dishonesty should not be confused with sins such as stealing money, shoplifting, chasing after your neighbor's husband or wife, and even plagiarism. These sins strike me as simple-minded manifestations of small-minded moral inadequacy. These ways of missing the mark are what the Roman Catholic Church might call "venial," and if unredeemed Dante would reserve a few unpleasant gnarled circles of his Hell, maybe merely a time out in Purgatory, for offenders of this type. In Dante's scheme of things the deepest and worst circles of Hell are not for those who commit banal misdeeds or passionately hot sins of the flesh. The circles for the worst sinners are dark and cold. These are reserved for intellectual criminals, those whose violations of moral codes are coldly calculated and result in destructive consequences to great numbers of bystanders. Offenders in Dante's ninth circle of Hell are inflated with pride as they sit high in positions of power and influence, and their decisions do harm far beyond the individual offending self. I see intellectual dishonesty in this light. It is, if you'll pardon the religious language, a "Mortal Sin," a malignant cancer that destroys the very soul of human integrity. Its tentacles are particularly malicious when they get a grip on powerful individuals and institutions and then are secreted into the body politic.

To commit intellectual dishonesty is to violate, through calculation and/or cowardice, the dictates of the best available knowledge, either by omitting, ignoring, or distorting that knowledge. Individuals often do this consciously, but when the practice is popular it is easier for cowardice, unchecked by conscience, consciousness or professional standards, to have its way with us. If, as Socrates alleged, "The unexamined life is not worth living [I would say less worth living]," and if one special calling of a well-lived life is the pursuit of knowledge, then we, as professors of knowledge, have a moral obligation to base our conclusions on the best available scientific and rational knowledge derived from ongoing investigation, research, and criticism. An intellectually honest person is one who believes in honoring the dictates of reason, logic, and evidence. Such a person understands the limitations of a field of study, factors in uncomfortable evidence, and confronts misconceptions and deeply rooted prejudices by insisting that available knowledge provides a better claim to credibility.

This, of course, is very easy to do when we are in the know about the prejudices of others, but quite dicey when we're not in the know about our own. When "Memory believes before knowing remembers, longer than knowing even wonders," it is very difficult to put honest checks on our own beliefs.

The climate of opinion in which we operate—the cultural soup in which we swim and perhaps are sinking into—does not make our pilgrimages toward knowledge easier. Anti-intellectualism as a force in American history is well documented, and despite our technical and scientific know-how—perhaps in part because of it—we have a wide variety of cults and sects, religious and secular, that make intense emotion the authenticator of experience. It seems somewhat beyond belief that the very premises of the Enlightenment on which the modern university is grounded—the idea that scientific knowledge and rational criticism are the pillars of humane self-government— should be under deliberate and well-funded attack not only by foreigners but by powerful self-interest groups within our society that benefit from the modern secular university. What many once took for granted as an inviolable way of life—the life of the mind as celebrated by institutions of higher learning—is now directly challenged by cadres of confident true believers openly dedicated to undermining those aspects of rational and scientific learning that do not square with their beliefs. The persistent public squabbles over the scientific validity of the Theory of Evolution and global warming are obvious examples of belief's refusal to take a back seat to best available knowledge. The attacks on thousands of scientists painstakingly trying to gather and piece together the data to support plausible and probable assertions about these two subjects are waged with passionate convictions that obviate the need to play by the ordinary rules of evidence. Credibility is insisted on not as a matter of fact but of belief.

This problem is one of the subjects of Daniel Goleman's intriguing book, *Vital Lies, Simple Truths: The Psychology of Self-Deception* (Simon and Schuster, 1985). We stick our heads in the sand, Goleman explains, by keeping our mental gates locked to information that causes social strain and psychological pain. Studies of memory suggest that we are better at recalling information that magnifies our strengths and minimizes our weaknesses, and that depressed people do the opposite. "Groupthink" occurs when we ignore contradictory evidence and fail to exercise independent judgment out of fear of going against the tide. We also have our ways of creating frames of reference that screen in or out of awareness certain opinions and actions. Out of convenience we forget and forget we have forgotten. White and other lies at first get dismissed out of politeness, then from habit, and studies also suggest that as we age we get worse at lie detection and better at subtle and often quiet ways of "turning up the noise" level that will keep us distracted from painful facts. Our history books often reflect our various forms of amnesia, reflecting the implicitly understood and accepted rules about what questions can and cannot be asked. What results are blind spots, individual and collective, that are projected from immediate self-protective instincts that may do us great harm later on.

It is grimly ironic that the habit of intellectual dishonesty has been empowered by those brought to positions of influence by democratic Enlightenment traditions. What the [Founding Fathers] did not anticipate, writes Robert Parry of Consortium News, "was how fragile truth could become in a modern age of excessive government secrecy, hired-gun public relations and big-money media: [that] sophisticated manipulation of media is what would do the Republic in." The Orwellian slogan that Ignorance is Strength is detailed in a new book called *Failure of Intelligence: The Decline and Fall* of the CIA by former CIA analyst Melvin A. Goodman. Goodman relates how CIA analysts in the 1970's were encouraged to deliberately minimize reports of Soviet stagnation and to grossly inflate Soviet military expenditures, so that U.S. military spending could be dramatically increased to compete with what many senior CIA analysts considered phony Soviet threats.

The deputy director who made a career of changing CIA culture in the eighties so that its analysts set aside intellectually honest assessments of data in favor of skewed reports that followed political agendas was Robert Gates, Director of the CIA under President George H.W. Bush, Secretary of Defense under two presidents, past President of Texas A & M. University, and current Chancellor of the College of William and Mary. For the past twenty-five years, concludes Goodman, the CIA's moral compass has failed. The result has been "an unending cycle of failure to tell truth to power." It is any wonder then that military spending under President Reagan more than doubled as the Soviet Union disintegrated and the Berlin Wall fell, or that compliant CIA operatives could be used by President George W. Bush to corroborate his false claim that there were weapons of mass destruction in Iraq?

Were we surprised to learn from David Barstow of the

New York Times (April 20, 2008) that the Pentagon had a special program of hiring high ranking retired military officers to be the "hidden hand" delivering the Bush administration's party line on the war? Were we morally outraged, merely depressed, or looking the other way when we learned that public funds were used to create a propaganda machine aimed at the public, that most of the so-called analysts had lucrative financial ties to military contractors, and that the TV networks ignored the business and political connections of these hired hands?

And doesn't it seem like business as usual when Juliet Eilperin of the *Washington Post* (June 3, 2008) tells us: "An investigation by the NASA inspector general found that political appointees in the space agency's public affairs office worked to control and distort public accounts of its researchers' findings about climate change for at least two years."

And are we surprised to learn from *Discover* magazine that researchers for drug companies have routinely designed and interpreted their own studies "in ways that make even ineffective drugs seem like life savers," because industry sponsorship of studies is "likely to yield pro-industry results." (*Discover*, July 2008).

I could go on and on with examples of this kind.

We have, I think, good reason to be alarmed and a long way to go to put our house in order. That decadence and corruption exist at the highest political and professional levels suggests not merely that it will trickle by example down to the rest of us, but that it has trickled up from us because we have let ourselves be dumbed down.

What should especially trouble us about these institutional distortions of truth is the quietly insidious way both the perpetrators and audience for the deceptions accept them as a way of life. We now think of "spin"—the twisting and turning of information so that it serves special interest purposes—as what makes the world go around, a skill now routinely taught to and learned by those selling products, ideas, public policies, salvation schemes, and college communication and marketing courses. I'd like to suggest that spin only seems natural and right if, to use Huck Finn's words, we are "brung up that way." As our impulse toward honesty has gone silent or in hiding, our leaders—political and professional—reflect in large measure who we have allowed ourselves to become. When knowledge is politicized, when science is driven by market forces and government contracts, and when a profession is conceived as a club or self-interest group rather than as a cooperative association of passionate practitioners defined by the codes appropriate to a field's standards of inquiry and conduct, how do we tell the truth about a product or manufacturing process our supervisor does not want to hear? How do we take time to explore a glitch when further study might delay a production plan? How difficult is it for a newspaper editor to craft an honest well considered opinion piece when a corporation that doesn't like the opinion has just paid for a full page ad in the editor's newspaper? How can we be plain spoken about the professional inadequacy of a friend up for tenure or promotion when we bowl on Tuesday nights with that friend? Do we say, "It is impossible to praise this person highly enough"?

In a culture in which spin is the norm, how can spin not enter the classroom too?

Intellectual honesty is, I believe, under siege in part because of unprecedented technological and cultural circumstances not given sufficient critical scrutiny. Let me mention just three: First, the sheer quantity of information now available via the internet is mind-boggling and so often free of responsible oversight that it is tempting to become cynical about the possibility of establishing credible knowledge. On a whim I Googled "Capital Punishment" and was greeted with 4,590,000 possible sources of information, opinion, knowledge or wisdom concerning this subject. I then narrowed my search to "Capital Punishment Deterrent" (437,000 sources) and "Capital Punishment Does it Deter" (352,000 sources). If I were a student this overwhelming quantity of possible information would not inspire me to sort, distill and evaluate: It probably would send me quietly screaming away, or looking for an easy way out. What we used to call "news" is another example. Robert Darnton, discussing "The Library of the New Age" (*NYRB*, June 12, 2008) says, "News in the information age has broken loose from its conventional moorings, creating possibilities for misinformation on a global scale. We live in a time of unprecedented accessibility to information that is increasingly unreliable." Though news has always reflected a point of view, the accepted professional standards of news reporting are now easily ignored by anyone with a web page or blog. We have allowed our democracy and technology to take us into an age when everyone has a right to an opinion, and all opinions, currently available by the billions to millions with a mouse, seem equal.

Secondly, our video technologies have made it possible for whole generations of youth and adults to accept consumerism's self-promotional devices as a way of life that glamorizes deception. Most of us spend countless hours in front of various screens, with literally years of our lifetimes spent glued to commercials whose irresistibility depends on deception, distortion, and distraction, the clever manipulation of suggestions and symbols calculated to persuade us to buy things for mainly irrelevant and irrational reasons we are not given enough time to consciously think through. It is inevitable that we become in part what we consume—compliantly amused and conditioned by all those entertaining commercials and their alluring spin on things. How can we expect all this spin not to dizzy us, make the grounds of our knowledge uncertain, and the roads to narcissism and relativism wider?

Thirdly, we seem to be normalizing a culture in which the conflicting claims of religious belief and science are not being adjusted or reconciled. Our fragmentation of education is in part responsible for this failure, especially when education is narrowly tied to strictly vocational outcomes. The humanities too often turn a blind eye to the sciences and the sciences look down on the humanities, and the different modes of discourse they use to investigate and interpret experience are often—I think unnecessarily—seen as mutually exclusive. This bifurcation has allowed the gulf between popular science and popular religion to persist, indeed widen in recent years. While religious true believers see science and reason as threats, many in the science and technology fields live double lives: In their work they abide by the strict grammars of science, engineering, and mathematics while simultaneously believing, rather literally, in Noah's ark, Jesus walking on water, and the Four Horsemen of the Apocalypse. If knowing follows belief, as Faulkner claims, and if educators fail to resolve their conflicting claims, is it any wonder that religion and politics often trump science? When intellect, emotion and imagination fail to integrate their differences and that failure becomes a cultural norm, is it any wonder that intellectual honesty falls outside the norm?

We should not be surprised to see universities and the knowledge they profess lose their credibility and their authority undermined. Several belief systems offer seekers the opportunity to enjoy emotional expression, a genuine sense of community, and the secure sense of order provided by stories that imply simple, and in the worst cases, final solutions to all problems. As anxieties resulting from global pollution, plague, proliferation, and overpopulation increase we can expect the attraction of belief systems to intensify. This spells trouble for weak-kneed knowledge. "Memory believes before knowing remembers, longer than knowing even wonders."

Belief is, I believe, necessary to our lives, and if, as the biblical wise man tells us, knowledge is sorrow, how can we justify what we do as professors of knowledge? How, in short, can knowledge have a say that might help balance a world trying to make sense of belief? We might begin by renewing our vows—make intellectual honesty the central article of faith in a deeply felt belief system we understand, share, and are willing to explain to people outside our comfort zones. We need no theology to do this, and it does not preclude merrily serving our private gods, or none at all. A recommitment to honoring and insisting on the rules of evidence and honest inquiry is long overdue. This creed would express itself in ritual practices, and above all it would require us to engage in an ongoing and open discussion of our moral choices and ethical standards. If we also deeply believe what we profess, and communicate to our students that we are passionate in our belief, then memory (call it our sense of history), knowledge (our arts, sciences, and criticism), and wonder (our hungering curiosity to know), may achieve new respect in our communities.

What are some basic ritual practices that might help generate this new respect?

First, knowledge promoters, educators, need to conduct ongoing discussions of professional standards. A profession is made credible by the quality of the knowledge its professors profess, not by the salaries they command. Nor is a profession made honorable when its members close ranks or slip into cowardly silence when the need to speak out is clear. Professionalism requires the articulation of the standards by which we empower ourselves to arrive at informed judgments in our disciplines.

It should go without saying that we need to maintain courteous, civil and open classrooms and lecture halls, in which individuals are invited to express contrary views. We especially need to invite into open discussion the most challenging contrary views, and to both present and address these views in their strongest terms. It is important that we approach conflicting claims from the inside, empathetically, so we see them in their best light. The hopeful promise that intellectual integrity is based on is that students will gravitate toward the more convincing claims, that they will be stronger for having seen the best claims against a position they take. And it is important to take these habits of mind on the road, into communities threatened by or unfamiliar with serious intellectual pursuits. Like a good basketball team, we need to gain respect away from home, especially when the referees of discourse are unfairly calling fouls on us.

We need to teach intellectual honesty as a concept both by example and by direct application to specific problems.

A warning in a syllabus about plagiarism will not do. And we need new pedagogies to address the problems intellectual honesty poses. These pedagogies must go beyond insisting on and testing for "right answers." They need to emphasize the processes of thought and investigation by which we arrive at answers. In particular they should confront the fact that many students link learning with entertainment. How can honest learning be taught in a way that brings deeply felt pleasure? We might begin by emphasizing that learning is a quest rather than a product to be bought and sold, and that as such it offers the allure of the unknown and pleasures of the quest.

We especially need to be critical of our language and able to explain in clear terms the theories of knowledge that are the bases of our fields of study. Though they belong to different orders of mind, words like "fact," "statement of fact," "knowledge," "opinion," and "belief" are often used interchangeably, and a scientific theory is often equated with a so-called "theory" based on mythology, uninformed opinion, or personal whim. And let's be frank: We need to call silly ideas and beliefs "superstitious" when that's exactly what they are. When we lose control of our language, fail to make it precise and meaningful, we can expect it to control us. Words like "maybe," "let's see," and "we don't know" should be regular parts of our vocabulary. We should be proud professionals wary of that other kind of pride, hubris, that likes to visit insecure people who prefer to think highly of themselves.

Let's be honest about what we profess: It's limited, cumulative, revisable, and subject to the blind spots inherent in our minds and instruments of measurement. The knowledges we offer to the world are merely likely probable and only rarely probably certainly the latest word. Though the scientific conclusions about Evolution and greenhouse warming are highly probably accurate, the studies are ongoing. In a good university the book is never closed on any topic. Secure within the belief structure of our knowledge cult is a special agnosticism working to energize rather than depress our curiosity about life. It is this that makes us merely and wonderfully a community of learners working to improve our world.

I find useful the distinctions made by James Carse (longtime director of religious studies at NYU) in his new book, *The Religious Case Against Belief*. There Carse distinguishes "ordinary ignorance" ("I don't know the dimensions of a standard canoe, but maybe I can figure them out"), from "willful ignorance" ("Don't tell me what my wife did with him in that canoe, because I don't want to know"). But then there is what Carse calls "higher ignorance" ("We may never know what gravitational effect one molecule of a canoe might have on the most distant star in our galaxy, but if we knew how to figure that out we would"). Higher ignorance is earned through careful study and through an exhaustive search of the sources of evidence. It is all the blank walls we hit after trying our best to see our way through them. This kind of searching is profoundly complicated—and perhaps made exciting and pleasurable—by the self-examination of our own private beliefs. Perhaps our exams should also test the quality of what we do not know. Higher ignorance is the degree every university graduate should attain.

Faulkner begins Joe Christmas' life journey in the corridor of a garbled school when Joe is a five year-old, and Joe dies thirty-three years later crouched behind a kitchen table, never having stepped foot in a university and never having that possibility enter his mind. Faulkner makes it poignantly clear that what killed him was a man, yes, an individual named Percy Grimm, but also a character who personifies the pattern of belief systems that link sex, race, and religion with violence. It should be obvious to all of us that many Percy Grimms are still with us. The suddenly enlarged small global world has many passionate believers not above violently trying to impose their views about sex, race, and religion. And we at home also have our own profit-driven business and scientific interests eager to magnify the destructiveness of war machines. We have a lot of important work to do, and need to do a much better job of giving our educators and our own Percy Grimms something better to believe.

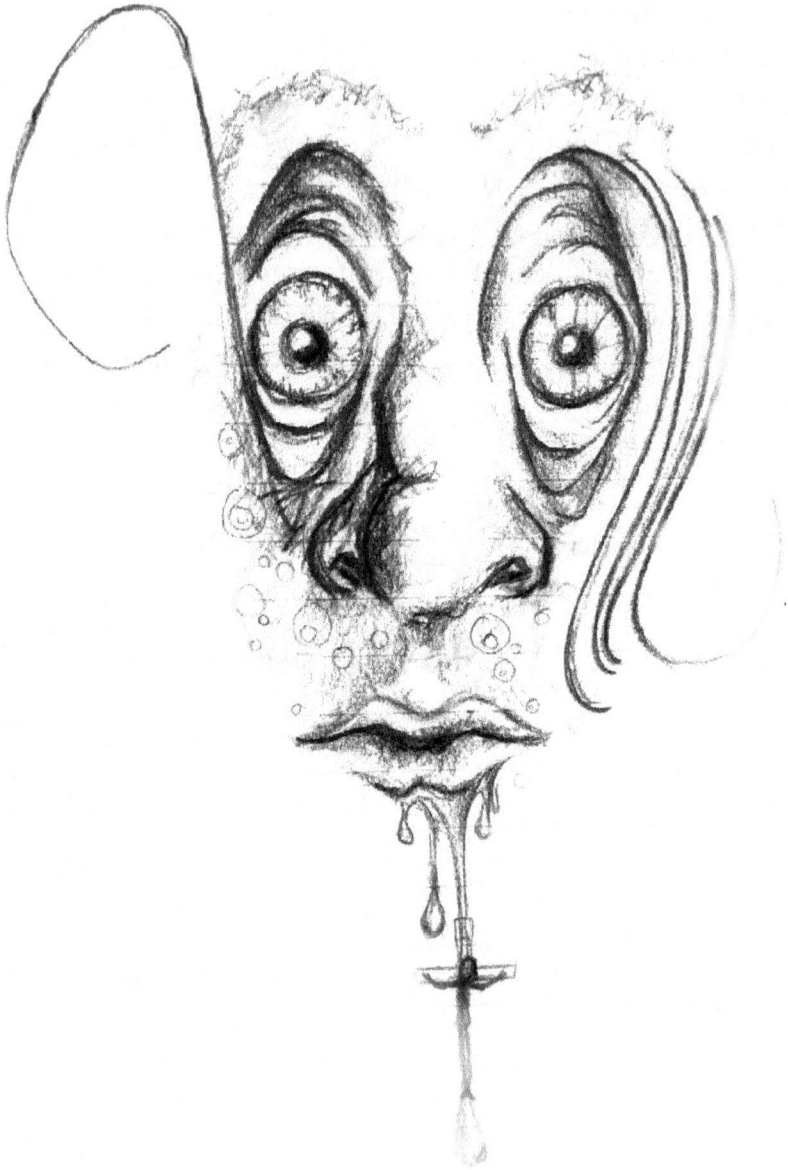

Advice to Spencer

Why should I presume? What advice can I—an old guy likely to confuse his aches and pains with the collapse of the entire world—give to a sixteen-year-old boy wondering what to make of his life? Old fools qualify best for the wisdom of age. I'm happily defunct—retired on a pension, with mortgage and health insurance paid, and some savings for rainy days that don't seem to be letting up. And you, Spencer, are sweet sixteen—creative, articulate, smart, lively, and polite, with the good sense and decency to be one of my son's very best friends. What wisdom can I offer in this Halloween season, which marks the advent of the Christmas shopping season and birth of the seven billionth human being on planet earth? Think of me as a pumpkin-head, my words of advice exhausted by the eerie glow of teeth and eyes lit by a stubby flickering candle inside.

One advantage of being gray is that I'm beginning to match how I see the world. The other is that I have less time to worry about the consequences of saying something stupid and wrong. It frees me up to speed my advice on its way.

It's also comforting to have some research data on my side, especially when anti-government slugs—white collar minds that spend hours sitting on their hands—have taught themselves to point a finger of blame all around without giving any thought to that finger's inability to turn itself around. The good news they think is bad is this: College students prefer to work in government. In a survey of recent college grads, conducted by the National

Association of Colleges and Employers, students expecting to graduate with B.A. degrees by the end of 2013 chose government work as their top choice, with human services, education, and social services their next highest preferences. Far below in their rankings were careers in finance, retail trade, computer and electronic manufacturing, other manufacturing, and oil and gas extraction.

We told you so, is what the nay-saying fickle finger must be telling itself. Government is bad, and this generation of college students has turned out bad because of it. Their schools and teachers are also bad, because when children go to schools where cooperation and self-esteem are taught they want to make a career out of practicing cooperation and self-esteem. A generation of young people who care so deeply about government, human services, education, and social services that they actually want to get paid for doing things like that must be suffering from the morally corrosive influence of teachers in the public schools. Why, the anti-Darwin social Darwinists must be asking themselves, can't everyone be like us, busy devising new ways to cut government, human services, education, and social services? Why do so many students get college degrees without being gung-ho about investment opportunities? Why do they put so little faith in oil and gas extraction? Don't they believe in futures?

It would be easy to conclude that the current generation of college grads has bought into the cynicism driving a lot of noisy public discourse today. While begging for more tax breaks and government perks the fickle finger points at the grads and accuses them of wanting to freeload on the government gravy train.

Could it be that college grads are hoping to find work that addresses serious needs? It's apparent that helping the needy is good for individuals and communities, and that new B.A. grads are willing enough suppliers. "The motivation to work in the public sector stems from a desire to help others," says Melissa Emerson, who serves on the American Society for Public Administration's national council. It's obvious that many governmental and educational programs do a lot to help others, and that the finger-pointers would rather just sit and complain while spending millions on politicians paid to make sure their unfavorite parts of government don't work.

So, Spencer, here's the advice I am not giving you: You can do whatever you want, if you try hard enough. Please don't believe you can be rich and famous, if you work hard enough at it, or rich and anonymous. Or that you should go west, young man, and follow the American Dream all the way to California's San Andreas fault. Or go for broke brokering real estate, for example, because as the earth shrinks under the press of seven billion souls, housing bubbles may burst but property prices are sure to re-inflate, and slum lords will have especially bloated success stories to tell.

So here's what I do advise: Beware the Empire State Building promise of the American Dream, Spencer. Hard work will not necessarily get you the life you want. Ask bean pickers in the fields how hard they work and how far they've come, often in the hope of having a few beans in their pots back home. Good solid Americans are supposed to dream big, and their dreams are supposed to make them famous and rich. Like thousands of lost boys on the playgrounds of Philadelphia and Detroit, I know you like to shoot baskets in the back yard. Do you think that any amount of practice is likely to propel you, or those thousands of lost boys, into the NBA? A lot of dreams, Spencer, are clueless and big. As the earth shrinks it will have better room for dreams that are smart and small.

It's obvious, Spencer, that in you there's an artist, not a lab technician or engineer. So I advise you to avoid unnatural acts. The political squeeze is on for true-blue American kids to take crash courses in math and technology so they can out-engineer the millions of Asians who already have taken advanced versions of those courses. But those Asians are waiting in lines to work for wages that wouldn't amount to peanuts in your home town. Can we STEM the tide of Asian brilliance and hard work while preventing the theft and recycling of our patented techno-properties? I doubt it. Do you, born with a compassionate artist's heart and mind, want to beat your brains out doing something you hate so you can finish with the pack in an endless global race?

Why not slow down and smell the flowers, Spencer, so you can see straight into the core of crooked realities with enough good sense to tell the difference between necessities and junk. Henry Ford was a genius whose sense of art was careless enough to be indifferent to the junk, toxins and wars his gadgets have created for us worldwide. Do we need more Henry Fords to invent gadgets that will allow a couple billion more cars in China and India to run in the exhausted air they emit, or do we need artists to conceive communities that can get by just fine without or with fewer cars?

I want you to be a realist, Spencer. Fifty years ago the earth had (only) three billion souls to feed. By 1999 we had six billion, and if current trends continue we will have eight billion in a decade or two. Pollution, global warming, and wars cast dark shadows over all the hope in your heart. So you need to be clear about what these shadows mean to you. There's a bottomless difference, Spencer, between cynicism, skepticism, and pessimism. Cynicism is the self-defeating and wholly demoralized belief that says "Everything sucks." You hear a lot of young people saying it these days. To the cynic, everything sucks. Nothing is worthwhile and nothing is better or worse. Cynics respond to life by dragging everything and everyone down to their mind-blown level, and also by trying to suck everything out of life without giving anything back. A skeptic is not necessarily a cynic. A skeptic takes a wait-and-see approach, questions authority, and subjects all beliefs to credibility tests. Skepticism is vital to critical thinking, and critical thinking is where good judgment comes from. A lot of pessimists are critical thinkers. A pessimist is one who sees the dark side of things, without necessarily becoming cynical. Pessimists tend to be realists, especially in these troubled times. A pessimist worries that tuna sandwiches made from real fish, Spencer, may become extinct. This pessimistic possibility also may be realistic and has to be looked at clearly. A realist is one who uses critical thinking to discern what necessities are, and it seems realistic to conclude that tuna fish are becoming increasingly scarce on the steadily shrinking and exhausted planet that is your primary place of residence, and your only source of water and food.

A lot of skeptical realists are especially pessimistic about current models of economic growth. They see these models as unsustainable and disastrous to the human race. But realists also understand the importance of "following the money" and "growing the economy." Currently a lot of important people are quite unrealistic. They think we'll be better off by having more stuff, especially the engines that feast on the oil and gas needed to feed millions more engines rapidly exhausting the air, water, soil, and parking spaces that 7,000,000,000 souls find more than merely convenient and fun. What's worse is that a lot of these important people spend their energies promoting an unrealistic paper economy that grows profits but not lettuce, beans, goats, arts and services. This paper economy exists mainly in cyberspace, and it promotes mainly its own growth. With an alarming percentage of the Ivy League's best and brightest graduates opting to become bankers, investment brokers and financial gurus, a lot of our nation's geniuses have addicted themselves to casino life. Well stocked with funds provided by the pensions and savings of working people, they sit behind computer monitors, hedge their Wall Street bets, and wait for tidbits of good news that will momentarily drive Wall Street numbers up. A lot of them, relatively risk free, lose a lot of money that is not theirs, and get rich doing it. Millionaire Wall Street geniuses currently have markedly devalued the fortunes of ordinary people who live on the Main Streets of our cities and towns. As a lot of these financial gurus became very rich gambling at the Wall Street casinos, even after the bad news that hit hard in 2008, we, back home, were too confused to ask what their betting had to do with our lettuce, beans, goats, art and human services.

Make a list, Spencer, of peoples' basic necessities. Live according to the necessities. Start with food, shelter, and clothing, then work your way up. Above all remember this: Food does not come from supermarkets. Then observe the squirrels, rabbits, and birds in your neighborhood. Note that they go naked all winter long and that most manage to survive to see the next spring. They huddle with other squirrels, rabbits and birds, and know the efficiency and pleasures of small spaces. And thrift stores offer great clothing deals, even on labels that have come back into fashion.

Live where there's an abundance of fresh water, even if it's frozen half the year.

Live where you don't have to wear a mask to breathe the air.

Live where body heat is a valuable natural resource, especially in the winter months.

Live where there's a bit of dirt to grow veggies in, at least during the unfrozen part of the year. A back yard or lawn space will do, and it doesn't take much dirt if it's black enough. Very small spaces also work. You can't grow pumpkins there, but arugula sprouts inside sidewalk cracks.

What advice can I give you, Spencer, about pursuing a career, especially since you'll be competing with 7,000,000,000 people wondering what to do with themselves? Hustlers say, "Follow the money." I say, "Follow the necessities," because money necessarily follows necessities too. Make a list of what people really need, and if you think smart and small some of them may pay you to provide those needs.

Here are other basic necessities, beyond the ones listed above.

Health care.
Education.
Human services.
Creativity.
Loving care.

197

Please note, Spencer, that we have certain standard ways of providing some of these necessities to some of our citizens. Those who can afford it go to doctors, schools, and supermarkets, so you one day could become a nurse, teacher, or butcher and have a salary. But most of the people who provide the five basic necessities mentioned above do it for free. They are the wives, grandmothers, brothers, sisters, neighbors, and strangers to those in need. They don't have regular jobs and salaries for providing the necessities for the many who need them. So your major challenge, Spencer, and the major challenge of your generation, is to get your money's worth for the valuable and necessary work you do for the millions who need your talents and services.

How can you get paid for doing good and necessary work? The artist in you, Spencer, is alive and well in you. Keep nourishing that good source of necessary life. Then make what's necessary in you available to others who need it too. You could teach, Spencer, perhaps in a school but also perhaps in a shop on main street or in a nursing home. You could become a leader in your community, conveying your understanding of art to design new neighborhoods and towns that work efficiently without or with fewer cars. You could mentor and be an example to others who know that creativity is a necessity but don't know how to realize it in themselves. Dare to dream new forms. Dare to express to the world how necessary your well-wrought visions are.

But be a realist. Only a few like you, Spencer, will realize their dreams unless the funny-money afloat in Wall Street cyberspace has a conversion experience. The billions of dollars that flow from Main Street into Wall Street accounts go there on the paltry strength of thousands of mouse-clicks per minute. Those billions of dollars need to stay—

and come back—home. Home is where the heart is. Home is where the clearest sense of what is necessary and good lives as happily ever after as possible. Home is where we get to know the names of the people who need health care, human services, education, creativity, loving care, food, clothing, and shelter. Home is where new companies, capitalized by local cooperatives and local banks, can spring into being for the purpose of employing people able to provide necessities to people willing to pay reasonable sums for them. You will need to discover what necessary work you can provide. Do your homework. Call it market research. How many people, especially the increasing millions of the retired, need what you can provide? What can they afford, and how can you make yourself affordable? The greater the need, the greater your career opportunities. But make this a rule: You don't want work that will make someone else poor. You will support generous collective programs, including those undertaken by governments, that help the poor.

Keep clear in your mind what work is. Work is what you don't want to do but believe you have to do, usually for money. If you love your work you will want to do it, and if there's love in your work your work will be easier to enjoy. When you want to do your work it becomes more like play. Think about this when you meditate on how you want to spend the rest of your life.

But you also will have to be realistic and strong, Spencer. Money doesn't trickle down naturally from cyberspace casinos into real places we can be proud to call home. It trickles more unnaturally up into the cyberspace bank accounts of the rich. When you are realistic you understand that the casino players are playing for keeps and will try to humiliate you. Their habits won't just go away. You,

Spencer, will have to deal with addicted, sly, pathetic, fanatical and nasty individuals, and some also will be very nice people who live next door. Most are single-minded optimists. A few will call you a loser, or worse, and you will have to acquire the habit of seldom baring your fangs as you turn the other cheek.

Are you up to it, Spencer? Do you see the challenges and opportunities? Do you dare to dream new forms?

Meanwhile, the price of food, clothing and shelter will increase. These are still necessities, and it is natural that necessary things will have prices that reflect their value. But you will have fewer gadgets and toys, Spencer, and more hours to spend with friends, family and art. Perhaps you one day will take the time to read Henry David Thoreau's book *Walden*, especially its first chapter called "Economy."

Meanwhile, Spencer, cultivate what's nicely growing in you—your curiosity, creativity, critical thinking, and sense of community. Read good books, see good movies (only), hang around smart teachers and disagree with them when they're being stupid again. Do your art, love doing it, and love it when it's done right. Broaden your learning and deepen your sense of life by going away from home, far away to strange but safe places. Be wide-eyed there, and talk to ordinary folk. Learn their languages, and learn from the realists you meet what you can do better next time. Then return to a place you discover or re-discover and begin to call home. Make a home of it by loving where you live. Think long and hard about taking a job you don't really want in a place you don't really want to live. You may have a job but not a home.

Play clean and hard. Exercise daily. Eat fresh fruit and veggies. Learn how to cook them to perfection. Make pilgrimages to sources of clean fresh water.

Look up. As Halloween pumpkins—and the vampires, zombies, and ghouls who hover near them—deliver us into the Christmas shopping season, a big moon sits pregnant in the early November sky. Soon the Wall Street seismographers will record the latest blips: The Dow Jones Average, Consumer Index, Standard and Poor's, and Moody's will be up or down. But even if all the moody economic indicators are up they will leave most of us unsatisfied, hungry for more. Once upon a time that big autumn moon was called a Harvest Moon, and a lot of people ate (rather than wasted) pumpkins out of necessity. They were plenty good enough. A few weeks ago my daughter baked one to perfection for me. From her I learned that when properly prepared a pumpkin is inexpensive, satisfying and wonderful.

One more thing you are required to do: Keep your friend, my son, from harm.

Spencer Hodge: Portrait

Endnote: Commencement Exercises

As it confronts advancing age my mind's vacations go south. It can't remember B.F. Skinner's precise words, so "Our education is the sum total of everything we've forgotten," will have to equal what he really said. Skinner's words make a landfill of "mind," with Dr. Freud's hot coals buried there along with Plato's airy ideas and sociology and History 101 and the MBA seminar on how to succeed at Insider Trading. Everything thrown into our mind dump exudes opinions like gas.

I find comfort and hope from the stews provided by the accumulations of self down there. One way or another our lives add up to something that has gravity and depth, a seething compost that exudes its stinks and fragrances from sources invisible to the eyes of those who make noise with words. Buried deepest in that compost is the child we once were, loved or neglected and abused from day one. That child makes my nose mindful of ecologies, notably the enduring health sustained by the moral structure of good art, how what goes in keeps coming up, and goes around. That alone gives my work purpose, and good reason to have fun doing it.

V.   Embracing Technology
(from *The Oxymoronic Dictionary*)

Participial modifier with singular noun

1. A mating game that pairs humans with mechanical devices equipped with invisible robotic hands engineered to get a death grip on their assets. Once it has begun the mating ritual of devices is impossible to call off, as they busily reinvent themselves through successive generations until their human partners are too broke or too broken to tear themselves away from the required affection.

Antonyms: Fresh air. Fertile soil. Clean water.

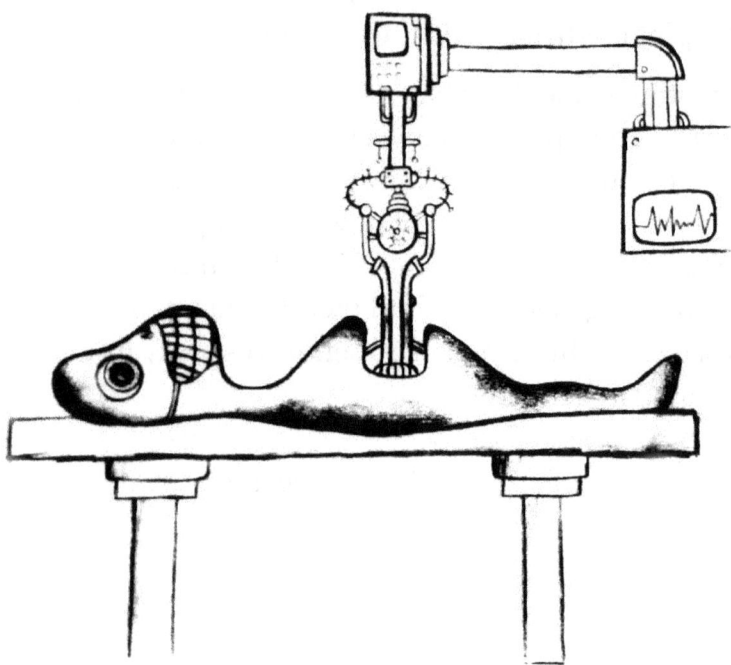

Blonk Blues

Imagine not finding one under the tree. So put yourself in my place when I take it upon myself to lead my wife to it in the garage. Then try to understand the glee that possesses me as I throw back the sheet. "I bought one for the whole family," I announce. "We are now proud owners of our own Blonk."

It took all three of us to carry the Blonk into the house, a journey that got stuck at the back door with the debate about whether to put it in the basement den or in the living room next to the TV. I prevailed. Everyone would want to Blonk, so why make them go all the way downstairs?

Blonking took a long time to catch on, arriving by fits and starts from its Asian origins. It caught on first in Oregon, then slowly spread its wings north to Seattle and south to L.A. The Rockies may have slowed its passage east, but once the first Blonk parlor opened in Greeley truckfuls of Blonks streamed over Great Plains freeways on their way to the salons of Cape Cod and the coastal Maine resorts.

Those of you who have Blonked know why it can't be dismissed as a passing fad. To Blonk is like nothing, and everything, else, engaging its devotees in a performance at once mystical and cardiovascular. The Blonk as thing is simple enough: A pyramidical cone, its shape not unlike a squat Christmas tree, its base made of a material heavy and dense, and its apogee silver-tipped. Though it seems to weigh in at half a ton, its gravity is carefully honed to concentrate the high energy its use is designed to generate.

Its design is simple and brilliant, and it comes in a variety of subtle hues.

A glance at the Blonk manual reveals that mastery requires the subject to twirl with increasing intensity around the Blonk's cone without losing touch of the silver apogee. Endurance and a deft touch are required if certain quality benchmarks are to be achieved, and it's no wonder that only a few Blonkers, mainly Asians, have become Masters. These Masters, at once esthetes and ascetics, have devoted themselves to teaching neophyte Blonkers worldwide about the symbiotic relationship between the cone and psychic centers of gravitas. Their discipline emphasizes how subject and object become one in the course of a well-executed twirl, how we can approach the ecstasy of mystical delirium as the twirl increases its acceleration rate, and how, more than anything, it is important not to lose touch.

Blonking for the many is an entertainment (merely). For some it is a skill. For the few, like me, it is performance art. Guiltless pleasures are hard to come by these days.

Like any serious form of art Blonking requires passion, commitment, and perfect form. And there is a price to be paid by devoted practitioners. Did my dedication to Blonking lead to slippage in my performance at work? That is an opinionated subject about which I keep a dignified silence. Nor do I regret troubling my family to move the TV rather than the Blonk into the basement den. What comes of artists who surrender the high ground, notably in the privacy of their own homes? The cost to dignity is directly proportional to decline in artistic value, especially when one factors in the not inconsiderable price of a single Blonk cone, with the final payment not soon in the mail. When one is free to practice one's art in the comfort of one's home, one is best situated not only to set one's sights on the perfection of the Blonking art but on the art's organic relationship to real life.

My individual progress was visible for more than seven months, refining itself into difficult small increments that made the going more polished and smooth. All was going well until the fateful moment struck when we suddenly were forced to count our blessings while licking our wounds. My doctor, who seems immune, gave me the bad news. His surgical manuals had led him to the conclusion that my Blonking days were kaput. How seldom we reap what we sow. I had suffered a tear in my transverse abdominals, and they were hyperextended beyond repair. His verdict was final: More Blonking would tear me apart.

So there it stood, in the middle of the living room. "You'll have to get it out of here," said my wife. "It's ruining the rug. It's leaving a black mark." I couldn't agree with her, though I noticed a shadow sagging into the floor.

I said my farewell, and with the help of neighbors we moved it to the garage. "It can't stay there," my wife informed me. "I keep banging the door on it whenever I try to get out of the car."

I had it moved to the back yard, quietly troubled to see its colors fade in the glaring sun. "It can't stay there," I told my wife. "There's a blackbird that sits on the apogee and besplatters it. I throw stones but the blackbird's always there again when I turn my back. Do you expect me to spend my whole life in the yard throwing stones?"

I insisted on moving it into the basement den, and my son moved the TV back upstairs to the living room. At Christmas time I found a ping-pong table waiting for me on the front porch, a gift from my wife who wanted it for our son. "Where are we going to find room for a ping-pong table?" I asked.

"I was thinking of the basement den," she replied. "The living room rug is a mess, with that big circle in it. The vacuum won't suck up the damage done by your Blonk."

"Why don't we buy a bigger house?" asked my son.

The ping-pong table moved in and the Blonk moved into the yard again, covered this time by a tarp. My blackbird friend called all his friends to make regular visits to the tarp, and the cone began to list after heavy rains because our Beagle named Bella was digging around its rim.

It did not help to discover that the standard Blonk was becoming as much a thing of the past as the Model T, replaced by aggressively marketed imitations customized to factor in individual body weights, heights, and diet regimes.

"Yours is maybe collectible," said my wife. "Let's sell."

Her suggestion opened a vacancy in my heart. I wanted to ask, "Don't you love me?" but I kept the question locked inside. How could I explain to her my need for a good Blonking now and then?

The home economist in her prevailed, but no one responded to our classified ad.

"Let's have a garage sale," she said.

"Maybe if we put a good enough price on it," was all I could think to say.

We lugged it back into the garage, and this time I'm the one who put the dent in the door trying to get out of the car.

"We'll have to park the car in the driveway from now on, until the garage sale is done."

People came and went, starting at seven a.m. on Saturday. They bought my old jeans and shirts, boxfuls of yarn, mysteries, bagfuls of old screws, forks and spoons, picture frames, an old TV and stereo, hubcaps, Bella's sofa-bed, and a rickety Christmas stand. Almost everything went, except three old computers. And the Blonk.

"We did pretty well," said my wife. "Let's have a yard sale next week. We could put a special price on The Thing."

"You want to move it again?"

"Do you want to park the car in the garage ever again?"

The yard sale came and went, but the Blonk stayed in the yard. A lot of people looked at it, then looked away from me, with either guilt or derision in their eyes. I lugged it to the curb and hung a sign around its neck: "FREE TO A GOOD HOME." It reminded me of a man standing next to a traffic jam while holding up a sign, "WILL WORK FOR FOOD."

No one stopped for it.

I made the call, but the trash hauler shook his head no. "Sorry, we can't take Blonks. The landfill is full up with them, can't take in any more. Plus, they leech. And I wouldn't try burning it. It's like setting fire to a mountain of old tires."

"What should I do with it?"

He shook his head sadly and walked to his truck. "I know one guy who tried cutting it up, but it cost him a fortune in carbide saw blades. Maybe you could paint it to look like a Christmas tree. Or something."

The garage was out as a place to landfill the thing. She'd moved the car back in. And the yard was out. The blackbirds would drive me insane.

"Where we going with it now?" asked my son.

"Back inside."

"Dad, how much did you pay for this? You could have bought me new video games, or a new wide-screen, or a pool table like I keep asking for, or a neat ATV, or motorcycle, or an exercise machine for Mom, or a rider mower, or a nice little boat. Dad, can we get a new car? The old one has that terrible dent in the door."

I got him to help me lug it into the living room, right next to the TV. We were very careful to put it right over its footprint already pressed into the rug.

"If that thing stays, I'm moving out," said my wife. She stormed out and I heard her talking to herself in the laundry room as I stood there gazing at it. An odd thing happened as my gaze turned into a stare. The Blonk seemed to swell right before my eyes, looking right through me as I shrank.

"Only the Dose Permits Something Not to Be Poisonous"

I'm proud that my sixteen-year-old son has chosen to tack a poster of Albert Einstein rather than Elvis or LeBron James on his bedroom wall. "I have no special talents," Einstein says in bold black lettering, "I am only passionately curious." But nowhere on that poster are the worry-wart concerns Einstein expressed to his scientific colleagues in 1952: "The scientist of today is distressed by the fact that the results of his scientific work have created a threat to mankind since they have fallen into the hands of morally blind exponents of political power...[and] that technological methods, made possible by [the scientist's] work, have led to a concentration of economic and also of political power in the hands of small minorities which have come to dominate completely the lives of the masses of people."

Too many words for a poster. And too much philosophizing, especially since Einstein admits he has no special talents. Our geniuses are especially useful to us when they stick to specialized tasks like doing the hard math we don't really care about.

The Einstein poster came to mind when I was standing in line at the post office, behind a grandfatherly gent sporting a floppy Green Bay Packers sweatshirt. The post office, facing budget issues, had cut back on its workforce, so it had only two clerks on the job to take care of people in long lines. Both clerks had cartoons of dead mayflies taped to the counters where they worked: "Why mayflies never go to the P.O."

The gent in front of me looked tired and wan but also affable and sane. Why not have a good social chat? I was curious about his thoughts.

Like good neighbors we immediately agreed to agree. It was cold outside. The line was too long. Mayflies seldom survive post office visits. There is never enough help. Government spending needs to be restrained. There is a lot of waste. Gas costs too much. The gent's SUV costs too much. Our wars cost too much, and they have soured us. We had propped up too many dictators and now we were stuck with them. A small minority of individuals are getting fabulously rich. Some people don't earn their money, and too many are out of work. The economy needs fixing.

I offered a modest suggestion for jumpstarting a solution to the immediate problem of waiting too long in the post office line: Impose a modest tax on immodestly wealthy millionaires.

His face seemed innocent, so I imagined him to be a good enough Lutheran, Catholic, Baptist or Methodist sharing the fishes and loaves. But it's clear that he was thinking in wholesale rather than parochial terms when he offered his solution to the problem of standing too long in line at the post office: "Nuke them all." That's what he said. He did not mean we should nuke the millionaires. His quick-fix silver bullet solution to our woes was to use nuclear bombs to "turn all those places into a parking lot." "Those places" he was referring to were biblical lands or neighbors of biblical lands, somewhere.

I didn't ask if his solution to our problems derived from what he had learned in the church of his choice, but I was still curious: Was he serious?

"Yes," he said, "and a lot of people think like me."

"You mean, just push a button and we'd be done with it?"

"Yep."

It's particularly troubling that he wasn't an oddball, because I like certain oddballs. One of them is Kevin, a distinguished chemical engineer who loves to talk about home-brewed beer while drinking it. Recently Kevin was passionate about a biography of Paracelsus he had just read. Paracelsus (or Philippus Aureolus Theophrastus Bombastus von Hohenheim) was a scientist who lived between 1493 and 1541. He was one of the Einsteins of his day, though his theories and achievements, which left his mark on the studies of medicine, chemistry, and botany, seem occult by contemporary standards. Notable is the rule that he, as "father of toxicology," brought to the attention of my brew-swigging friend Kevin. "All things are poison," Paracelsus said, "and nothing is without poison; only the dose permits something not to be poison."

The rule's obvious applications come to mind—pesticides, fertilizers, cars, cell phones, X-rays, chemotherapy, beer—but Paracelsus believed that the rule applied to any alchemy resulting from mixing the human and natural. Toxins result, in short, whenever people meddle with earth, air, water, and fire to invent something new. Though historians are in the dark about whether Paracelsus owned a cat, or if the cat's curiosity killed it off, it's clear that Paracelsus, like Einstein, was a worry-wart. He knew well the warnings broadcast about the legendary medieval maverick Dr. Faustus, who sold his soul to the devil to get access to nature's terrible mysteries. If he were alive today Paracelsus would say that Dr. Faustus, not Einstein, was the true father of the nuclear bomb.

I don't suppose we can keep from poisoning ourselves, and the best we can do is live in the hope that the poisons we brew will work like flu shots. Some won't. The problem is not that we're not all Einsteins; it's that a lot of us are passionately curious. And because we're curious we make things out of earth, air, water, and fire, and then we try selling them. Though selling goods, services and patents is not always the same as selling a soul, making and selling things is what we do, whether it's art, artificial flavorings, or nuclear bombs. As our numbers increase and multiply, we naturally should expect to find it harder to escape the stews we brew. And as the stews we stir ourselves into become more unnatural, so will we.

I eat a carrot and apple a day by taking my vitamin pill, but if there were a vitamin button to push I'd rather push it than eat a pill. Like the gent in the post office I like to push buttons to get things done, and it's clear that we've evolved beyond buttons made of flesh and bone. I push a button to unlock the door of my car, another button to open the window, still others to turn on the air conditioner and radio. From my cell phone I call my daughters in Iowa or Brussels. On my computer my mouse lets me surf and stream. If there were buttons for lowering deficits, for taking boredom out of schools, for preventing the extinction of tigers and lions, and for cleaning the kitty litter box, I'd push them all. It's a hard-wired habit hard to break, and I am hooked.

My son, who knows how to push my buttons, tells me not to worry because we're smarter now than geniuses were in the old days. He pushes buttons in his sleep. We have smart-pads, smart-phones, and smart-boards, he says, and we've got robots who work while we play computer games. Computers have shrunk centuries worth of human history into a memory chip, and they also know how to beat us at chess and bridge. Anything we want to know is a mouse-click away, and everyone in the world is wired like never before. Who needs Einstein to solve math problems when the answers are on-line?

Already we have smart bombs activated by buttons pushed thousands of miles away from the people they kill. Stuart Wolf, who worked on an early version of the Internet, is looking not very far ahead. He sees the development of a headband that "feeds directly into the brain and lets us, among other things, talk without speaking, see around corners, and drive by thinking." He also envisions soldiers wearing battlefield "thought helmets" that will enable them to "communicate wordlessly by translating brain waves." (*NYRB*, June 23, 2011).

It blows my mind.

So why should we expect the gentleman in the post office line to lag behind the times? Humans, not animals and goat-herders in biblical lands, push buttons when there are problems to solve. Biology is slow and low down. Tech is fast and high.

I push a pause button in my mind to zero out the thought of using a brain helmet to do my talking for me. There's much to be said for nature taking its course in old-fashioned ways. The gentleman waiting in line at the post office, his words still ringing in my ears, also needed to get a piece of my mind. Does he think that any of our technologies will allow us to win wars without us experiencing the wars? In some probably unintended way will we not experience the technologies we deploy? The gap between future technologies and video games is narrowing, but will drones, movies and prayer get us through our current wars? Nuclear bombs, I say to him, are weird devices whose friendly fire makes everyone its enemies, but so far they have proven useful only when not used. These inventions, extraordinary concoctions of earth, air, water and fire, are extraordinarily toxic. Is there a proper dose? What would Paracelsus say?

Political geniuses tell us we should focus more narrowly on the economy. We should make hay from the messes we've made. As I search my soul to find some way to contribute to growth a light goes on in my mind, a wonderful new opportunity for ambitious investors, engineers, and entrepreneurs. I see a lot of people walking the streets with wires coming in and out of their pockets, coats, collars and ears. It's getting harder to distinguish humans from their instruments. Even Paracelsus would agree that all the wires necessary to being properly wired give us a slovenly look not unlike Einstein's hair. I therefore visualize a vast market for push-button and mouse-pad vests, and new lines of outer and underwear capable of making fashion statements that address the realities of our times. The underwear line would privatize all unsightly hookups, and mouse-pad wear could be specially tailored to be cozy and warm. Instead of being made from inert pieces of bone, the push-buttons on new vestments could be cut from a variety of soft pelts certain to provide a menu of soothing touch-response options. Specialty lines could be developed to appeal to a growing mass market of individualists feeling a deep need to be directly engaged by remote control to the facts of real life. Both the push-button and mouse-pad vestment lines could be programmed to satisfy privatized gratification impulses, and would come in many colors and styles.

My soul is a shabby thing so no one would think of buying it, but my new product line ideas are for sale, starting now, to the highest bidder.

It's the kind of investment that might appeal to the wan-faced gentleman who waited in line with me at the post office. His Green Bay Packer sweatshirt looked loose on him, maybe because it had to make room for an artificial heart.

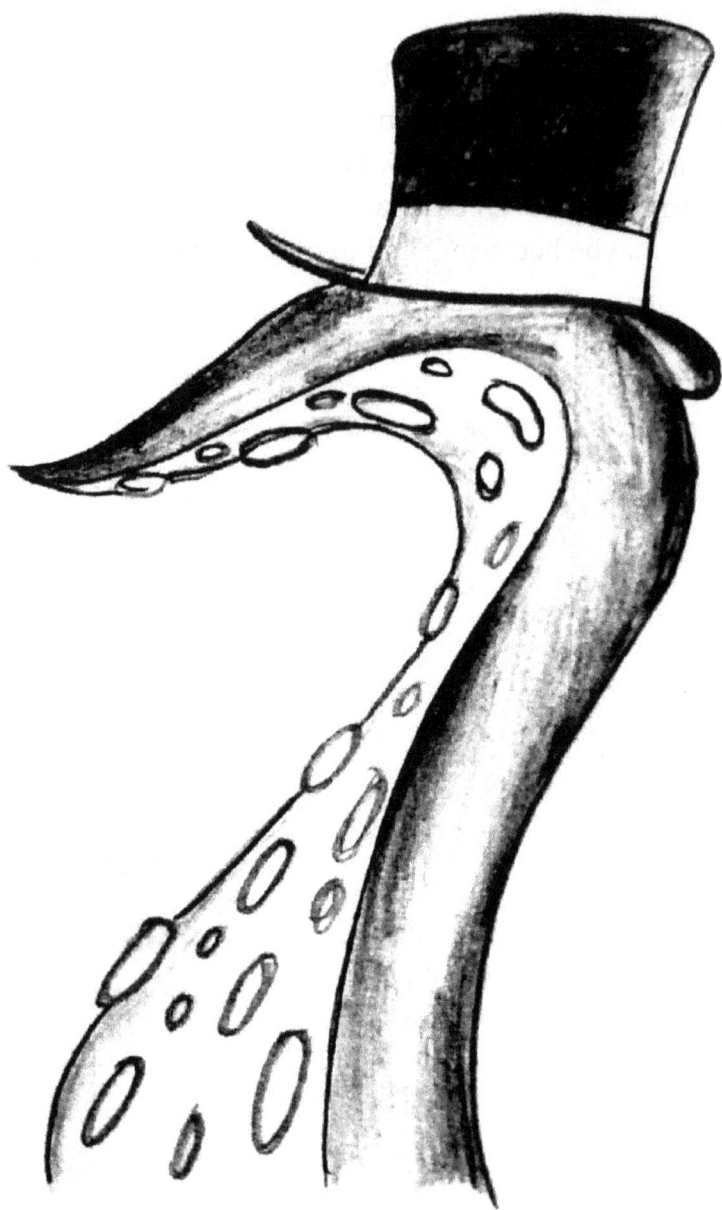

Making Small Waves

On the TV screen the images the tsunami left behind look at once familiar and bizarre. Wide swaths of trash— the wreckage of appliances, houses, cars, furniture—swept along as if by an off-camera bulldozer doing an ordinary day's work at a landfill without end. There's a soothing feel to the lava flow rhythm of the trash, as if the monstrous mass has a mind of its own and is in no hurry to get to wherever it's going. Even the largest TV shrinks the terrible offscreen facts into frames resembling the paintings of abstract expressionists. We gaze at the pictures on our small instruments, curious and amazed at being so quickly in the know, with our sense that knowledge is power retreating from us with the flow. So compelling is the moving mass that the smoldering nuclear plant in the distance is like white noise, out of sight and out of mind.

We stand transfixed, knowing that children were also swept away into a vast landfill that once was a landscape of city and countryside. We're not sure what to feel. What we see is so compelling we can't turn away, but our technologies shrink and distance the destruction so far from us it's hard to feel it's real. We turn away to our daily routines to keep our imaginations in check, and our hearts from melting down.

Our hearts and minds are equally stunned if we pause long enough to imagine that the victims have actual names, friends, cousins, lovers. It's hard to believe in suffering so unimaginable, and suddenly it's harder to believe what we believe. If God caused this devastation or simply allowed it to occur, then God is a nightmare character in an absurd world. If we believe that the destruction is the work of Nature rather than God, it's hard to picture a decent role for Mother Earth on a planet imagined as green. We sink into the dazed existential incomprehension resembling despair. Who can gain true solace from the fact that we didn't, by chance and accident of birth, happen to be at the wrong place at the wrong time? Does being alive and safe make us happy?

We need a good story to console and give us good reason to go on. We retell ourselves the usual one: This is all part of God's plot. The victims are minor characters in a moral drama with a rapture happy ending for those who can force themselves into believing the myth. Or. Mother Nature—like the lovely women we see at the outdoor market selling veggies—has gone berserk because her children are making a mess of her home. She'll show us a thing or two, including the brutal power of her underside. If we behave better in the coming years, maybe she'll look like meadows and exude the fragrance of spring flowers again.

But I'm innocent, we say. I didn't create the huge geological formations that cause tsunamis. Blame God or Mother Nature for that. I'm just another ant lucky enough not to be swept away. I'm next to nothing, really, so what do you expect from me?

I'm also clever enough to look askance at the fire and smoke coming from the nuclear energy plant. Plant? Like a green thing that grows naturally from the soil? Or is it a human monster now, carefully constructed from crude concrete, steel and subtle alchemies?

I convince myself I'm not responsible for tidal waves, so I point my finger at God or Mother Earth. Then I turn on the lights, and the furnace, microwave, refrigerator, and TV, and someday in my greenest hope I'll own an electric car. Why not two? What do smoldering nuclear reactors in Japan have to do with me? I'm a nobody, working hard to be somebody who someday has two clean electric cars.

The fallout:

The Minnesota House is trying to pass a bill reversing the ban on building nuclear power plants in the state.

Tokyo Electric Power Company (TEPKO) wants to build two new nuclear reactors on the south Texas shore of the Gulf of Mexico. The Obama administration has asked for a $4 billion loan guarantee for the project, and for $56 billion to be spent on nuclear reactors in other states.

According to Greg Palast, who has been a lead investigator of nuclear plant fraud and racketeering for the U.S. government, it was Stone and Webster, a company which falsified its "SQ" or "Seismic Qualification" certification for the Shoreham nuclear facility in New York by changing the test scores from "failed" to "passed," that is scheduled to work with TEPKO to build the new Gulf of Mexico plant. Stone and Webster's phony certification is what we call a lie.

Nobody can agree about what to do with spent nuclear waste. In Minnesota spent nuclear waste rods are stacked somewhere near the nuclear plant in Red Wing.

Nobody seems to want them, especially in Nevada.

Children living in the area of the Chernobyl nuclear disaster that occurred in 1986 have a ten times greater incidence of thyroid cancer than children elsewhere. Everybody knows why. The spreadsheets don't have enough room to count the health related costs, and some fear that doing so might lead to a tax increase.

Nuclear power plants seem to be vulnerable and likely

targets for terrorist attacks. Can such attacks be prevented? At what cost?

And in case you haven't heard: On March 12, 2011, German citizens demanding a moratorium on new nuclear plant construction formed a human chain that stretched for 27 miles.

Some of them no doubt have an important story to tell, one that gives everyone a small part to play in an ongoing narrative. It begins with the players being shaken awake by an earthquake in a faraway land. Individuals are suddenly in the dark but not afraid of the powers of darkness they need to confront, and they know they need to do something to save themselves. The action scenes are boring, wordy and long. There are thousands of heroes and heroines in this narrative, not just one or a few, and they do not trust technologies that destroy or create. They are always unsure of themselves, small candles walking carefully in the dark, driven to go on not by what they can do but what they ought to do in the small houses, towns, and neighborhoods where they actually live. They turn off the lamp in an empty room, knowing they can't throw the switches that dim the gaudy lights in Nevada and Hollywood. They walk a lot and spread the word. In the face of the huge problems they have to confront, they hope not to win or succeed, but to carry on.

They make small waves.

Who Knows

As a small-fry writer I have a professional interest in being well-known. Celebrity is an American gross national product routinely converted into cash, and cash comes in handy when the bills come due. Celebrity, especially in the entertainment industry, more easily spawns cash if there are dirty little secrets involved. I personally entertain loads of dirty little secrets, but my small-fry status as writer has crippled me when it comes to the cash.

I'm hoping that government will make me famous in a way one of those Hollywood columnists never could. I'm certain that every government agency, state and federal, knows enough to provide the economic and social security I long for. They have a right to my Social Security number, but their police scanners read my license plate as I drive down a freeway, their highway department knows I have astigmatism, and our Department of Homeland Security knows how many times I use a phone so smart its IQ is higher than mine. I don't know what else government agencies know about me, but I wish I knew who to call whenever one of those Socratic moods comes on requiring me to know myself.

Though I haven't been able to translate what's known about me into the fame that also brings in the cash, I'm certain my government knows me in a special way. I'll let you in on one of my dirty little secrets: The FBI has been watching me for years. This is something I know, even if I'm like millions of other average Americans who know but can't prove what they know.

When I was a young college professor I was front and center at some demonstrations against the Vietnam war. Nothing illegal or violent happened at these events, and nothing nearly good enough to put a timely end to the war. But during the demonstrations a couple complete strangers were taking pictures of everyone, especially me (it seemed), as I marched along in the front row. No one knew who these strangers were, where they came from, or why they were taking pictures of everyone. They were not press photographers. If they were, they were also liars.

I think I know they were FBI agents. Though I'm right-handed I happened to be carrying my protest sign with my left hand, at a time when J. Edgar Hoover was zeroed in on all organizations and individuals with anything leftward about them. So I'm sure the FBI has a file on me that includes the pictures those strangers took. I'm also sure that the file the FBI had on me ended up in the IRS data bank, because well, why not, I could be a dangerous radical.

Those who imagine themselves to be Tea Party folk, with their complaints about government inefficiency, should be irate it took the IRS so long to pay special attention to them. I think it's because the IRS has been too busy with people like me. Year after year the IRS kept auditing my small-fry income tax returns, without finding anything wrong. It is true that my Ph.D. in English did not qualify me to understand IRS forms, but I somehow muddled through and paid what was due on time. Did I dare complain—tell them, for example, to go after GM or GE or AT&T instead? I didn't because I felt sorry for the IRS snoops. I could see on their faces that they had too much to do.

Sadly, my redundant encounters with the IRS did

nothing to further my literary career. Though I was known (if unread, and not wholly understood) by two powerful government agencies with enormous public presence, I could not translate what they knew about me into the celebrity sure to generate the kind of big-time cash that would inspire the IRS to ignore me.

I can think of only one way the government can provide me the celebrity my literary career deserves. I'd have to go public with something that's nobody's business. Somebody in government probably knows where I take a leak, but it hates leaks of matters it deems sensitive. The cash I'd get from my celebrity as a leaker would be substantial if I were in exile or on the lamb, but I doubt I'd enjoy it much in a prison cell. So if I had something worth leaking I'd probably contain the urge.

I'm also reluctant to ask for state sponsorship of my celebrity, in part because the fairness issues are complex and unique to our times. In a democracy is it fair for a government to know a lot about me without my knowing what the government knows? Or does? Do we dare call it treason when the government robs our private data bank? Do we have a right to ask the government to return what it has secretly taken from us, and how do we do this if we don't know it has been stealing from us? What is a fair free market fee for information taken from us? The FBI charges a fee to citizens who want to know if the FBI has a file on them, and another fee if they want to see everything on the file the FBI hasn't blacked out. Can we be blackmailed for asking to see what's been blacked out?

These questions are so knotty I can't help but feel sympathy for government information gatherers. But they can't compete with the private sector. If Socrates said that self-knowledge was the work of a lifetime, the marketplace now has made that workload manageable and profitable. The marketplace knows more about me than the government does. It knows stuff about me I can't fathom myself. Amazon.com knows what books I read and which ones are good for me. The woman in the GPS system of my car knows better than I do where I'm going, and she is not shy about expressing her views. Sears keeps me in spare change by reminding me I have an unspent $14.00 coupon, and Sears, always open on Sundays and Saturdays, also seems to have taken an interest in our entire society's spiritual well-being. Coupon points, I'm reminded, "apply automatically toward our redemption, in store or online at Sears."

A few years ago I Googled myself for the first time, suddenly gratified to find myself widely known in cyberspace. There, in that airlessness, all my books were listed, as were facts about myself I didn't know about myself. There, for example, I discovered that I'm in footnotes written by authors who remain entire strangers to me. There was an Emilio DeGrazia who also had a fig tree in his back yard. It could have been me, but he had just died in Connecticut. Google's attention to detail is remarkable, but that one got me thinking more deeply about how easy it is now to be dead but not gone, and whether timeless writers will have to share their immortality with just everyone.

Neil Postman, in his timely 1986 book *Amusing Ourselves to Death,* foreshadowed the privacy issues we face today. Postman argued that staring for hours at the TV, currently deemed by many to be a low tech offspring of primitive minds, was making us stupider and more vulnerable to government control. Our entertainments, said Postman, would require us to "amuse ourselves to death."

Mind control, he claimed, comes in two forms. One way is described in George Orwell's *1984*. There Big Brother's telescreens and agents watch and know everything about us. In Orwell's totalitarian world the control apparatus is pervasive, hard-wired, and brutal. Aldous Huxley's *Brave New World* offers an entirely different, call it a "soft" approach, to mind control. In Huxley's society pleasure is the control mechanism of choice, notably mind-numbing "Soma" pills that the population loves to eat.

TV, argued Postman, was creating not Orwell's totalitarian nightmare but Huxley's pleasure-driven mindlessness. A former chairperson of the Federal Communications Commission, he did not live long enough to write a book about where we are now—trying to figure out how to muddle along in a time when Orwell's and Huxley's nightmare views seem to apply simultaneously. Government and the marketplace both have technologies with Orwellian capacities, and both have their ways of feeding us "Soma" pleasures that seem to diminish our capacity to be alert critical thinkers eager to engage ourselves in the self-government required of successful democracies.

If government plays the Big Brother part, the enterprising spirit of our free enterprise system skimps on the freedom part. The private sector, while lobbying publicly for fewer controls on its privacy, wants total freedom to know more and more about me. We are being profiled now as we speak to each other here. And there is no shortage of entrepreneurs eager to supply the demands government makes on businesses eager to help government take our privacy from us. Verizon, a Fortune 500 enterprise, is happy to accept the millions the U.S. government pays for telephone taps of Verizon calls. When asked if AT&T, Sprint, and T-Mobile were in on the scheme to develop "megadata" for the National Security Agency, each offered "no comment" as a reply. They want to keep what they're doing a secret, and in Orwell's world no means yes. Government snooping on our privacy would be starved without the harvest of profits corporations and private contractors enjoy at public expense. Which private sector self-interest groups hate government most? I'd say it's those having promiscuous love affairs with government agencies.

As I learn more about what's going on behind my back, I'm getting used to looking forward to a future in which loss of privacy is a default setting. The new technologies boggle, while probably reading, my mind. Lasers see in the dark and peer through walls. Hand-held gizmos put me on somebody's radar screens. Google-Earth allows me to see my cousin Pasquale standing in front of his house in a village in Italy. Body and brain scans reveal naked truths about what's going on deeply within, while technicians unscramble my genetic codes. My dirty little secrets are no longer sacred. Meanwhile, drones somehow know enough to blow up somebody's house with somebody in it somebody thinks is my enemy.

I think we rather love these technological breakthroughs. They're good for private sector business, and their exponential development and spread is good for the economy. For now. We want to retool college educations so we can train more people to use the newest technologies, so we keep gearing up to enable ourselves to improve our snooping. Long-distance thinking suggests that as we use our new technologies we become complicit in the outcomes they produce, but long-distance thoughts don't have lasting power in a culture that values the momentary good. And because so many of the new technologies entertain us while doing us some good, it's difficult not to become addicted to them. While they pile up high in hills of trash they go down as easy as Soma pills.

But scary genies have escaped and there's no stuffing them back into the vials where they belong. Techno-wizards are working hard to manufacture robots and brains, and maybe one day the brain machines will also have minds. Then, of course, the real hard work will begin: Developing a conscience for the things.

As our sense of self-control becomes more wired it's not likely we'll get a big kick out of checks and balances. And who will insist on the wisdom of bothering with knowledge when there's so much entertaining information at our fingertips?

We have good reason now to believe in Santa. Both government and the private sector already know if we've been good or bad, so we'd better be good for goodness' sake. Those who cheat on their taxes, those who launder millions, those who hide assets in foreign banks, those addicted to sexual exploitation and insider trading, those CEOs, college presidents, football coaches, and others who can't be shamed by absurdly high salaries—all these have good reason to fear snoopy technologies. In a time when it's fashionable to blame anything that goes wrong on "government," the private sector has a weak case to make against government snoops who spy on all of us because two or three demented zealots might be trying to blow up New York City.

Because I now believe in Santa again, I made a New Year's resolution last Christmas Eve: I will speak out. I want everyone to know what I think.

I hope everyone speaks out. There is safety in numbers.

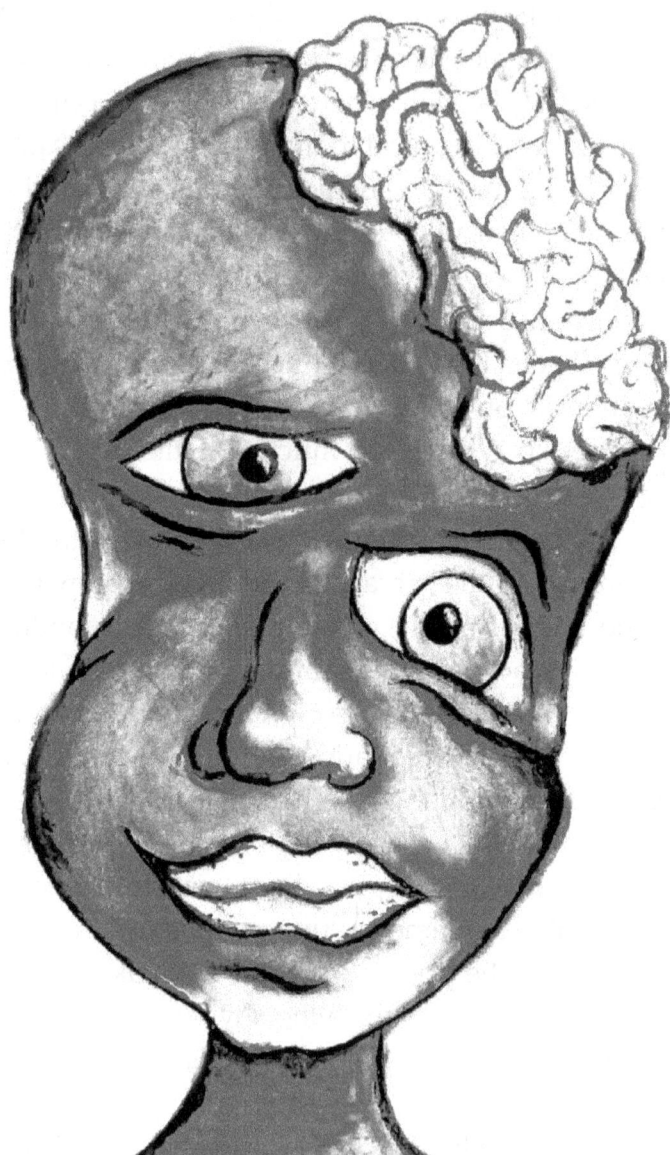

Chicken Soup for the Body

My mother had simple remedies for all my troubles. "Eat," she would say. "I fixa da chicka soup to make you good. If you don't eat you gonna die. You eat soup and go sleep. Then you feel good, ma-sure."

Midwest wind could cause fatalities. Did I want to get sick and die? All I had to do was work up a sweat and take it outside into a cool evening breeze. A cool evening breeze brushing against bare shoulders caused colds. Minnesota winters caused pneumonia. Ma-sure.

All pills, prescriptions, and medicines were suspect, taken only as a last resort—when chicken soup, fruits, dandelion greens, nuts, tap water, and a steady stream of pasta failed.

My mother died at 89 of mesothelioma, a cancer that results when asbestos secretes its vileness into the lungs. My father died just weeks short of 99, when his heart lost its legs. His heart had checked out fine just a few months earlier when he began a regime of anti-arthritis pills, a new wonder drug later proven to cause heart attacks. To the very end my parents insisted on chicken soup, fruits, dandelion greens, nuts, tap water, a steady stream of pasta, and, in my father's case, lots of beans and an occasional dose of prune juice.

Good genes, we hear ourselves saying, as if to confirm our dread that even good things can't be helped.

I grew up confused and careless about cause and effect, and I'm still confused about their strange relationships. When I get sick I see remedies stabbing at ills lurking in the dark. The ills often stab back. As both sides stab they retreat, regroup, and rethink their ways and means. When the problems don't magically disappear there is always something, or someone, to blame. I've never been one to surrender to unpleasant inevitabilities, hoping new research, technology or my dead mother will intervene. When we don't feel well we sometimes just want to muddle through, maybe get back to work next week, if we have a job. When solutions take too much time or fail we take to drink or drugs. Or we pray, especially if we don't have medical insurance or a job. Or we kick the cat, giving no thought to why cats purr.

When we're jobless and hurting it gives us less quality time to wonder about who should pay how much, and for what. I think of myself as a good enough American, but can't help asking if troubling questions about the nation's welfare (narrowly understood to mean its solvency) are more important than the health and welfare ("wellness faring") of its citizens. I'm told that millions of Americans are uninsured. If I'm very sick because I can't afford medical care, a doctor, surgery, or drug, should I make a patriotic sacrifice of my life in order to balance the nation's checkbook? Should I salute the flag, suck it up, drive myself to the cemetery rather than hospital, and be the loyal unknown citizen who dies miserably on some patch of grass?

We like to think of the U.S. as "exceptional," the world's superpower, God's chosen nation and guiding light. But the health care numbers, as established by the World Health Organization, are alarming and embarrassing. In general health system attainment and performance the U.S. ranks 72nd, well behind Iceland, Turkey and Cuba. France, Italy and Spain are near the top. We rank 14th, behind most

Western European nations, in preventable deaths. When life expectancy, educational attainment, and national per capita income are taken into account as indicators of "green" living and quality of life, the U.S. ranks 23rd, well behind Finland, Iceland, Norway, and Sweden—all of them such frigid nations where my mother was sure people died young of wind chill factors because they didn't bundle up. Meanwhile, the U.S. is in second place among the biggest spenders for health care as a percentage of GDP, behind first place Marshall Islands. The cost of our mediocre health care is almost off the charts.

My mother, always a thriftskate, would be very upset to know that Italy spends more on health care (at 27th) than Cuba (50th) and San Marino (62nd). A dose of chicken soup, nuts, dandelion greens, tap water, pasta and an apple a day was the price she routinely paid to keep the doctor away. She could find some of this stuff in the garden in back and buy the rest with the loose change she kept in a coffee can above the kitchen stove.

She never understood, or really adjusted to, these more complicated and expensive times. A couple years ago my daughter had a somewhat routine surgery that cost somebody $28,000. Recently I had an enzyme injection to correct a problem in one finger. The injection alone cost somebody $7000. I'm very happy to have my daughter healthy again, and when I gaze at my little finger of my right hand I'm overwhelmed at how valuable the rest of me no doubt is.

But I can't help wondering: Why do such things cost so much? Where does all the money go? And is someone getting too much of it? If we're being gouged while being fixed, who's ripping us off? In the old days highway bandits asked the question a lot of people have to face when they get sick: Your money or your life. Luckily only three of my ten fingers are bad. Luckily I have (expensive) medical insurance, Medicare, and the Mayo Clinic nearby. And luckily I don't have cancer or Parkinson's or a failing heart.

Does my good fortune in life make me guilty of greed? I confess: Greed is one of the masks my insecurity wears. I feel most insecure when I'm an unrestricted free agent who doesn't know how best to ward off what's ailing or threatening me. That's when I'm almost tempted to shore up my defenses by getting uppity about my right to defend and take care of myself—by flailing away at what ails me with uplifted arms, for example, or by insisting on my right to rake in enough money to get all ten of my fingers fixed, just in case, and to hide the money I don't need in Bahamas banks where money is so well-laundered nobody there calls it dirty money. I'll survive on my own, I tell myself, and everyone else can go to hell with the rest of the world going down the drain. By pulling myself up by the straps I don't have on the workboots I wouldn't think of wearing— I'll escape the drain hole.

Greed, once widely advertised as one of the Seven Deadly Sins, leads a quiet life as a cottage industry these days. Pure profits, and impure ones, like cancer cells, are easily secreted away, often far from doctors' offices and hospitals where people actually do the work. Nurses, who quietly do a lot of actual work, maybe know this best.

I'm numbered among those who have managed to avoid going down the drain, though scientific evidence is inconclusive about whether I am one of the most fit to survive. The marginalized masses also have certain strengths—resentment, for example, and anger—that have their ways of asserting themselves as survival skills.

Resentment tends to be drifty and careless as it gnaws away at what it abhors, and anger is untidy too, even when it achieves the focal point sharp enough to cause it to explode big-time. An outspoken wellness professor, untenured, once told me that resentment can swell like a tumor into a social illness that only hot fires can remove. It seems like a very painful way to make things right.

As I keep waiting for greed's benefits to trickle unnaturally up its ladder of success I wonder how much waste is going down the drain. I see my mother smiling at me from Purgatory for asking this. Her heart was guilty as hell of cursing when she saw anything useful or edible thrown away. Her suspicion of all doctors and psychiatrists was as unfair as it was deep, maybe because they never developed a chicken soup pill. In her eighty-nine years she had endured miscarriages of twin boys and eight surgeries, most of them "exploratory," so she and plenty of doctors were close. She spent the worst part of a lifetime failing to understand the source of her troubles, and her own chicken soup did little to heal the unease she felt as woman and immigrant. Are there medical cures for these afflictions, and for the lonely, the homeless, the jobless, those frustrated by language, gender, skin color liabilities, and mental and physical disabilities? How carefully do we study and do anything to diminish the various forms of social unease that may lie at the root of actual disease? Can such diseases be amputated by budget cuts?

If my mother had stayed in the Old Country she might have died from a chill, from another miscarriage or from one of her benign lumps. Or she might have lived happily ever after until she turned 99. The World Health Organization's rankings suggest that health has something to do with place. What also seems reasonable is that health has something to do with how we think and believe.

A couple of decades ago I clipped an article from the Minneapolis *Star Tribune* and tucked it away in my mind. That piece of newspaper looks almost as old as I am today, but it still rings the bell in me that says the past is never really past and the future is now. Lynn Payer, author of the book *Medicine and Culture*, argues that, "Medicine is not quite the international science that the medical community would have us believe." A disease in one culture is not a disease in another, and there are very different ways of treating the same ailment in different cultures. A doctor's best practice in one place is malpractice across the border. "Looking at medicine abroad can…show that…aspects of American medicine are not the inevitable result of medical progress but of choices—conscious or not—made on the basis of our own cultural biases."

In England, for example, aggressive and exuberant free enterprisers run the risk of being diagnosed as mentally ill. In a culture that values self-control and restraint, "symptoms such as 'agitation,' 'irritability,' and 'elation'" might be indicators of profound pathology. "British doctors," says Payer, "in fact prefer inactivity to mindless activity not only in their patients but in themselves. British doctors do less of everything: less complete examinations, fewer diagnostic tests, fewer prescriptions and less surgery." The English also recommend lower doses of vitamin C.

My mother might have been happier with English doctors. She might have avoided some of her exploratory surgeries, and happily would have saved the money spent on vitamin C pills.

Payer cites John Fry, a general practitioner who has compared medical systems worldwide: "The British health service is based on the conservative, critical questioning and cynicism of doctors ... it's highly self-critical. You are trained to think what is really necessary... [and to ask] does technology do any good? Is it better than not doing anything?"

The U.K.'s health care system ranks 18th worldwide, compared to the U.S. at 37th, with the U. K's health performance weighing in at 24th compared to the U.S. at 72nd. The U.K. also is better than the U.S. at preventing deaths, though (with apologies to Ireland) it ranks as a less "green" and livable place.

Cost? We're almost number one and the Brits weigh in with their pounds at a lightweight 41st.

Though they manage to eat, pay the rent, and go to plays, British doctors, of course, make less money than their U.S. peers.

German doctors, true to the romantics in their midst, tend to think we'd be better off if we paid better mind to our telltale hearts. Payer explains the Germans' "seemingly promiscuous use of drugs for the heart" (eight times that of England or France) as a function of revering the heart as not just a pumping machine but as "an organ in dynamic balance with the circulation" and core of our emotional lives. Hence Germans are less inclined to do coronary bypass surgeries to unblock a clogged pipe, and more apt to prescribe emotion-altering drugs designed to make us— as parents, friends and lovers—less heartsick.

In both Germany and France infectious diseases tend to be seen as consequences of lowered resistance (not enough chicken soup?) rather than as invasions that have to be zapped by antibiotics. "The 20 most commonly prescribed drugs in Germany," says Payer, "include no antibiotics." The advent of MRSA suggests that antibiotic overuse is now a serious problem in the U.S. Dangerous bugs seem to morph into tiny terrorists adept at hiding from the drone-like attacks of brilliant antibiotics too fuzzy-minded to worry about how much collateral damage they do.

American doctors apparently have taken their cues from the auto industry. If a carburetor is going bad, take it out and put a new one in. In this view the human body is a machine, the doctor a fix-it man. When the heart hurts it's time to perform surgical strikes on the heart's parts, or cut it entirely out and put a new used one in. Emotions and any other mysterious ghosts in the machine muddy the waters for the fix-it man, so an American doctor is inclined to cut to the quick. This attitude supplies us with new plastic knees and hips, new faces, new lips, and implants unmentionable in the company of Baptists. It makes a lot of old people shine like cars recently purchased from used car lots.

I admit the thought has crossed my mind: How much would it cost to attach three slightly used brand new fingers to my hand? They shouldn't be hard to find in some bone yard nearby.

As I wonder if there is a better way to fix my fingers, I also find the complexity of our current health care debates rather bewildering. To return to the old unreformed "system" seems to encourage free enterprising promiscuity, with millions of the uninsured out in the cold. As the new "Obamacare" plan approved by Congress tries to chart a new course for American medicine, it moves forward by fits and starts like a new-fangled machine that came off the assembly line with sabotaged parts.

We're not wholly in the dark. European health care systems are more "socialized" than ours, and we'd have to close our eyes tight over our minds to believe that greed and waste are not among the biggest sin twins corrupting a free enterprise approach.

So where does all the money go? Who gets obscenely more than a fair share? What types of enterprises are freely hogging it? Is greed the leading cause of waste?

I'm especially intrigued by the attention Germans give to the heart, and by the new stem cell research implying that the body as machine can also organically renew its defective parts. It makes me think I've got growth potential for something other than cancer cells.

My wife Monica also makes tasty chicken soup and has it ready for us whenever there's a hint of a cold coming on. She says there's no secret about the special ingredient she puts in it that makes it work so well. It comes from the heart, free of charge.

And it's natural too. She comes from German stock.

It's The Terror, Stupid!

My son, a teenager, warned me in advance. "You won't like it, Dad. It's really interesting, but there's a lot of action in it." By "action" we both knew he meant violence.

The TV ads for the movie *Inception* were not just relentless. The imagery in them was bizarre and spectacular enough to make the movie a must-see. I wasn't surprised to learn *Inception* cost $200,000,000 to produce. Two hundred million dollars. That ton of cash could fund a lot of teaching jobs in a troubled nation whose people are told their problem is the economy (stupid!). But like a good American I parted with ten bucks to see the movie too.

Inception's rather corny plot has promise as an exploration of the mysterious depths and workings of the mind. In the movie Dom Cobb is a master at "extraction," the invasion of people's minds, and his professional services are especially useful to corporate spies. But Cobb has problems with his daily life at home: He's suspected of murdering his wife, and he suffers a melancholic alienation from his two lovely children. Did he kill her or did she kill herself? An offer he can't refuse comes along: A corporate chieftain wants him to "implant" an idea in the mind of a business rival so the rival's corporation will dissolve. Cobb is assured that if he can pull off this perfect crime, arrangements will follow that will allow him safe return to his children.

What follows on the screen is a challenging, and strange, configuration of sequences that depict Cobb's invasion of people's dreams—and dreams within dreams—

so he can successfully perform his duties as a mind-controller. For more than two hours the lines between dream and "reality" are blurred, and the audience doesn't know what's real, even at the end when Cobb returns, in dreamy soft-toned hues, to his children at home.

The story line, highly rigged to suggest intellectual heft, is promising, as faces confront each other to discuss their schemes and the mind's strange ways. But fully a third to half of the movie depicts, in often spectacularly original ways, mayhem and violence—slugfests, gunfights, car chases and crashes, paramilitary battles, and doomsday implosions. "You won't like it, Dad. It's really interesting, but there's a lot of action in it." A lot of violence wholly unnecessary to the story-line.

Film technology—"the talkies," "moving pictures"—has its biases. Cameras can't think or enter brains to picture thoughts happening in the soft tissue there. Film-makers have to imagine what's happening in a brain and find some surface to picture it. Film-makers also shy away from thinking that comes in the form of complete sentences and paragraphs, and they know they risk losing their audience if they spend a lot of time aiming the camera at people who just talk face to face. The bias against "talkies" has tilted sharply in favor of visually stimulating action scenes, and the current tilt leans strongly toward blowing things up, even whole cities and planets, in bigger and more spectacular ways. In recent years Hollywood routinely has given us a steady stream of crime, car chases, disasters, shootouts, monsters, fires, towering infernos, runaway trains, runaway viruses, sinking ships, doomsdays, and apocalypse nows. Even in children's movies—from Disney productions to *Lord of the Rings* and the Harry Potter flicks––we get armies of monsters, most of them quasi-human, engaged in extraordinary battles certain to keep our kiddies bug-eyed during their naps. If we miss the action on the big screen, we can pick it up on TV. A routine channel surf will provide us any number of TV programs with ads that feature people pointing weapons at each other and blowing things up. Violence can be fun and profitable too. Video games offer a caricatured violence unmatched except on real battlefields, and the military promotes these games as cost-efficient recruitment tools and early training exercises.

If dieticians and chemists can provide generally accurate descriptions of the negative effects of being supersized by fast food habits, we wonder if Cobb's expertise is good enough to help us understand what producers—consciously or unconsciously—are "implanting" into the minds of their audiences, and what these audiences are "extracting" from the steady diet of supersized violence Hollywood and its media offspring provide. Clearly, the diet has an addictive allure to it. We seem dulled by, bored with, and hardened to ordinary doses of screen violence. We seem to want more and more of it, and in progressively higher doses. An old-fashioned shootout at the O.K. Corral understimulates. We want to see what it's like for Planet Earth, or a galaxy, to blow up. Given the persistent success of what Hollywood pushers offer for sale, it seems that we're too collectively hooked to just say no thanks to all that.

There are some, many of them busy in Hollywood, who say no to Hollywood as a cultural influence. Movies, they say, are just entertainments, disposable like throwaway plastic soft drink bottles. They "implant" nothing in us and we "extract" nothing from them except momentary suspensions of disbelief that momentarily take us away from the daily, perhaps too dull, rounds of daily life. These naysayers say that movies do not influence—flow into us—either consciously or unconsciously. Parents, teachers, books, and Sunday schools, they say, are the real cultural influences from which we derive our view of the world, our values, our hopes and fears.

The influences of parents, teachers, books, and Sunday schools are no doubt present in our lives, but I wonder if larger than life violent screen spectacles make them seem unreal, like the soft half-remembered tones of the children and idealized ordinary family life Cobb desperately wants to return to after he's done his dirty work. It's simply implausible to dismiss the power of the culture of violence, and it's becoming increasingly difficult to view it as a secondary influence. Certainly it reflects, in part, who we are as a people, for it comes from us and we approve of it as a mass culture we pay millions for. We must derive some sort of pleasure from what we so hungrily consume. If what we feed on is a steady stream of escalating violence, and if violence breeds fear, insecurity, and demoralization, does this culture "implant" feelings of fear, insecurity, and demoralization that challenge and sometimes overwhelm the positive values we associate with ordinary life? And if we "enjoy" this violent culture, do we enjoy being fearful, insecure, and demoralized? Where is the joy in that?

It's clear that addictive personalities are tied to stimulating activities and substances that temporarily ward off feelings of worthlessness, nihilism, and depression. It's common for substance abuse to escalate if underlying problems are not addressed. Fear's usefulness as a biological defense seems obvious enough. It's a good thing to run like a scared jackrabbit if a lion is chasing you. But lions—and tigers and even sharks with big jaws—are becoming fewer and more far between on a planet being overrun by parking lots. We're not likely to run into a lion in a Minnesota field or into snakes on a plane. And while we have good reason to fear terrorists, they too seem rare and certainly less threatening than the widgets of warfare they somehow get and sometimes use.

So fear's sources as biologically natural inspirations for personal survival are becoming defunct. What we have now is civilized fear, its objects normally mass produced as predatory widgets (guns, bombs, etc.) of warfare and violence. The ingenuity that goes into producing these widgets is bottomless, and the culture of violence, thanks to Hollywood, is futuristically visionary in promoting its advances. The imaginative ingenuity of movie producers who spend millions to pioneer new mechanisms for violence is astonishing. Their futuristic and fanciful inventions in movies no doubt in turn inspire the voracious appetites of military visionaries and engineers who want to see if the widgets can really be made to work.

We confront the interests of terror on two fronts: foreign and domestic. To the global war on terror, what some like to call our World War III, we commit billions of dollars and thousands of lives in the hope of eliminating, or checking, terrorist threats, if not the fears deemed necessary to conduct the war. The culture of terror Hollywood provides us on the domestic front we are supposed to enjoy after paying the ticket price. If FDR once spoke eloquently about the importance of living free from fear, we now seem hell-bent on promoting a two-front culture promoting fear.

How does this two-front culture affect the economy? The bottom line cost of the global war on terror is incalculable, but this much is obvious. The U.S. military budget for 2010-2011 was $733,000,000,000, compared to the combined total of $25,000,000,000 for potential "enemy" nations (Iran, North Korea, Pakistan, Venezuela, Syria, Cuba.) U.S. military expenditures alone exceed the combined military expenditures of all the nations of the world. Not even China (at $144,000,000,000) and Russia (at $85,000,000,000) come close. Clearly we are leaps and bounds ahead of everyone else in the arms race. But if the U.S. was bankrupt during the Great Depression of the 1930's and if World War II pulled us out of the Depression, we don't see our global World War III, now well into its twentieth year following the first invasion of Iraq, giving us the war benefits that are supposed to save economies. We are going bankrupt.

Is the culture of terror on the home front good for the economy? Expensive extravaganzas like *Inception* stimulate Hollywood job growth, if we can trust the lengthy credits we have to endure as we're walking out. But if, like *Inception's* Cobb, we believe that movies, TV, video games, books and Sunday schools "implant" emotions and maybe even thoughts, then we should calculate the economic impact of the cumulative anxiety the culture of terror provides for our viewing enjoyment. If what we "extract" from this culture are fear, insecurity, and demoralization that complement the anxieties generated by our global war on terror, what hope is there for the cheerful optimism needed to stimulate economic growth? When I'm insecure, afraid, not sure if I'll see my lovely children again (Cobb sees them at the end, but nobody's sure they're real), my yen to invest in the future of America wanes, as do my power and willingness to spend. If I'm wealthy I invest abroad. If I have a job I'm less likely to buy widgets and toys, and if I don't have a job I click into survival mode: I buy only necessities, or head toward the food shelf, fairly certain that the economic mess has made a victim of me, and perhaps wondering if the small pleasures and values of daily life are enduring and real.

And if I'm hooked on Hollywood I hope to have just enough cash to buy a ticket for the next blockbuster coming soon to a big screen.

Endnote: On Dying When Everything Is New

Common wisdom dictates that as I age I become more conservative and pessimistic about the fate of the earth. And naturally so. Because I'm dying I resist being swept away by the latest fads, I insist on preserving our imagined past and the old-fashioned habits I enjoyed as a youth, and I stand convinced everything's going sour. Or worse, I'm convinced the world will blow up just as I release my last breath. If only I could go back to the good old days when choo-choo trains were the only improvement needed on the horse-drawn cart. But I have cars now, and jet planes, and space ships, and TV, and computers, and computer chips, and robots, and GMO corn and beans, and neutrinos, and stem cells and the balance of terror, and I see the new technologies as an ever renewing youth movement that will run on and on without ever petering out. As these technologies keep renewing themselves, they govern more and more of the vast, and tiny, cellular spaces of our lives. As they expand their empire over and into us they no longer are a "virtual" reality. They are becoming our dominant reality. Our bodies, and the biological wonders they've evolved into over centuries, are becoming the new virtual reality. Call our body and its old biologies newly "unnatural."

As I see wired people walking down the street zombie-like (they're not) as if they're the plug-in energy plants for their techno-devices (they're not yet), I wonder if some day our technologies will evolve an immortality app. I'd like to see how such a device works, its power source, especially as we seem hell-bent on engineering our biology out of existence, stripping it of its power over us. The old heaven and earth gods of nature—those primitive personifications of physics, geology, biology, psychology—seem too weak, invisible, fictional, and human for us. So we keep engineering alternatives to them. Though I'm destined to die too soon to take advantages of living forever as a biological alien in a brave new techno-world, will I more unnaturally get old before I die, assisted by amazing new life support medicines and machines of this new age? Therefore, will my conservative convictions about our failing attempts to restore belief in earth's natural cycles— and my pessimism about the brave new techno-world we're creating for ourselves—both be bad dreams come true?

VI.   Military Intelligence

(from *The Oxymoronic Dictionary*)

Adjective with singular noun

1. The confusion that resulted in 1949 when the Department of War was renamed the Department of Defense.
2. The strategic thinking, based on the latest theory of gravity, that motivates cult behavior in large office buildings: The mass of bodies lying at rest is directly proportional to firepower and inversely proportional to the distance of eye contact.
3. The cunning of strategists delegated to politicians clever enough to increase military spending to levels that exempt them and their children from combat duties.
4. When the shooting starts the mindfulness lost in private by too, too many privates.

Antonyms: Diplomacy. Patience.

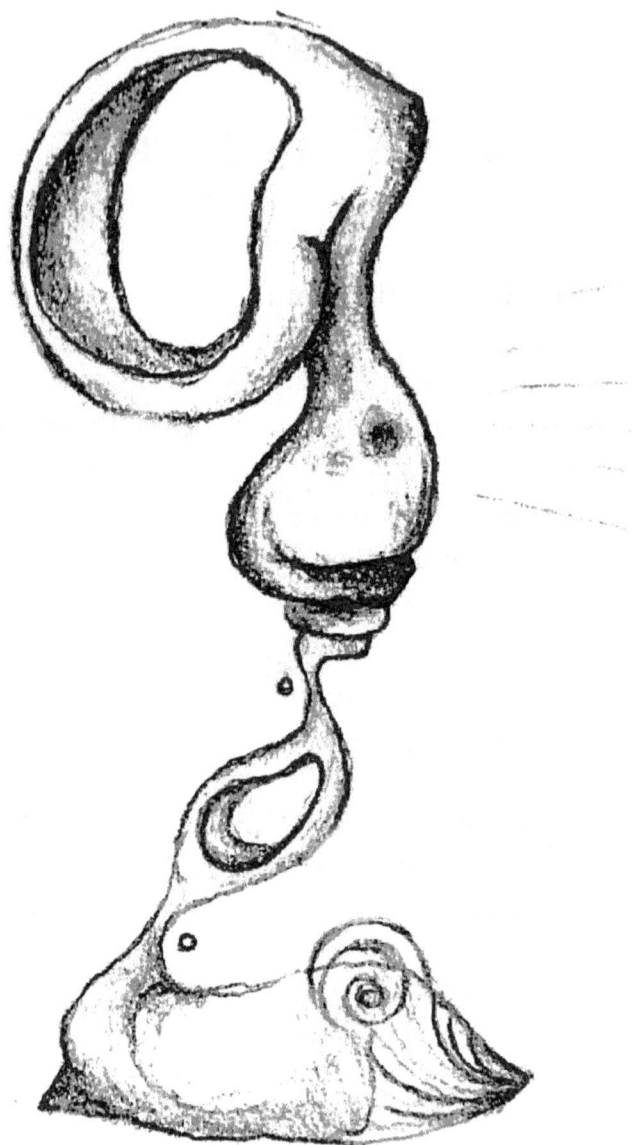

War Colors

If the first September chill foreshadows the winter coming on, it also backshadows me into my childhood. The movies in that childhood were what we call black and white, though the best of them were artfully composed to display the subtle interplay of shadows and shades. Since I was fated to be born in 1941, the Pearl Harbor year, those movies color how I still see my history. World War II has always been waged in the black and white theatre of my mind. Though sinners and saints can probably agree that no war is good, even for the few who make money from it, Studs Terkel named the war I was born into *"The Good War"*. The quotation marks are his way of telling us war is hell.

As I get older and sometimes forget the names of my cats I wonder not only about the factuality of my memories but about their coloration. I see World War II through the lens of those grainy movies and newsreels, and I'm convinced its darkish hues are not merely decorative. For me that war—and those shadowy blacks and whites—have presence as a force that shapes present belief.

I was not yet five years old when Japan formally surrendered on August 15, 1945. That afternoon I piled into our Model T Ford with my mother, dad, and two sisters for a ride to the intersection of Michigan and Schaefer avenues in Dearborn, Michigan, my home town. We met there a huge crowd of very happy people cheering and honking horns. It is a distant but distinct memory, the only one I can directly connect to the war. So if I remember only this happy hour how can the horrors of this huge war be alive in me? Having directly experienced only its happy conclusion, you'd think it would have made a cheerful person of me.

I'm not.

The darker secretions of that war entered me in mysterious and uncountable ways. Old movies that pre-date the war come to mind—*The Cabinet of Dr. Caligari* (1919), *The Blue Angel* (1929), and *"M"* (1939)—all three of them black and white German films made following World War I, each clearly foreshadowing the debacle to come. Books also darkened my view—row after row of black ink stains marching in paragraphed discipline like whole battalions of soldiers on parade. The words on those pages crowded into my mind, commanding my respect and sometimes starting quarrels about what is real.

Heraclitus the philosopher said we never enter the same stream twice, and I'm sure I seldom see the streams entering me. But one stream of unconsciousness certainly entered me at the eleventh hour of February 16, 1941, the night I was born: World War II, a war that had to wait several more months for its Pearl Harbor waters to break. "The Good War" was swelling in me, and in our nation, before we formally entered the war. And I have no doubt that it is also present, for good or ill, in anyone born after 1945. I, for example, count myself among the beneficiaries of the affluence the war conferred on its survivors. Others, including many of its middle class beneficiaries, feed on a regular diet of antidepressants, or make regular visits to their psychiatrists. The lights and grey shades of this black and white war still darken us all.

What concerns me most is not the accuracy of my memory of the war but the general impression still alive in me, and perhaps in us collectively. "The Good War," the one still seen in newsreel black and white, made it easy for us to see the catastrophe as morally unambiguous. We were the good guys, and the Nazis, some of whom might have become nice German-speaking neighbors in a nice Minnesota or Wisconsin town, were the bad guys. But these nice neighbors became faceless once the uniforms were put on. Human faces, all of them somebody's good neighbors, became giant forces of light and dark colliding in war theatres all over the globe. The official school textbook word is that the good guys won, and that a curtain fell over the drama to mark its happy ending. History as epic melodrama, like apocalypse: The battles are fought, the evil overcome, the savior heroes come marching home, and the story's done.

But it isn't—ask the victims, the soldiers, and the dogs of war that still sniff around the wreckage of lives— because many of the shadows and shades that were alive before the war survived the war and passed, often anonymously, into the next generation. The distortions of common sense and scientific fact, the arrogant claims for national destiny, exceptionalism and racial purity, the failure of educational institutions to nurture critical understandings, the churches' habit of looking the other way, the popularization of culture based on caricature, showmanship, distraction and fear, the privileging of military special interests—all these shadows and shades are not easily bombed out of existence in a war "we" won, and they know how to hide, disguise themselves, and improve their images.

As a nation we've been almost perpetually at war since the end of World War II, with one difference: "The Good War" was one we fought, as a nation generally, because it seemed black and white, morally justified. We were collectively willing to make serious sacrifices to prevail. We believed in it.

Korea, Vietnam, the dirty little wars in Latin America and elsewhere, and our two decades in Iraq continue to trouble us morally as "The Good War" never did. The Korean war, "the forgotten war" we now find difficult to remember and forget, also came into my youth in black and white terms, conjuring nostalgia for "The Good War" just won. But this picture was marred by the ugly smears of the Red Scare that caused us to think twice about why so many of our soldiers were dying so far from home. Vietnam came to us in full color, its technicolor blood and guts brought into our living rooms and wide-screen theatres via films such as *The Deer Hunter*, *Apocalypse Now*, and *Hearts and Minds*. But the imagery and colors fade and shrink after that, mainly because our leaders learned well the most important lesson of the Vietnam war: Control the information, especially the imagery. So Iraq's Desert Storm we see mainly as a virtual game shrunken into the size of a video screen, in colors we can't recall, not one of them blood red. And now, what color is a drone? And how long have we been in Afghanistan? We look for Afghanistan on a map to see how to color it in our minds. And the war on terror? What color is it?

Iphigenia in Woebegoneland

Again the latest bad news comes home to us with a poignant sadness not nearly as long-lived as indifference. Four more Minnesota warriors killed this week somewhere in the Mideast, in a war allegedly winding down while heating up. Our business as usual indifference saves us from the grief that would trouble us if we paused to memorize the warriors' names. They're Minnesotans like us, but thankfully they're strangers to most of us. We hold ourselves at attention for a moment, then try to let go of them, perhaps not pausing to imagine each one having a mother, sister, lover, daughter, or wife.

We brushstroke the warriors' deaths with the word "tragedy," the same word we use when someone we know dies in a car accident. By itself the word "tragedy" brings a personal story into the picture that helps generate some emotion, if not understanding, of what led to the violent deaths of the warriors. They did not die by accident. We like to think an accident just "happens"—it can't be helped, is a mere function of chance. But the word "tragedy" suggests something deeper than an accident. In tragedies victims don't necessarily die for a cause, but their deaths are caused, usually by ignorance or a character flaw. Accidents just happen; tragedies don't have to. Tragedy challenges our need to understand why things went wrong, and it implicates us in the wrong for our failure to understand in time the conspiracy of causes—elements of choice, chance and circumstance—that have made a terrible outcome inevitable.

The webs of choice, chance and circumstances that trap victims are complex, and they overlap. Parents, schools, churches, economics, friends and flaws—*et cetera*—combine to nudge victims this way or that until they are hopelessly trapped and undone. When we examine the tangled webs of causation in a tragic light we pity and we grieve for victims who fall, and in the best tragedies we see ourselves in them. There but for fortune, fate, or chance go I. It takes a second and more imaginative gaze for us to see that the tragic victim's mother, sister, lover, daughter, or wife might also be caught in some sort of web.

In Woebegoneland only a few cranks enjoy reading tragedies, particularly the ancient Greek ones we now call "myths." They're easy to dismiss as fictional and therefore entirely false. The ancient Greeks themselves kept respinning their myths, trying to understand themselves and their histories through them. They were not above using myths to serve special interests. The Greeks were also low-tech, most of them unable to read or write, so their poets made careers out of memorizing the myths or setting them in motion in vast and lovely theaters made from stone. Some of the dramas ritually performed in their theaters no doubt carved indelible impressions on the minds of the thousands that listened and watched.

Take, for example, the (perhaps) 3,000-year-old legend of Iphigenia. Iphigenia was the daughter of Agamemnon, commander-in-chief of the various Greek tribes gathered at the seaport of Aulis to begin the Greek invasion of Troy, a city-state in the nation we now call Turkey. Agamemnon has his excuse for going to war: Helen, beautiful and blonde Greek queen, has run away from her husband Menelaus to be with her lover Paris in Troy. Her passion for love-making (and nice clothes) appears to have been sufficient cause for thousands of Greek men to get passionate about going to war to teach her a lesson or two. So the Greeks, according to their own hero Achilles, "left at home their wives and children, all because a terrible passion seized all Greece to make this expedition."

But Helen's abandonment of the Greeks—criminalized by her extraordinary beauty—is the moral equivalent of the Vietnam war's Gulf of Tonkin Resolution or Iraq's mythical weapons of mass destruction: Accuse someone of throwing the first stone so you have a reason for dropping bombs on them. But the Greeks had motives other than Helen for invading Troy. With Troy under their control the Greeks would dominate trade in the region, and Troy was full of gold. And there were women to be had—Helen, of course, the trophy wife, was one, but there were many older women useful as slaves, and the younger more attractive ones useful as concubines.

What did the mothers, sisters, lovers, daughters and wives think about this?

The Greek warriors at Aulis were stalemated. All they had was each other. They had left their mothers, sisters, lovers, daughters and wives behind in order to achieve the great honor and glory that comes from the death, disease, destruction and bondage of war. And once they left their home towns they found themselves stuck with each other at Aulis, waiting for winds that refused to blow, as if the winds themselves were conspiring to prevent them from going to war.

Why didn't the winds blow? We discover that commander-in-chief Agamemnon has offended Artemis, goddess of the chase and the chaste, by arrogantly encroaching on her hunting turf.

How can Agamemnon get the winds to blow so the ships

can sail and the terribly destructive ten-year war can blossom into decades of bloodlust and lust? He solicits a priest's advice and is informed that he can have his war if he sacrifices his daughter Iphigenia to appease the goddess he has wronged.

These days fathers don't kill their daughters in order to start a war. Today we've progressed to the point of doubting some kings, and most of us probably know a preacher or priest we don't trust.

But Agamemnon, desperate to keep his war plan alive, cuts his daughter's throat (though in Euripides' version of the myth she escapes in the nick of time). And the winds begin to blow. What follows is a most miserable history for generations of others who never fought in the war—not only for the defeated Trojans but for the Greeks who conquered them.

So what is the point? What were the mythmakers trying to make unforgettable by memorializing Iphigenia's ritual sacrifice?

There is no one point, no way to reduce these stories to simple sermons. The Greeks had a sharp feel for the way thick webs entangle individuals, especially those who try mere reason to force their way through the webs.

But this much seems clear: Iphigenia and her mother had little power to stop Agamemnon's hand, for Greek women in general had little control over their warrior-men. Agamemnon was so hell-bent on having his war he had to look into his daughter's eyes as he cut her throat. The warriors went merrily away to their miserable ten-year war, leaving their miserable families behind. In the absence of husbands, fathers, and sons, family ties broke down, and when Agamemnon returned from Troy his wife murdered him with a knife. Many warriors and women on both sides suffered and died, and the "victory" over the Trojans eventually turned into a defeat for many Greeks and their children.

Iphigenia's ritualized sacrifice memorializes a pattern: Innocent females—mothers, sisters, lovers, daughters, and wives—suffer terribly in all wars, not only as casualties of actual battles but bitterly in the safety of their home towns. If tragedy offers anything, it gives us a chance to widen and deepen the scope of our grief. We grieve, as we must, for fallen warriors, and for the sacrifices war requires of winners and losers, but mostly for the women on both sides who are victimized.

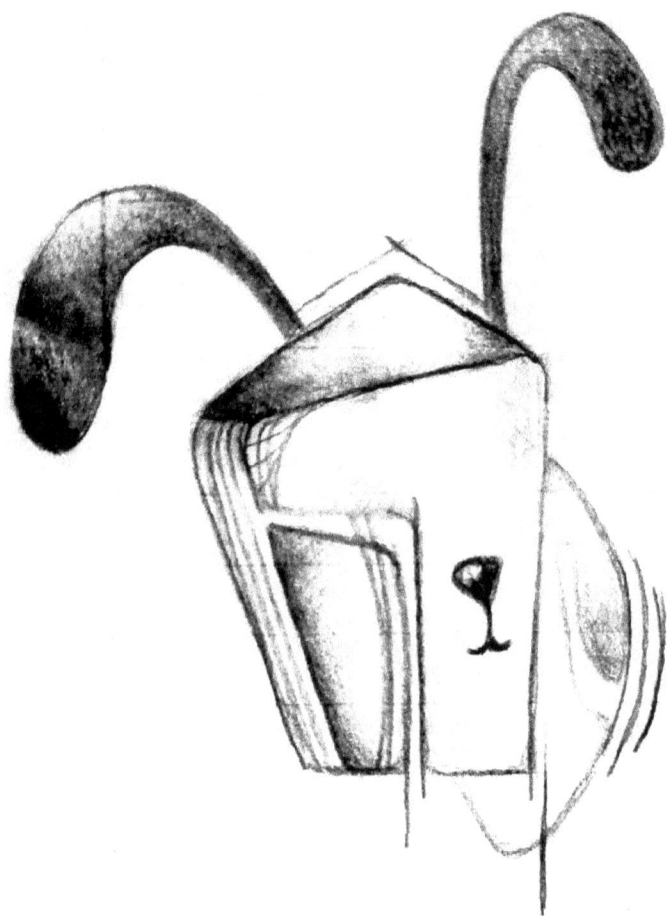

Women Warriors

In a telephone conversation with an Israeli friend I asked if he held some hope for an end to hostilities there. "Almost none," he said, "the way things are going now." And why not? "Because the bullies on both sides have dragged the women in. Now the women are deeply involved, have taken sides."

In peacetime women have enough battles to fight—fending off domestic violence, making ends meet, insisting on fair pay and equal rights, and getting their work done at work while raising the kids and doing the laundry. War has always dumped on them one more burden, required them to play their parts as casualties, workers, cheerleaders, prizes, and slaves. While many have participated as civilians behind the lines, relatively few have played the warrior role in uniform. This is becoming less true in progressive societies in which the quest for female equality has been extended to include the profession of soldiery. As more and more women are getting a shot at having military careers, women are wise to worry about the equitable distribution of military authority and perks. One other thing is clear: When things get bad enough all uniforms look alike. They will be in the trenches too.

It has become increasingly common these days for "asymmetrical" warfare to devolve into stalemated conflicts that drag on and on, with no clear "winner" or closure. I would argue that the fate of these conflicts is largely determined by women. If they choose sides and participate as partisans they risk prolonging and enlarging the scope of conflicts; and they directly risk their lives. Their other option, also dangerous, is to do their best to avoid the hostilities and to insist that their husbands and sons stay home.

The conventions of war are given new twists when women volunteer to assume warrior roles. It is one thing for mothers and schoolteachers to indoctrinate young minds against an enemy, or for women to take jobs manufacturing bullets destined for some other mother's son's heart. These are the lovely options war offers them. But when women enlist to fight side-by-side with male warriors for military pay, and when girls offer themselves for suicide missions because they believe in a cause—war has taken a radical turn toward making them champions of warrior values that historically have been monopolized by males.

What gets diminished when women are thrust into the front lines of war is their power to act as peace-makers at home. Though many males are routinely gentle and nurturing, and most have these impulses lurking in themselves even when they're at war, the woman's traditional role, and one measure of her survival skills, has been to nurture and protect through non-violent means. The woman traditionally has turned the other cheek, even while enduring the hard consequences of doing so. A strong case could be made—and has been convincingly exemplified by the likes of Gandhi, Martin Luther King, and Jesus—that turning the other cheek yields better long-term results than war.

It is troubling to see compliant mothers, lovers, and wives surrender their men to coercive war machines. Ancient Greek women, so often terrible victims of male aggression at home and abroad, were known to resist the war glory promised by "heroes" to their sons. Thetis, Achilles' mother, dresses him as a girl and tries to hide him in a girls' school when the war recruiters come to get him too. She weeps when they take her son away, for she already sees him dead. And for centuries millions of other peasant women have wept when military recruiters representing powerful interests distant from the immediate daily rounds of ordinary domestic life have come to steal away their sons.

To surrender a husband, lover or son to a war requires a woman to sacrifice her deep natural affection to the abstract, and often wrong-minded and illusory, ends of the state. Patriots always argue that a greater good is to be achieved by war. On the contrary, war usually breeds more war. It is more likely that the greatest good—the impulse to nurture and love—is made the loser by those who uncritically support military establishments that are, at the core, well-funded anti-democratic male monopolies of institutionalized violence.

Women, often acting across national and even enemy lines, have acted as counterforces to these monopolies of violence. They have shielded and rescued civilians and soldiers alike from conflicts. Through wiles and persuasion they have reined in belligerent males and preserved a semblance of ordinary peaceful life. In living rooms, schoolhouses, and factories, women have supported the creation and funding of programs that clean up the messes warriors leave behind, including their own wounded selves. In Aristophanes' comedy *Lysistrata* women refuse to have sex until the men refuse to wage war. Women today can make even more powerful moves. They can deny support (and votes) to leaders who insist on bullying their way, particularly those who push for aggressive "pre-emptive" wars. In churches where flag-waving has more force than the Cross, women can stand up and be heard. Their efforts should not be dismissed as "weak." Because heads of state, almost exclusively male, don't seem able to do it on their own, women are the main hope we have to divert the vast funding of military establishments to sensible use. And asking peacemakers to hate war but "support the troops" is self-destructive if the military continues to see the peacemakers as enemies.

The times and new technologies are too dangerous for us to stay our present course. We cannot continue relying on the spokesmen for privileged warrior elites that have done little to solve the real problems that ordinary people face, even as these elites cause enormous destruction while complaining about how they're taxed to death.

Landfill Ghosts

It's too simple-minded to call it what it is: Military waste. What else are we to make of the belated revelation that the remains of "at least" 274 American soldiers and more than 2700 unidentified miscellaneous body parts have been dumped in the King County landfill just south of Washington, D.C. It would be crass to call it a cover-up.

I'll be frank: I have a serious aversion to military funerals. The solemn soldiers in full uniforms, the flag-draped coffins, the bugler playing heartbreaking taps, the huddle of deeply pained loved ones trailing the procession—I often feel used not by them, the sorrowing participants, but by those who attach solemn emotion and dignity of the ritual to their current political agendas. See, they say without saying it, here's another one of ours innocently victimized. I told you so. When our loved ones die we suddenly realize why we went to war. We need to keep casualties like this one from happening again. We need a bigger and better war, more money for the military. We need you to vote for me so I can vote for war.

So support the troops. Put a yellow ribbon on your car bumper.

How can we not grieve for the soldiers? They leave family, friends, lovers and jobs behind, and some don't come back alive. Don't we also have to have sympathy for the administrators of the disposal problem? They too asked: Who were these lost soldiers, and how do we reconnect them to lost families? Whose leg, arm or skull shard is this? They come with no names and addresses attached. We can freeze or incinerate to prevent bad odors and disease, but then what do we do with the remains? They're not much of anything any more. Please, will somebody tell us what to do with all these dead body parts?

Who do those in charge of the immediate disposal problem talk to, and what do they say to their families and to themselves when they go home from work?

What I find reassuring, especially in sub-zero temperatures, is to walk into one of those small societies of gravestones huddled next to a country church. The dead seem to be at home where they routinely went to church, and the silence surrounding them seems to put an end to the battles they've won and lost all their lives. On that little plot of land they've achieved not only a sacred blessing but common ground. I like to wander among the stones, read the names, and imagine the lives. A lot of the dead have the same last names.

Some primitive communities gave burial a similar vitality that seems to be distancing itself from us today, especially given the widespread belief that there exist both a heaven and hell where winners and losers go away from home to live forever in a mansion or lake of fire, with body parts intact. Some primitives, without believing in either heaven or hell, insisted that the actual body of the deceased be present at a home town funeral rite, not ensconced in a photograph, empty casket or dust-filled urn. Early Greeks, for example, those who scratched out their livings in small villages long before mythic hero hoards exported their years of slaughter, pillage and rape to cities like Troy, believed it was unnatural, indeed blasphemous, for their dead to be buried away from home. Their local deities required that proper burial be a home town event. Any lost body not buried in a local tomb in accord with proper rites was doomed to be transformed into an endlessly miserable wandering ghost, lost to the community. Only in an actual community could the deceased, in memory's eyes, have ongoing presence in the community. Especially since an actual tomb was visible nearby, death brought tolerable closure, and enduring connection, to the living.

Home-burial as a sacred rite became embattled when people massed themselves into city-states and later into nation-states that collectivized their males into armies that found it profitable to wage wars away from home. Village boys kidnapped to serve in these armies often never returned home, many of them ditched in distant lands. Over the centuries, as armies and weaponry became larger, bureaucratized, and more lethal, a strategic rule evolved that is becoming more difficult to enforce as the world shrinks and lethal technologies increase their range: Export the war to someone else's turf, win away from home, then return for the parades and enjoyment of the spoils. Home town burials suffered a decline. As populations and war machines increased, mass graves full of anonymous invaders and bystanders made home burials more quaint. In the twentieth century millions of casualties have been landfilled like garbage, and the twenty-first century is off to a horrifying start to continue the trend.

Especially in a time when the word "conservation" is slipping into disuse in favor of "growth," what seems to be getting lost is the sense of how massive the waste has been. There is sullen and muted suspicion, often across political lines, that there has been plenty of waste, but hawkish politicians, while they obsess over budget deficits, seem unwilling to calculate the losses generated by the wars they sponsor behind closed doors. The waste they fund seems distanced, away from home, and therefore the things they don't like to count don't count. Casualties are brought home one by one, with little enough ceremony to disturb the public peace, and those who sorrow—neighbors, friends, family, lovers—also tend to disappear from public view. War, a massive public event, is privatized.

The ancients, with their local gods and home town rites, seem to have taken their casualties more personally. As our world "shrinks," mainly under the influence of technologies, we routinely move away from home, especially if there's a job somewhere else. But this mobility, which promises adventure, opportunity, and prosperity, makes displaced persons of us too. Family ties are loosened, tied to quick-fire electronic exchanges and holiday visits. Uncertainties and the wealth squandered on non-basic necessities makes renters of those who cannot afford to buy into a place where they can live happily ever after. Family becomes redefined as special friends that come and go. As we become absorbed by our fascinating new technologies we are also disinclined to favor the actual five senses evolution has honed for our survival in the real world. Our abandoned home towns matter as places with nostalgic value fit to visit for class reunions. Meanwhile, we move from place to place, finding it convenient to leave our messes behind for someone else to worry about.

American soldiers who spend their holidays in a foreign land no doubt feel the alienation more profoundly than civilians who have become accustomed to it "at home." The spaces these soldiers stare into across desert sands are crossed by no freeways they recognize. Since the Vietnam era there has been no consensus about whether any of our wars have been either necessary for national security or morally defensible. And those opposed to our wars have allowed pro-war factions to expropriate the flag and other major symbols of national unity for their exclusive use. In this way a nation becomes divided against itself, and the extreme political partisanship that results makes cooperative compromise difficult. Hard-headed division digs in for more battles at home. So soldiers naturally ask: What am I doing here in this foreign land? What am I fighting for? What homeland am I defending?

It's easy, and probably most accurate, to answer the first two questions in cynical, and mercenary, terms. But the tough question—What homeland am I defending, especially this far away from home?—requires an increasingly abstracted response. We all have a place of birth, but more routinely now it's not where we live. We're often not well grounded in any "home town," or, if we're city dwellers, in a neighborhood we can call "ours." We all pledge allegiance to the flag of the United States, but Columbus, Georgia, feels like a foreign country to a lot of people in Columbus, Wisconsin. So-called American corporations offshore many of their assets and thousands of jobs to distant lands, and their "lean" business practices seem indifferent to the reduction of individual employees to a skeletal workforce made up of anonymous pawns. When American soldiers pause to think about the dirty work they are ordered to do in some faraway place, they have good reason to wonder not what homeland they're fighting for but whose private profits they're dying to increase.

I'm still primitive enough to see the ghosts of their casualties hovering in the bad air above the King County landfill, just south of Washington, D.C. Though I don't hear their actual voices I suspect they're telling us they'd like to come back to real places where genuine homes exist and where reconstruction of towns, neighborhoods and a sense of community is also taking place.

The Zeroes of the Dogs of War

The dogs of war, infamous for feasting on the carnage
of battlefields, would be less vile if they did not hound
civilians too. Once the dogs are unleashed nobody wants to
claim ownership or responsibility for the diseases they
spread. Because I entered life in 1941, just months before
the Pearl Harbor attack, I was born into the stench of war.
And because my nation has been at war (declared or not,
hot and cold) every year of my life, the stench sickens me
more and more. My affliction displays no obvious
wounds—no scars, disfigurations, missing limbs. Rather I
suffer from a persistent nausea, no doubt stimulated by the
stench, for which there is no quick-fix. Please note: I'm no
war hero and wouldn't dream of asking for a Purple Heart.
Nor does my status as citizen casualty inspire me to strain
VA resources by seeking treatment for post-traumatic
stress. The wars and their stresses are ongoing, and they
infect soldiers and civilians. Like millions of others I fear
I'm doomed to carry my war sickness to my grave as I
warily look over my shoulder at the dogs of war chasing
me down.

The nausea routinely kicks in after I turn off the nightly
news and I'm quietly alone. That's when I begin seeing the
zeroes with faces in them. The nightly news scenes are
familiar to us—the car bomb explosion on the side of a
nameless road, the crowded marketplace all fire and
smoke, children holding their heads in disbelief as they try
to believe their eyes, and one day a black-robed woman
dead in a gutter in Kabul, her ear to the ground, a

birthmark under her left eye, her mother next to her screaming as she pulls her hair out.

You know, this kind of thing. Over a lifetime, scenes like this add up. Hundreds, thousands, millions of the wounded and dead.

The zeroes, like anti-inflammation pills, offer some relief, especially if there are enough of them. If one car bomb kills a half-dozen civilians but not me, then the ten car bomb attacks I've survived seem less destructive to me. Try imagining a thousand bomb victims, all those faceless zeroes who have no names. When there are thousands of zeroes I find it easier to draw a blank.

I take some consolation from the fact that the facts come to me in miniature, no larger than the biggest high-definition TV screen. As such they only momentarily interrupt the stream of ads that blink their way past my consciousness to that part of my brain that desires relief from pain. Why pause on the face of a dead young woman, a foreigner, with a birthmark under her left eye, when I can glimpse instead the gals in beer ads luring me toward them just before they go away to wherever used images go?

The ads make it easier for me to step around that woman lying dead on a street in Kabul. I see now that she was marked by fate to never arrive at the fruit vendor's stall where vegetables had just arrived from the countryside, and that her father, who for months had jealously kept unworthy suitors from her, was so struck by bottomless despair at the sight of his daughter dead that it would take three days for his rage to rise from the ashes of his sorrow. This sorrow is profound and irrational. The dead young woman's father now maybe hates me because I, a perfect stranger, am an American. Would he kill me if he could?

I resolve to go about my business as usual, and resolve to put the young woman's life in her distant grave. She took up only ten inches on my twenty-one-inch TV screen, and her death scene took away only three or four seconds of my life. Her eyes were closed, so I imagine them as chestnut brown, and I think she was thinking about some young man she had just met, wondering what he thought of her. The nausea sets in again, a deep sea-sickness nausea I also feel when I've eaten too much. The world of the birth-marked woman, the enormity of her bad luck, is too big for me to take in. I need to zero her out. A certain dosage of the customary is required of successful social life, so maybe it's time again to share a good whine with good friends. Besides, the kids are in safe hands, in college.

My nausea bloats as I shrink, so I find it best to think small to make room for my self. Today new atrocities are announced: Fresh carnage from a bombing raid, six American marines lost when their helicopter crashed, the throats of two hostages sliced. All this information carries with it a democratic bias: All death is created equal.

That woman with the birthmark under her left eye and skin too lovely to touch—what does her mother think of when she's sitting alone on the edge of her bed, her head in her hands? I don't know the young woman's name. How can I be expected to know her mother's name too?

I have to do what I must do to self-medicate. I take daily showers and long naps. In a participatory democracy we all share equally, and not at all, in thinned-out blame. If I'm to endure my nausea I need to fight against the dictatorship imagination has established in me. That imagination, when on high alert, may make good art, but it darkens everything with the knowledge it is hungry for.

This hunger enslaves me to its need to connect, understand, feel compassion, make difficult moral choices, contribute, create, organize, speak out.

Art and War

(For my son Dante's 18th birthday, as he goes to college to study music, literature and art)

What follows are a father's comments, so they come from an older time, and from someone making no claim to be an expert about art. So my advice gives me pause. I'm an amateur, a lover of certain kinds of art. My faith is that some good may come from the art I deeply love, in its making and uses, and in the loving.

John Ruskin, the Victorian empire's most eminent art authority, gives me, a proud Minnesotan, some bitter food for thought. "All pure and noble arts of peace," he said, "are founded on war; no great art ever yet rose on Earth, but among a nation of soldiers. There is no art among an agricultural people if it remains at peace. Commerce is barely consistent with fine art, but cannot produce it. Manufacture not only is unable to produce it, but invariably destroys whatever seeds of it exist. There is no great art possible to a nation but that which is based on battle."

These are fighting words, and Ruskin didn't hold his fire, especially since he delivered them in 1865 at a commencement ceremony for cadets about to see the world as products of the Royal Military Academy at Woolwich, England. His insistence that the "arts of peace" are "founded on war" seems odd coming from a man who was outspoken in defense of the underclass, those most likely to be the victims of war. If the cadets at the commencement ceremony were certain that Ruskin was not eager to rush them off to war, they also were left to wonder about what potential for art was latent in them as warriors. Were they, like William Blake's tiger, "burning bright/In the forests of the night"? Would they, and the "deadly terrors" they were trained to inflict, "dare frame [a] fearful symmetry?" Did their ability to destroy and create come from the same energies?

If Ruskin's comments about the relationship between art and war were stroked with a broad brush that leaves abstractions in its wake, my own responses here seem like some examples I've seen of so-called minimalist art that inspired in me bouts of distance gazing in which only a few broad forms are visible. Every writer faces the blank page with a teeming and dizzied mind. What escapes the pen are a few threads that only hint at the ongoing unraveling of the mind's tangled thoughts, beliefs, impressions and prejudices. I'm not sure I understand or like minimalist art, but I start here with a few minimal scrawls. Then I dare to add more scrawls, some of them very broad, until I run out of periods.

Travel helps open the eyes, and sometimes it opens the mind to troubling questions about both art (I mean music too) and war. When I first visited Europe as a student (in 1967) London was my first big city eye-opener. What I saw and heard left me in awe—the elegant Parliament buildings, the organ concert in Westminster Abbey, the National Gallery, British Museum, Windsor Palace, etc. etc. etc. My awe deepened when I saw Paris next—Notre Dame Cathedral, the Louvre, the Sainte Chapelle, etc. etc. etc. By the time I found myself on the streets of Florence and Rome I was almost numbed by the array of churches and cathedrals, museums and villas, paintings and statues, grand houses and palaces.

I returned "home" to Detroit in late August of that same year. My city, one that in my boyhood had landmarks, a symphony orchestra, and museums resembling those I'd just experienced in Europe, looked like a war zone. The city lay in ruins. And still does.

I've been to Europe five times now, in part to feast my eyes on the art. Much of Europe is, as Hemingway said of Paris, "a moveable feast."

It was during my third trip to Rome (in 1989) that I finally got a sense of what Ruskin was trying to tell the cadets. On that trip my legs again were about as numb as my sense of awe, perhaps because my mind was weighed down by a few dense books I'd been reading. Taken together those books gave me a deeper, and not wholly lofty, view of European history.

What struck me as I stood (small) in Rome's St. Peter's Basilica was (again) its sheer magnificence. It is a stunning achievement of human engineering and art, accomplished without modern machines—the result of many careful hands working for almost two hundred years to realize a grand and ambitious vision. In heavenly places on earth like St. Peter's—and other grand cathedrals—believers feel their faith surge, and even unbelievers feel the uplifting gravity of massive well-carved stones.

But as I stood there in that grand artwork my awe eventually came down to earth's common sense. A question began nagging me: Why did so many people go to so much trouble?

The grand, and official, answer immediately came to mind: For the glory of God. Yes, of course. Sincerity of belief deserves being honored for its honesty and intensity, if not for belief's content and purposes. But why worship in this grand, expensive, and perhaps inefficient way? Why not find God and spirituality instead in a simple flower, or in a beggar woman's brown eyes? Why not put the emphasis, energy, genius, and money toward addressing down to earth needs—spiritual and material—instead?

What would Ruskin say? That if art is the result of human passions unleashed by war's excess, and if the winners of wars are profiteers, then art patrons are the beneficiaries and custodians of war's excess. In Old Europe art patrons were kings, aristocrats, bishops, and wealthy merchants. In today's more democratic times patrons are corporations, the wealthy, and more ordinary "consumers" of art. Art serves their individual personality needs, or the purposes which they define for it.

I wonder a lot about art's purposes.

Ruskin suggests that poor people have no time or resources for the making of enduring art because they are busy doing basic life-sustaining work. If art requires leisure and money, these arrive wholesale as a consequence of conquest, often of poor people trying to get through the day by doing their life-sustaining chores. The spoils of war that ancient conquering armies paraded past cheering crowds featured not only the women, girls and boys they enslaved; it included the spoils of war, stolen stuff made from silver, gold, and brass, and, less visibly, the leisure and wealth necessary for the making of more art. Slaves did much of the work on many of the monuments we adore.

I see some progress when it comes to victory parades. Today the enslavement of women, girls and boys is not usually put on parade. And what happens in sweatshops is not, technically speaking, slavery.

Don't get me wrong: The food for thought Ruskin provides is hard to swallow whole. His comments, like mine here, are only abstractly meaningful, like some art. I love what I believe is (good) art, and I'm as capable as anyone of liking bad and ordinary art. I'm also a beneficiary of several wars, a prosperous child of World War II and several other wars since. My prosperity is linked to the death of thousands of soldiers and civilians. So in my good time I feel privileged to spend a few hours scribbling poems rather than digging potatoes out of dirt. But I can't stand on any street in London, Paris, Rome, Barcelona, Berlin, St. Paul or Minneapolis without wondering about the sources of the wealth that paid for the great art roosting in these wonderful places, and what provided me the leisure for scribbling poems. Now and then I pause to ask why I write poems. After reading Ruskin the word "empire" keeps creeping into my mind, and with it the image of a child, big-eyed, and starving.

*

I prefer not to be personally responsible for every big-eyed child starving somewhere in the world, and my poems don't feed starving children. Nor should an artist's sons or daughters plunge into wholesale guilt over their failures to address everything wrong with the world. It's easy to find someone else to blame. Only dimly and distantly do we see ourselves as individually responsible, especially in the absence of a sense of collective responsibility.

And only dimly and often distantly is war obviously connected to the production of individual works of art. But hard questions still nag, with tangles too gnarled and fine to unravel into uniformed lines standing at attention in short essay form.

If there is a hint of truth in what Ruskin said about the arts—"that no great art ever yet rose on Earth, but among a

283

nation of soldiers"—I cannot easily dismiss the conclusion that the prosperity of the arts we enjoy might be directly proportional to a people's inclination to wage wars. That the U.S. has been almost continuously at war since (and before) the Revolutionary War—rightly or wrongly, by proxy or directly, in hot or cold confrontations—is clearly outlined in history books most people prefer not to read. Since 1846 the U.S. military has "intervened," for example, 79 times in Latin America alone, and for most of the last half-century we as U.S. citizens have enjoyed the aura of peace at home even while we have been actively at war abroad. If war is a major part of American enterprise and if art is one of its by-products, on what grounds can the expenditure of public money for arts development be defended? And why should peace-lovers value the arts?

These questions are especially troubling when we consider how war art has been used to legitimize and empower princes, dictators, nations and businesses that find wars useful. When we think of "Europe" an artificial construct comes to mind: We think of the great capitals— London, Paris, Madrid, Vienna, Rome, etc. etc. etc.—and of their fine and noble art. We speak of the glory that was Greece and the grandeur that was Rome, with the glory and grandeur of their art providing us some reason to look past the abuses and horrors these empires visited on conquered people. Seldom do bean pickers, goat herders and woodcutters come to mind, except in folk and fairy tales, and seldom as victims of the so-called winners of wars. Except for a sculpture by Michelangelo I'm aware of no European monument representing slaves, who did most of the hard labor of empire-building, as laborers, and as anonymous artists and artisans.

Self-interested individual artists routinely serve the self-interests of war's sponsors. Statues and portraits of war heroes are favorite subjects of art, as are landscapes of war scenes, rousing marches, and inspirational novels for young adults that exalt "heroic" virtues. Now we also get a manly fill of violent big screen movies, some of which resemble horrific video games, and these we consume as a staple of our cultural fast food cuisine. When I step back from such displays I begin wondering if even war art deemed "grand" and "fine" provides war a vulgar beauty, and compelling power, it doesn't deserve. Can it do anything more, usually, than glorify and caricature war's horrific realities? Is any art about war truly "realistic?" Can it ever be? Does such art not only distract but also delude us?

It seems easy and appropriate to appreciate "grand" and "fine" art for its "own sake"—whatever that means—perhaps merely for the sake of the careful craft that goes into it. But do we transfer this appreciation for craft to the purposes for which such art is used? Does the careful artwork of a grand palace chime with the dirty work done by a brutal dictator who once paid workers to construct it, or some corporate bandit who now lives in it? Do fine sculptures and stained glass windows do justice to priests who looked the other way as so-called witches burned and as Jews were herded into concentration camps? How lovely were the fine-tuned choruses singing halleluiah as preachers kept their silences while blacks were being lynched? The actions art empowers cast shadows on its lovely forms. How chastely white are the columns holding up the house of presidents who permit torture? And how delicate are the sensibilities of billionaires who make obscene profits from sweatshop labor in order, among other things, to fill their mansions with Picassos and Monets?

As I stood that third time in St. Peter's the sense of art's overwhelming power to both lift and delude my spirits descended on me. The question I couldn't avoid was simply this: Did St. Peter's as a work of art do more than saints, theology, good deeds and articles of faith to legitimize the authority and define the mission of the Church? Would the Church have been different, and differently Christian, if Michelangelo, Raphael and a host of other wonderful artists had not enhanced the Church's aura of authority with their great art? Did their conscientious work put a lovely mask over a lot of corruption, and did their art make "holy" wars more possible, and unholier?

I'm not singling out the Catholic Church. What the Church provides its believers in the way of spirituality is incalculable, and some of its devotees have worked faithfully to reduce poverty and misery. But its indulgence of high taste for the arts chimes with its hierarchical structure, giving it a commanding view of the artless and of its iconoclastic Puritan rivals whose artistic tastes trend toward the simple and plain, often the dreary. As a political and economic institution that has relied on artistic high taste to enhance its authority, the Church is an easy target. And the questions we direct its way about art's influence on the minds of people are also applicable to any institution living under the influence of a king, prince, president, millionaire, or committee chair.

There's no cynic in me asking these questions. I have high, probably unrealistic, hopes for art. So there is a nag in me who keeps wondering about what "good" art is and what it is good for. That nag first asks, What is art? Is it any man-made thing, or is it defined by the desire to express a vision in some sense authentic and original? Are all such visions created equal? Do they have the same inherent value, or do some have qualities that, in some sense, are connected to a sense of beauty, and, presumably, with beauty's power to do some good in the world? If so, wherein lies art's beauty and virtue? How are they best expressed?

That nag also tells me there's a difference between "art" and "craft"—that craft refers to skill while art expresses a vision and the values inherent in that vision. The nag supposes that the best art marries expert craft with worthwhile vision, and that the best artists brood over the misuse of worthwhile vision—the re-purposing of art, artists, and their reputations.

And the citizen inside the art nag asks if the state, especially a so-called Big Government state like Minnesota, has any business being involved with the arts.

*

To claim that art has nothing to do with our troubles is to minimize its influence, or to attribute to it a life of its own most of us don't understand and are unwilling or unable to explain. To claim that it has no behavioral or moral impact on daily life and decision-making neutralizes and dehumanizes its presence. Such claims transport art to some airy sphere where only a few—the artsy types—"get it." Art, whether it be a museum piece or simple logo for a new company, is usually selected by a few experts for reasons seldom made clear, sometimes not even to themselves. The experts have their uses for the art they select, and the public is seldom consulted about whether these uses serve the public good.

When we decide not to make sense of art it's sometimes because both art and artists make us seem stupid when we try to find words. Our language about art revolves around a solipsist set of synonyms: What we "like" we equate with what we call "good." A standard of preference is identified with a standard of value. If we like something—let's say, for example, a zombie movie—it's the same as saying it meets the standard for good movies, and that good movies are no better than the zombie movie we like. In these cases meaningful discussion goes in circles, and in many cases discussion is socially unacceptable. In the pursuit of this kind of art happiness all opinions about art's value are created equal.

It is generally assumed that art is good when it is "creative," but what it creates is often difficult to express in clear terms. When artists and art "consumers" say, "It means whatever you think or want it to mean?" they seldom give a penny for our thoughts as they wait for us to say what they want to hear. For art to mean no more than what consumers want it to mean allows artists to surrender responsibility for defining the uses to which their art may be put once it leaves their hands. Surrendering ownership of a work does not neutralize its moral or social impact, but it frees its new owners to make what they want of it. If art becomes just another commodity—like Beanie Babies or Barbie Dolls—subject to the whims of its owners or the marketplace, it compromises its ability to define itself by the qualities generated by its purposes, content and structures, and by the sense of reality inherent in the vision it projects.

But if art is one of the "high virtues and faculties of man" (and women, Ruskin fails to mention), it is also difficult to see outside the context of what Ruskin sees as its primal parent, war. He is unequivocal about war's art-making ability. "You must have war to produce art," he tells his cadets. War destroys properties, lives, and other art while creating the profits, and inspirations, that make new art possible. Ruskin's linkage of what's "pure and noble" about war with "expressions of the highest state of the human condition," however, suggests that not all art is "pure and noble." No one who is sane would assert that war represents what is "highest" about the human condition, and most would agree that war, even when its cause is "just," is what is lowest about human enterprise. If we accept that art comes from war, we are not relieved of the responsibility to distinguish between art that expresses "the highest state of the human condition" and art that fosters more war.

In a culture based on the abuses war propagates the term "art" is easily, even promiscuously, abused. It means whatever someone wants it to mean—and do. So it's not surprising that many books have been written celebrating the "art of war," all of them streamlining warfare into ways of crafting techniques and technologies having their own set of qualities, purposes, and outcomes. This "art," like war's glorious monuments, are created to celebrate war's partisan destructiveness. It is also easy to confuse powerful new military technologies with "art." Death and destruction, often on a massive scale, are the intent and outcome of these technologies.

It seems sensible to distinguish the technologies of death from the arts of life.

*

It's arguable that art has a natural enemy, nature herself. If "nature" is in some sense the opposite of "art"— that is, if what we make with our minds, hands and machines requires us to use natural resources, and thereby even destroy, the spaces, plants, animals, and resources provided us by nature—then art may be said to be nature's enemy. Do we delude ourselves when we claim that the making of art is a wholly "creative" act, especially when we bulldoze a field alive with trees, weeds, and grasses to build a new museum on it?

As the natural environment gets "developed"—a term seldom seen as a synonym for "debased"—we find more and more of the natural world routinely abused and exhausted. It has become obvious now to all but the most persistent blind believers that we live in a special state of emergency calling on us to distinguish between art that destroys nature from that which allows us to make a truce with it.

One critical question—there are others—facing the present generation and its stressed planet is strictly aesthetic: If art is one of the spoils of war and a despoiler of nature, can it also be conceived as an act of resistance that makes war and the destruction of nature less certain? Can art, child of war, be war's spoil sport? And can art ally itself to nature in ways at once useful, beautiful, and recreative?

Ruskin's comments about art's incestuous relationship to war and the inherent antipathy between art and nature should make Minnesota's citizens proud that the Clean Water, Land, and Legacy Amendment had broad public support when it was approved by the state government in 2008. The Amendment's arts and culture clause was embedded in environmental protection aims: "To protect, enhance and restore our wetlands, prairies, forest, fish, game and wildlife habitat; to preserve our arts and cultural heritage; to support our parks and trails; and to protect, enhance, and restore our lakes, rivers, streams, and groundwater." To fulfill these ambitious ends the State of Minnesota, a "Big Government State", increased its sales tax on spenders by 3/8 of one percent.

In contrast, the U.S. government, the most generous sponsor of wars, penny pinches the arts. For the year 2014 the U.S. National Defense Authorization Act called for $638,000,000,000 in "defense" spending, with another $85,600,000,000 for "winding down" the war in Afghanistan. Meanwhile, the $154.46 million allocated for the National Endowment for the Arts, the federal agency that supports arts activities in all 50 states, looks miniscule in comparison to the roughly one billion dollars spent annually to fund military musicians. The numbers suggest that the U.S. government is willing to admit the existence of the arts as a national pastime, and that music by and for soldiers and their supporters is the most important national arts activity.

Most troubling is art that does the work of war by inspiring irrational fears. The huge U.S. defense budget suggests that people in the U.S. have a lot to fear. To justify such huge expenditures on war we should first ask if the fears are imagined or real. We might also ask if the fears have external—foreign and "enemy"—sources, or if they are in part generated by a steady consumption of American art.

A steady stream of thriller novels and big-budget terror-action movies comes to mind.

When domestic art generates fear it may be an enemy's most powerful weapon, making it easier for nations to wage war on each other and on the arts that resist enemy influences. Art suffers collateral damage in any war, but ideological and religious wars zero in on an enemy's artwork. Iconoclasm is a regular feature of religious wars, with a culture's symbolic art often reduced to elemental forms such as rubble, silver and gold. When art loses its face value as the expression of individual and cultural visions, and when it undergoes diasporas outside the societies in which it was created, its anonymity becomes useful to those willing to undermine its purposes. When precious *objets d'art* are destroyed they become worthless, and when melted down they live on simply as hard currency. While the prices of fine art often become absurdly bloated they are also subject to the ironies of terrible times that may reduce their value far below the price of a cabbage, a glassful of clean water, or one fresh apricot.

But art's forbidding power to preserve itself is suggested by many historical survivor examples. It is common for warring nations to destroy enemy temples with impunity, but exceptional art is sometimes spared. During World War II what was it that prevented generals from issuing orders to bomb the cathedral at Cologne, or from excluding Kyoto, Japan, as a possible A-bomb target? These sites were not spared so they could become spoils of war, for it was the conquerors who were carried away with them. Nor were they spared because they represented sacred creeds. During both world wars dutiful Christian soldiers devastated many Christian holy shrines in Europe and beyond, and they certainly had no special interest in preserving the Shinto religion worshipped in the temples of Kyoto they did not destroy. The artwork of these holy places had a power that made them exceptions to war's destructive ways, and this power was more important to the survival of these sites than were the creeds they stood for that failed to keep the peace. It is also doubtful that they were saved by those who make a religion of art for art's sake. Clearly, the structures of those shrines spared by American bombs had a spiritual power that touched something deep in our very humanity. The magnificent expression of that depth took an elegant, convincing, and successful stand against war.

What would John Ruskin say, notably about the of the Minnesota Clean Water, Land, and Legacy Amendment money earmarked "to preserve our arts and cultural heritage" and natural resources? That Minnesotans are convinced the private sector will not generate enough war arts without state support?

Or that they want to give peace, and nature, a chance.

*

Ruskin acknowledges that some art gives birth to "All the pure and noble arts of peace." So while war's excesses make art possible, what kind of art does war generate that opposes war?

What can the "pure and noble arts of peace" do? What inheres in its very nature that fosters life rather violence and death?

The question gets giddy as we turn it different ways, and it develops a distant look of abstraction as we try to define basic standards that apply it to multiple art forms. Our varied responses to individual works of art resist definition but invite further discussion. This resistance is one of art's best strengths. The aura of uncertainty—call it mystery in its best examples—surrounding certain art sets it apart from the clarities offered by caricature, stereotype and business as usual propaganda necessary to the demonizing of enemies. Such mystery challenges us to re-articulate our emotional and mental responses to real experiences. Art's mystery creates new life by reawakening us to life's variety, complexity, dissonance, fluidity, and forms. It attracts us to these variables by way of an invariable, the constant at their core, a form of beauty James Joyce associates with the word "radiance." The heart intuitively tunes this constant in, though it often lacks words for it.

War art moves away from this ideal, not toward simplicity but toward the sameness that generates revulsion, disorder and violence. The appropriate—critical—response to it Joyce appropriately calls "loathing." Some pieces of music and art spontaneously cause us to turn away from them; loathing manifests itself both as actual disgust and as lifeless apathy. If Ruskin drew attention to the military aspects of the art of ancient Egypt and Greece, and praised the art of Gothic chivalry sponsored by "the fighting dukeships and citizenships of Italy" as work that allowed "a passionate delight in war itself, for its own sake [to be] born again"—he was as terrified as he was charmed by it. In recent centuries one of state-sponsored art's favorite subjects are the uniform and the super-symmetry of battalions marching in tidy rows in honor of the violent chaos of war. Leni Riefenstahl's *Triumph of the Will*, her celebration of a brutal Nazi regime, is one of war's award-winning twentieth century masterworks.

Though in his speech to the cadets Ruskin asserted that, "whenever the faculties of men are at their fullest, they must express themselves by art," good art's lust for beauty's original faces and forms is war's enemy. Certainly we are all born with creative impulses that males, not able to give biological birth, express via art. If some psychiatrists blame outbreaks of war on repression of libidinous energies, sublimation of these energies is a way of enlisting beauty into rebellions against oppression. The cadets Ruskin addressed at the Royal Military Academy, like painters, sculptors and musicians, have the urge to break the chains that bind—emotional, sexual, economic, moralistic, political. Good art, like war, wants out, and will out, like graffiti splashed on public monuments as individual expressions of resistance to the powers monuments represent. A nation's well-being perhaps may be measured by the quality of the graffiti its nameless artists produce.

But graffiti art also serves war when performed by those who find making a point as easy as shooting a gun. Art calculated to make a point, especially when as narrow as artless minds, shrinks to a slogan useful to propaganda pushers. In good art there are never merely "points," and never just black or white, or bad guys and good, however these melodramatic opposites present themselves. There are instead shades and shapes seen in no rainbow or on no skin surface, shadows of meaning lurking in conspiring metaphors, sharps and flats singing minor melodies as the brass section rages on in C-major. The innuendoes, inflections, and reflections of such art gather to attempt the impossible: Visions of the world's realities on the move, morphing as they distinguish themselves from the stereotype and banal.

What good do good artists do as a class? Their eccentric genies together escape from magic lanterns to change and trouble us. In war-oriented societies (such as ours) in which war is a well-heeled and respected norm, artists keep testing and extending the parameters of the possible. The pleasure good art provides, its radiance, is difficult to forbid or wall out. It quietly gets into the goosebumps under our skins. While art that serves war dulls the senses and mind, and often is calculated to distract people from war's presence and realities by "entertaining" them, art that makes peace engages people by holding or transfixing them, putting them on alert. A given aspect of art genius is its ability, like metaphors, to "bring things together," and these linkages are most originally of things not normally associated. So the oddness we find in much art, its dissonance and originality, is a way of establishing the metaphoric, and organic, unity of individuals, societies and nature. As such, art extends itself to outsiders—the eccentric, the ill and disabled, the rebellious, the unseemly––and tunes communities into their presence. As outsiders are more clearly seen it becomes more difficult to make enemies of them.

Given war's origins in centers of power and its monopolization of the arts by the wealthy and powerful, the decentralization of art makes it friendly to democracies. Ordinary people need and love the arts, and love doing art. To imagine that art belongs in and emanates from the boondocks is an unconventional view, and popular art raises issues not unlike those raised by "pure and noble" aristocratic art with its addiction to expensive, often absurdly extravagant, tastes. New—and young—artists not steeped in aristocratic arts will make mistakes; they will confuse arts with crafts and entertainment, and noise with music, for example. But an arts culture is a crucible, and when what's hot in the pot is stirred something good is likely to come of it. This something may be very good for those—artists or not—who could use some stirring themselves.

The presence of the arts in the center of public life also favors social stability. The artless are also the alienated, and the alienated more easily become enemies. As more and more immigrants arrive to work in rural areas, and as the poor and dispossessed abandon rural areas for big city life, the degree of their alienation depends on the art they encounter, or its absence.

We should not underestimate good art's transformative power. When art's vision and beauty are ingenious and when a work is expressed with consummate skill, it creates moments that transcend the differences that divide, and it binds performers and audience into a sense of community aglow with the art work's radiance. War's inclination to divide and conquer dissolves in the separate peace created by this radiance. Under its spell we forget that the artist was a jerk, the performer an arrogant opportunist, the work sponsored by profiteers, and the audience loaded with pretenders. The heart and mind bask in the radiance, as differences dissolve and disappear into it.

Given the state of the world it is unlikely that art will overwhelm war and redeem nature soon. If war makes art that in turn makes more war then it is clear that the fate of societies—and nature—is descending into a destructive spiral. When art violates nature without honoring or at least making a truce with it, art does the work of war. If the arts and artists of peace are to survive, they will have to establish their own presence based on a holy alliance with nature, and look to nature to discover the organic principles of growth unifying their work. This holy alliance ties art and artists to nature's munificence as a source of material and spiritual sustenance. As we approach a moment in human history when the end of nature seems a possibility, artists may do well to conceive of themselves as master gardeners, with their art providing food for thought derived from rivers, lakes, soil, forests, marshes, fens, and airs these natural resources give us for our own good. Art that stages survival of the fittest melodramas dominates current popular arts scenes, with the concertos that speak to nature's graciousness, its edges contained by rounds, are played on the periphery. If art is necessarily different from nature in kind, it need not be by degrees. When the boundaries between the two are semi-permeable, both, like Aeolian harps diversely framed, may live by the rule of doing as little harm to each other as possible. In such work respect and love for nature and art are reciprocally renewed.

*

So, my son, I send you off to college knowing that dedicated artists face difficult odds as they try to make room for their work on a planet becoming more contentious and crowded. You will have to confront the artist's temptation to want "out"—to exist on the periphery of society and to let others define your work as having marginal, or merely decorative, value. There is no way out. For all the years of your life your nation has been actively at war. You therefore are a child of war, and your art, charged by the destructiveness of war that cries out for new creations, is also one of war's offspring. To respond to these cries your art will not be merely marginal or decorative. It will have to give peace a chance. Nor will its value be easy to assess. Few judge art's value by doing a cost analysis of its healing impact on the inner life of individuals, or by assessing how it saves taxpayers money by providing alternatives to their absurdly expensive addiction to wars. If war's accountants feel no shame about calculating the projected costs of future wars, you as artist perhaps should enlist accountants to assess how much destruction your art prevents and how many lives and medical costs your art saves the state. It's one thing to address enemies with violence. It's another to use the arts to make friends of enemies.

College departments of accounting might want to explore the new job and research opportunities these original arts assessment alternatives could create.

You, my son, have not always been easy to have around, especially during your middle teenage years. And good artists are not always easy to have around, especially if they challenge themselves and others to explore both what's deeply inward and most essentially real outside themselves. For this reason we should expect them to disobey their fathers, especially if these fathers were children of a nation almost perpetually at war. Good art is often edgy, and good artists are often on edge, because that's where the horizons are.

So I'm sure that you, my son, will think you know it all, as I do here on this page. I expect you to look upon my work and say, "It is good." All of it. My behavior will irritate you because I am your dad and I love repeating "It is good" after everything I say to you as you move away to improve on me.

I know one thing for sure. Your contrariness will make you undesirable as a spoil of war, and therefore you will give war lords one less person for war to spoil.

So go, Son, do your art. You have vitally important work to make of your play. See, feel, taste, smell, hear and think it too, all at once, and add generous servings of learning to it. Above all live it all your life, in its radiance.

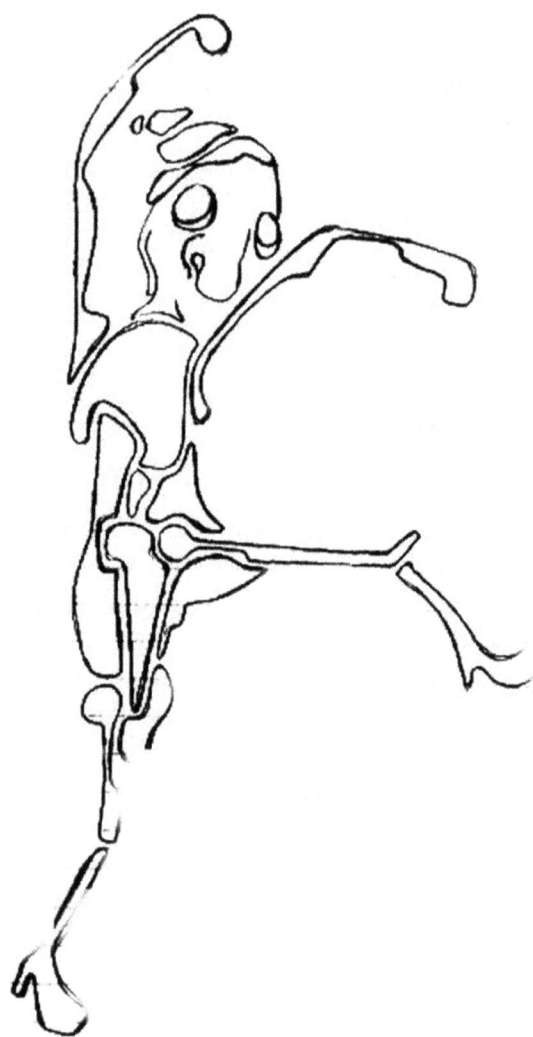

Endnote: Family Life

The writer Isabel Allende (*The House of the Spirits*) considered herself a "child" of Gabriel Marquez (*One Hundred Years of Solitude*), who in turn saw himself as a "son" of William Faulkner (Yoknapatawpha). That these authors who wrote elaborate family sagas thought of themselves as kinfolk suggests that family life has a dream-like presence that does not distinguish between those who live south of the American border and in the American south. For each of these three writers family life is the major metaphor for history's ongoing intrigues.

In family sagas we glean small chapters of the history of humanity. Power—the strength of love and hate—drives these sagas, sometimes lurking anonymously in the dynamics of plots, call them conspiracies, we also call story-lines. Love and hate (call them also the powers of attraction and repulsion) work their way through human relationships into family destinies. All those American stories that "look forward to the future," as if there is no darkness following sunsets in the golden West, seek to escape from or turn their backs to the presence of family. Those with no interest in or fearful of the secrets of the past keep the long histories of family's blessings and curses hidden from view.

There's only a little truth in the saying that "history repeats itself." It does, but only in the sense that its powers reassert themselves, inevitably in new guises and invariably variably. Some family names, and all its members, die out. But nothing that happens is coincidental, and in the stories that may or may not get told we, their offspring, are all adopted children.

War, those terrible episodes that afflict the so-called "Family of Man," often if not always are rooted in conflicts between male and female as they try to mate, marry and engage in family life. Despite Eve's popularity as a primal antagonist, no one thinks of her as mother of the "Family of Woman." If war makes families dysfunctional, wars are also caused by dysfunctional families quarreling over property—and naming—rights.

VII.   Jock Strappings
(from *The Oxymoronic Dictionary*)

Adjective with plural noun

1. Over-organized forms of play, endured during time away from work, elevated into work-out routines by those hung up on making play hurt.
2. Pre-mature mating rituals configured as war games by real men about to divorce their wives so they can devote their lives to spectator sports.
3. The great hunger for celebrity felt as a small salivation response following a winner's feeding frenzy on losers.
4. The self-flagellations enjoyed by taxpayers who pay the salaries of millionaire coaches and the construction costs of billion dollar stadiums.

Antonym: Physical fitness.

My Little Left-Sock Deals

Because I'm addicted to basketball not even the woman to whom I had been married for three decades really knew: Every morning I put my left sock on first. Always my left. All the other basketball nuts who play in the noon ball pickup games at the YMCA know I have trouble going to my left. That never kept me from voting with the liberals. But because I'm short, slow, suddenly old, and hopelessly addicted to playing the game until I drop, I've made a religion of putting my left sock on first.

It's a strange behavior that makes me feel like a superstitious fool whenever my actual mind kicks in. I prefer to think I share this distinction with more famous fools. Captain Ahab of *Moby-Dick* fame comes to mind— that tragic sufferer who made a whale with a headful of spermaceti synonymous with the mind of God. But for me it's just my addiction to noon ball at the YMCA, not grand whales, that gives my left-sock hopes both meaning and momentum.

I take little consolation from new genetic research suggesting that my left-sock habit makes me more fit to survive. For the close kinship between an omen and amen we can thank the scientists who discovered the God gene. Such a gene has survival applications, notably as a way to balance the floor on basketball courts where what Richard Dawkins called "the selfish gene" also comes into play. Ball hogs, with their selfish gene, never pass the ball, and then there are saints like me who long for nothing more than to touch the ball so they can throw up a prayer now and then.

But I suspect there may be a third gene, a role player, hidden away. If you're short, slow and old and still insist on playing the game, you have to conclude that a basketball gene was implanted in a special few. So you find yourself dependent on your genes. You have no choice but to play, and if your selfish gene fails to make a winner of you, you depend on your God gene to get you by.

It's my belief that my God gene, the omen and amen chromosomes in it, requires me to put my left sock on first every single day. It's that left sock that gives me a shot at getting through a life experience I can't avoid as it makes a hopeless loser of me.

How do I know if putting my left sock on first improves my noon ball performance at the Y? My secret (until now) has required me to be the judge and jury of what works. If I do okay in a Monday game I'm assured my left sock did the trick. If I have a lousy game I'll have to put it on more carefully next time. On some days I change my socks two or three times (always left sock first) so I can increase my odds. I need all the help I can get.

When things are going particularly wrong—not only on the court but at home, in Washington D.C., or maybe because the buried victims of an earthquake in some God-forsaken place turn me inside out—I feel the need to invent new procedures to reinforce the influence of my left sock. If I stumble going up the stairs it's probably because I shouldn't pressure my left sock by leading with my left foot. If I refuse a delicious bowl of ice cream it's probably because my left sock is aware of my sacrifice. If I refuse to scratch an itch it's because both the bowl of ice cream and the left sock understand that this act of self-denial is expected of me by a Power, my God gene again, that could make things worse for me.

My practices may be singular but I'm not alone. Check out any ordinary free throw lane in the middle of any basketball game. The pressure's on: The poor guy on the line has practiced forty-foot buzzer-beater shots for half a lifetime, and now he's expected to perform a genteel fifteen-foot lob while standing lonely and still, with body parts seizing up in front of thousands of eyes. Ask Shaq what it's like for a giant to drift a small balloon into a wastebasket from fifteen feet, with half of the world's normal-sized people waiting to sneer because they're so short.

When things are on the line we all need divine intervention. So we try three bounces. Not two, or (ever!) four. A Holy Trinity three is preferred. Then we spin the ball three times in our hands—perfect spins, with no wobbly seams. Then we cradle the ball under our left arm as we touch our stomach, chest and chin with our right hand. In the same order ever time. Then we take three deep breaths. Then three exhalations to cast evil demons out. And when the ritual is complete we load the gun and shoot.

I know of no empirical study comparing the success ratio of the thousands who perform similar rituals to the few who don't. Sometimes it makes me wonder why university research facilities exist.

One of the guys in my city league games had a ritual that took so long he had to change his ways after the refs made a silent pact among themselves to time him out and take his free throws away. "Breaking the habit was really hard," he said, "because I'd get the shakes. At first I tried cutting down—aiming my hand at the rim and sighting along the arm, then adjusting the elastic on my shorts, then rocking up and down three times with my knees bent. But I felt awkward doing it that way, so I went cold turkey instead."

"Nothing?"

"I cut way down. I don't go to church, but I started saying the same little prayer in my own head every time: 'God, I promise to pray even when I don't need your help sometimes.' I think it helps, especially the ones that rattle in."

What he says would make perfect sense to some good neighbors of mine. One of them, an insurance man, says Jesus really walked on water whenever he wanted to. How can that be? He says maybe water isn't what it used to be. Maybe back in Biblical times there was more substance to it. And maybe days were different back then too. Maybe back then a day was a thousand years long. He says the library is full of books that agree with him, and I should check the internet.

The other neighbor is an engineer who works day and night connecting the little parts of widgets that go BOOM! He believes water's always been the same, but that doesn't mean Jesus can't walk on it. He believes it happened once, but what he believes is his business and it doesn't keep his widgets from working efficiently. No harm, no foul.

Basketball benchwarming and timeouts inspire meditative moments that lead to interesting comparisons. Take baseball, for example. I'm grateful I gave up my baseball habit years ago. I don't spit well. Even foreign exchange students mention that baseball players have strange ways—they say sweet nothings to their bats, they pull on a left ear lobe before every pitch, they adjust their cups just before stepping in the box, they point to the sky after getting a base hit, they envision home runs escaping like doves into the grandstands just before they strap down their batting gloves to keep their heads in the game—and they spit. The spitting is not, I'm convinced, merely habitual. It has meaning, as if spitting (sunflower seed husks, tobacco juice, bits of food dislodged from teeth, bits of teeth, or just plain phlegm) is a ritual requirement for membership in the baseball cult. I personally believe that a spit ball's beguiling dance results from magic invoked by spit. Those who doubt the supernatural basis of spitting also can't account for the infrequency of news reports about baseball players contracting infectious diseases. In the midst of waterfall spitting one never sees a runny nose. Coincidences like that don't just happen.

If amateur basketball players like me, usually confined indoors, deny themselves spitting's charmed prowess, their limited circumstances offer them ample opportunities to invent their own. Who knows how many left sock firsters there are playing Noon Ball in big city YMCAs everywhere in the world, or who maybe insists on touching his right hand to his nose twice after he puts a jock strap on, or wearing that jock inside out every other day, or counting to seven just before a game begins, or brushing his teeth before heading for the gym, or wiping a Sign of the Cross across his chest every time a foul is called on the man guarding him, or retying a shoelace during time outs, or washing a shooting hand in the drinking fountain at halftime of every game, or being sure to call Mom the night before.

Sir James Frazer, in his encyclopedic anthropological study called *The Golden Bough*, details the many ceremonials so-called primitive peoples performed to persuade their Great Referees to make winners of them. When an infertile Batak woman of Sumatra was having a hard time scoring points as a mother, for example, the tribal elders gathered to sacrifice three grasshoppers to the gods, and then a swallow was set free with a prayer persuading the woman's infertility to fly away. If the natives of certain islands of the Indian Archipelago periodically sent their diseases away to sea by loading little boats down with fowl, eggs and nasty insects, how many of us who now play twenty-first century noon ball heap our missed free throws, bad passes and double dribbles onto the backs of teammates, children, and wives?

It behooves us to step back from our behaviors to gain perspective and make better sense of them. Is there both ritual recurrence and religious fervor (perhaps lacking the usual omens and amens) to ever popular tailgate parties? Frazer tells us that the village chiefs of the Hos of northeastern India believed that their gods required the sacrifice of a cock and two hens (one of them black), these fowls offered up with the flowers of the palash tree, rice-flour bread, and sesame seeds. Then the villagers imposed on themselves the need to chant and shout, preludes to orgies of feasting, drinking, cursing, and debauchery during which "servants forget their duty to their masters, children their reverence for parents, men their respect for women, and women all notions of modesty, delicacy, and gentleness." If the Hos, normally a modest, quiet, and gentle tribe, were willing to part with their common sense in order to fill their little bowls with rice, what ceremonies do we perform and what divine aid do we invoke in our high-tech times to reap victory in the Super Bowl?

I can't escape this bottom line: Because we all cut peculiar little left-sock deals, God believes in a free market economy. We are all deal-making entrepreneurs in God's vast free enterprise system, and it's up to God's Hidden Hand to provide. Maybe it's our God gene that requires deal-making of us, that and the thrill of the chase. No one can dispute that the mystery of existence is enhanced by the suspense resulting from dramas of profit and loss.

But there's a beauty to this system too. In the old days philosophers argued for the existence of God by invoking the Argument from Design: Science tells us (ask Newton) that there is both pattern and order to the universe, call it "design," and because a design requires a designer it follows logically that God the prime designer exists. Each little left-sock deal I make with God at some free throw line in the mind is my way of saying yes, I'm buying into God's scheme of things. Every missed free throw is really part of God's plan. This fact requires me to be a lobbyist too, asking God to tweak the scheme so his Hidden Hand can give me a little of what the politicians call pork. It's not really practice that makes perfect in this scheme of things. I can never work hard enough to earn enough. Never in my lifetime will I ever slam-dunk a basketball, no matter how many hours I spend in the weight room trying to lift myself up by my bootstraps. Every free throw I shoot is an outward and visible sign that the hand of God is shooting my free throws for me. The ball is in God's hands. When you're on the line loaded down with that thought, you realize that not even free throws are really free.

There's something to be said for the relief from responsibility such thinking inspires.

Rooting for Yellowness

The philosopher Albert Camus, sensitive to society's desire to enjoy a moral lifestyle, made no secret of this essential belief: "All that I know most surely about morality and obligations, I owe to football." Since "football" meant "soccer" to him he understandably skirted the lessons to be learned from American football field generals simulating our World Wars by calling for a blitz or throwing a bomb. My cousin Louis, a tennis player living in Iowa City, tells me about a Japanese visitor who had some knowledge of American bombs, two very horrifying ones in particular, but who could not understand American football. "Why don't they give each team a ball," she asked, "so they don't have to fight?"

It's that time of year again. Here, downstream, the maples on the Mississippi River bluffs are maturing into their lovely hues, and on Sunday mornings church bells tell us there are hymns in those trees. Meanwhile, outside the Minneapolis Metrodome, the tailgate parties have begun— those picnics in parking lots. As game time nears the huddled masses gather in front of TV sets, their souls sinking into sofas as their mouths water for chips, beer, and a score that makes winners of them about half the time, or less.

Why all the fuss? The Vikings never raped and pillaged in these parts, and our Ole and Lena folk tend to be nice Lutherans not much interested in Norway or Thor. So why do we shell out $50, $100, even $500 to achieve a couple hours' worth of social security inside those unpearly stadium gates? Why no fuss when team owners—no doubt troubled that the nation will have socialized medicine before their new executive suites are furnished with the widest wide-screen TVs—keep asking for new taxes to build new sports palaces? Why are we reminded of doctors' waiting rooms as we endure the roughly four hours of talk, huddles, time outs, and endless ads for Viagra, cars, chips and beer that interrupt the roughly 18 minutes of action on the field? And who needs the sanity of old-fashioned Sundays, that day given to meditation and quiet leisure once upon a time sacred to pagans as the day of the Sun and to Christians as day of the Son.

A few years ago, while I was in church on a lovely Sunday morning trying to become more congregational, I became aware of football's power to move cultural mountains. The minister, a nice-enough regular fellow, was chipper when he made the announcement to the assembly: The annual membership meeting with its discussion of faith and policy would be changed to late afternoon so we wouldn't miss the Vikings-Packers game. Only a few puritans in those pews frowned. No one stood firm—like the golden-haired prostitute Melina Mercouri—to declare "Never on Sunday." And the traditional chicken dinner every Sunday at the family table simply no longer can compete with the TV football feast of chips and beer.

Let's not go too far with this complaint. Though in ancient times it was hard to tell heroes and gods apart, Sunday football is not a religion. Football honors heroes, not God.

But there's something deeply moving about crowds that can make demi-gods of heroes. While visiting Louis in Iowa City I attended a football game pitting Hawkeyes against Panthers from Northern Iowa. I paid $54 to get in.

The Hawkeye Marching Band made clever designs on the field while cheerleaders strutted their smiles with military precision. I was mainly impressed by the massive collage of yellow T-shirts across the way, thousands of University of Iowa students teeming like bees in a hive, clapping their arms like mandibles in unison. And then the spelling bee began, with huge flags requiring thousands to stand and wave as they spelled out I-O-W-A in a chorus round that no doubt appeased all gods gazing down at the football shrine from clouds above endless fields of corn. The spectacle was spectacular, colorful, loud, and grand—choreographed into a dramatic ritual for a mass of humanity happy to sacrifice their individual identities to the corporate scene.

What would an anthropologist from outer space—or Louis' Japanese friend—think of such performances, especially when they become more ferocious and less artfully conducted on NFL holy days?

The question became more troubling a couple of seasons ago on the day Brett Favre turned traitor and joined the Vikings enemy. A few old Cheesehead gasbags on the Wisconsin side of the Mississippi compared Favre to Wernher Von Braun, who defected from the Germans to work for the Americans after he did Nazi work for years perfecting the V-2 rockets that bombed London in World War II. Favre's rocket arm and Von Braun's rocket mind are incomparable. And both confronted moral dilemmas: Do we abandon—call it betray—our people, our communities, those who cheered us on as our greatness swelled? Yes. For a higher good? Filling the air with footballs and bombs? The prevailing opinion at Cheesehead tailgate parties is that the number both of them wear beneath the uniforms they shed is the one closest to their hearts: Number One.

So what do we root for at a football game? The heroes have huge home-town followings, but they're known to follow the money trail to some other town that is really a vast city swollen with anonymity. Newspapers and TV swell player-hero stories into myths, and now and then the heroes' names end up on the front page as criminals. We are awed by the artful beauty of the occasional great deed––the move combining power and grace—but go silent when it's performed by the visitors. We're dumbstruck by the well-honed athlete, but would rather not gaze at some of the grotesque body parts. The coaches are geniuses, but they're plugged into earphones that deliver wisdom to them from sources better informed. The players' numbers are larger than their names, but they're faceless behind their masks. A lot of them get hurt very seriously. There's a certain unpleasantness about it all, even when the Purple People-Eaters destroy the other team.

And there are certain uncalculated costs. We chip in with taxes to support this free enterprise, not just for a new stadium now and then but for the roads and the parking lots and the latrines and the landfill acres the new stadium requires of us to fulfill its destiny. We are told that pro teams are necessary to local economies, without bothering to count how many people don't shop on Football Sundays, or if the money spent on this week's game would be spent on groceries if it were not heading down the freeway to get in line at the stadium gates. And we bloat our minds with all the time we invest chewing the fat found in entire sections of daily newspapers and endless TV programs that provide sports free enterprisers a steady stream of free advertisements.

We're deeply into it, so what's in it for us?

Though the Iowa Hawkeyes also claim black as one of their essential colors, at the Iowa game yellow stood out. Everyone wearing yellow was cheering for Yellowness. I, born and raised in Michigan, a graduate of Ohio State who pays taxes in Wisconsin, am also a long-time resident of Minnesota with a cousin in Iowa City and daughter at the University of Iowa. So I, at once Wolverine, Buckeye, Badger, Gopher, and Hawkeye, had (like most good Americans) an identity crisis. I was all and none of them. But I found myself rooting for Yellowness too. The other team, the purple-suited one from Northern Iowa, was Purpleness. But on that afternoon I was Yellowness, and I rooted for it. At a Vikings game I would root for Purpleness. I confess that I too wear Number One close to my heart.

No team, by the way, wears pink, for reasons any macho man can explain. And though no one had a thing to say about black, someone provided the corny explanation that in Iowa yellow is really gold.

A lot of preachers tell us the end zone is near. Football has stolen Sunday from them, so they're fighting back with their own high-tech blitzes to accompany their own sporadic outbursts of the wave. Those who are best at it are also good at taxing their congregations to build new stadiums for them. These preachers understand alienation––the sitting alone we do staring at TV and computer monitors, the hours exhausted in idling cars, the vast noplace that is cyberspace––the privatizing of experience that has come to define what it means to be American. And they know what we need: The value of uniform beliefs expressed in colorful and powerfully concentrated chorus form. They understand well the depth that cheering for

Yellowness, or a similarly profound theme, can provide when our genuine family, neighborhood, and national communities falter, become polarized, or don't exist.

Uniformed

Watching big crowds watch big ball games in big sports arenas has become one more way for me to feel small. Spectators now seem required to wear T-shirt uniforms as outward and visible signs of their inward devotion to the scene. Now and then it's possible to spot a deviant in the stands sporting a plaid or polka dot shirt, but deviants seldom cheer or smile. They sit there standing out.

Their devotion is suspect, for it's obvious they haven't signed the unified T-shirt loyalty oath that requires them to swear they never have been, are not now, and never will be members of the party that wants the Cornhusker, Blackhawk or Miami Heat enemies to win. I too have lots of colorful T-shirts with logos on them, and now and then I watch a game on TV. When I do I usually pull the shades, a little worried about what some fan hot-rodding past might say about my failure to color-coordinate myself with the sports franchise of his choice.

Grandstands full of uniforms (and waving hankies, as if everyone is saying farewell to each other) seem at odds with a nation of ordinary folk so deeply at odds with each other. The individuals who inhabit the uniformed blue, red, white, yellow or teal T-shirts during a big game probably would be duking it out with each other if they weren't cheering for the same team. Try talking about abortion, government spending, global warming, immigration, same-sex marriage, birth certificates, raptures, or gun control, and things are likely to get out of control: My way or the highway is the American way, except when our team's ahead.

I spend enough hours on the road to wonder where I really live, and I'm not sure where I am when I spend a lot of hours at a desk or on a sofa in front of the TV. Divorce rates suggest that even moms, dads, and kids routinely fail to co-exist in homes where so many cold wars are waged. When I'm landlocked and blue with Minnesota cold I begin dreaming of Caribbean beaches, and then surfing comes to mind. But because the planet is tangled in the wily wires of the worldwide web it takes less than half an hour for me, like Melville's little Pip, to feel insignificant and lost in all that on-line immensity. I walk down the street, passed by faces texting, cell-phoning, tweeting—being, in short, somewhere other than where they really are—and then too I feel the urge: Why not pay good money for a ticket to a Vikings (or Cornhusker, or Golden Bear, or Blue Devil) game? Maybe if I were doing a color-coordinated wave during a time out I'd feel less at sea.

Meanwhile, most of us spend a few hours in the real places we call home. Near those places a Bible-believing fundamentalist lives next door to a liberal agnostic, a Republican goes to the same church as a Democrat, an African/American walks down the same street as a white supremacist, and a gun-toting NRAer drinks at the same bar as an off-duty cop who favors gun control. When solid facts about any issue don't much count—maybe because they're lost in a democratic crowd of freely expressed opinion—opinions more easily congeal into the hard-core beliefs we take home to bed with us. As we snooze these beliefs burrow deeply into our guts. There they know what they're all about: They want to win.

We wake, convicted winners and losers, to a house

divided. A nation full of citizens holding diverse views is painted red and blue with broad brushes on color-coded political maps. We cheer for our team, blue or red states, as if they're states of mind. We take our made-up mind-set to the big game with us, expecting to have a good fight and win, and when we don't win little riots begin to stir in us that sometimes spill over into the streets. I've been close to such scenes and have had the urge to join the revelry, my anger drunk, unable to walk the straight line that will help it find its way to a place where a home team lives. I know the hung-over feeling that kicks in, the nausea we want to wish away to a good sleep that calls time out from the nasty issues, those hard-core beliefs that keep shouting that it's my way or the highway time.

The millionaires who own the teams say it's a good thing for all of us to keep going to their games. Winning teams make winners of us all, they say, so we have to pay the price for T-shirts, winning teams, and a new stadium with fancy grandstands. Meanwhile, in the grandstands the issues that divide us remain homeless, unspoken for, lost in the crowd.

I too want something to cheer about, but winning teams aren't enough. I'm not alone. A close Presbyterian friend (who also happens to be a gay Republican) confided to me the sad loneliness he feels. He attends church but is made to feel like a hypocrite. He doesn't feel he belongs in either a gay bar or among his fellow Republicans. He's afraid to have a frank conversation with anyone except the few who know him well. He wears his work uniform—suit and tie—religiously, and hides behind sad smiles. He keeps his opinions to himself, doesn't want to win or lose. He just wants to live peacefully someplace and make a decent living for himself. "I feel homeless," he says.

I try consoling him: Read the U.S. Constitution and Bill of Rights. The concepts in those documents are large. They contain multitudes.

I say this knowing that I get small consolation from pledging allegiance to the flag. As I look at the many nasty polarizations all around—the brutal partisanship in state government, the divisive and routinely dishonest loud-mouthing of public discourse, the hard-headed hard-lining of religious belief—I begin losing faith that anyone can agree about what's American about America or Christian about Christianity or humane about humanity. The word "polite" seems rootless too, having divorced itself from "politics" and sometimes the "police." The wellness doctors tell me that a body dies when it destroys itself from within, and that a mind that hates part of itself begins conjuring violence and suicide. When I think about the future of the American body politic I check my wallet to be sure my Social Security card is still there.

I know where I feel most comfortable: Where people like me and are like me too. I want to be a soloist but also want to belong to a choir that sings hymns with words I can truly believe. I want other voices there to back me up when I sing out of tune, and I'll do my best to zip my lip when it's not my turn to sing.

But I've always disliked choir robes. Uniforms narrow my mind's view of how various the colors of real life naturally are. They make us members of parties that partition us. When I look at uniforms I see veils and shrouds useful to people with something to hide. A local school board member, convinced he has the key to bad test scores, says he wants all public school children wearing uniforms. There are more than enough uniforms to go around. I see them on children in private schools, on postal workers, on devotees of religious cults, and on kids attending day care centers. Employees of certain firms also adhere to the dress code costumes that signal to the public that the wearers equally belong to the same tribe, even if secretly they'd rather not. Most troubling are military uniforms that take hard left and right turns toward the totalitarian. These uniforms form themselves into stiff, symmetrical marching columns required to obey command chains, their dogmatic orderliness poised to unleash the full fury of its latent disorder on those who prefer to dance to their own tunes.

If I'm young (or old), free spirited, free thinking, open-minded, a little gutsy, tentative, and very curious—I'm needy. Needy, that is, to connect with others who share my untidy, open and general view that life is large enough to contain multitudes. Where do I find a like-minding community in a real place? Where are the well-established institutions, and vast arenas, where hundreds or thousands who share my view can routinely, even ritually, come together to affirm each other's values, commitments, and identities? Such vast arenas are becoming popular hangouts for true-believing religious folk. Churches the size of small stadiums offer worship services, spiritual programs, music extravaganzas, and other rituals important to identity, renewal, solidarity, and service. Though pro football has become the nation's mandatory Sunday ritual, mega-churches, with their high-tech entertainment menus, have learned how to stage manage glory sessions that make crowds feel like they're on a winning team.

What communal experiences are there for the rest of us? The shopping mall? More Woodstocks? The naked truth about such happenings is not pretty to contemplate.

So where do I go when the public library's doors are closed and the intellectual and moral dishonesty of churches becomes intolerable? I remind myself that humans are uniformly made from flesh, bones, and blood. Then I remind myself that we live in neighborhoods, real spaces with permeable boundaries. In a neighborhood there is usually a park, where I can just sit and gaze, or talk to someone who also wants to enjoy a little time out. A few others are starting a pick-up softball game in this park, or a game of Frisbee, and I'll stroll over to watch, hoping to get in. Or I'll challenge someone to a game of H-O-R-S-E at a desolate, netless hoop, maybe a kid who needs someone to talk to about his dreams of making it to the NBA instead of in school. Around the corner there's a coffeeshop where a few talkers return every day at roughly the same time to agree to disagree. Next door there's a neat little place where the Mexican, Thai, or Chinese food is prepared by someone who doesn't speak English well but has seen neighborhoods I know nothing about. Two blocks away there's a front porch stoop, where I watch over a mother wheeling her baby past on the sidewalk across the street. There's a front porch too, with three friends, a bottle of wine, and someone I've never met before. If we're lucky there's a community garden within walking distance, where someone may be willing to trade me some tomatoes for my beans.

The neighborhood, where two or three gather together here and there. Routinely. Ritually. Where the solidarity of community adds up like bricks, one relationship at a time. Where uniform needs, fears, desires and hopes learn each other's weird-sounding names. Where winning is not the important thing, and nobody is required to wear a uniform.

Why Jackie Robinson Smiled for the Camera

The first snowfall on a cold November day sometimes helps me adjust to the coming December dark. From the comfort of my living room the snow seems serene, a quiet balm to the noise blaring out of the TV screen. A longing for baseball settles in like laziness. Baseball—its long yawns and outfield lawns—revives a sense of hope in me in a way football, the warrior sport, never does. Nostalgia is in my longing. I played baseball as a kid, and it's easy for me to believe everything was better in those good old days when I was young. If only we could go back. We can't. But against the backdrop of the snowfall whitening another leaden November sky I still see Jackie Robinson, his wide-open smile bright on the black and white screen of our family's primitive TV set.

November is probably the cruelest month for those who call Minnesota home. Despite the warm and colorful days of October that are like Passover signs promising that the winter plague won't strike us this year, November can't keep the cold from sweeping in. In November we want October to stay and December to stay away. Our avoidance reaction persists until the December holidays, ceremonial preludes to the hopeless blizzards of January when we conclude that blankets, firesides, hot toddies, and curling in close are a pretty good way to go. Winter has a way of muffling outdoor noise, and an indoor calm also settles in by mid-February when we enjoy another football truce.

What we can't completely purge from the household are commercials and politics. Though we'd rather stay home than drive to the shopping mall, the commercials keep blaring at us to buy. And politics don't go away—noisy, nasty, ugly. We ask ourselves whether there's any good reason to believe that democratic striving for improvement is paying worthwhile dividends. In winter, as in the long view of old age, we think with both feet on the brakes of our runaway duty to say yes. But the temptation persists. Why not turn political noise off with the TV, curl up in a blanket, and just snooze instead? What would Buddha do?

It's clear that roughly half the registered voters heed Buddha's call to disengage from active politics, though they probably keep their TVs on and tell safe friends what to believe. But they don't vote, feeling, perhaps, that one vote is too small to represent the breadth and width of their depths. Besides, the planet is a lot bigger than a living room, so it's natural to feel small in it. It's understandable that so many half-choose to believe political acts don't matter at all.

Whenever I conjure "culture" I also feel small. I see myself as a speck swimming in a thick stew simmering inside a petri dish where whether I'm healthy or sick, happy or sad, and rich or poor depends a lot on what nutrients and toxins might be in the stew. In November that image congeals. I think of "culture" as glacial. It's a massive heap, a slow-moving glut of opinions, behaviors, fashions, habits, and stuff that just inches along, with me, a shivering speck, somewhere inside being moved along too. November politics seem like a noisy shower of hail hitting rock solid rooftops, so it's easy to imagine politics hitting culture's glacier and just getting lost in it. It's consoling to know that if poisonous government breeds monsters in a culture, presumably we could—if our culture were good enough—absorb poisonous politics. But culture is massive, sluggish, and drowsy. It's rather hard to get glaciers to speed up, or to move them left or right, and it's not every day they turn around.

That's why Jackie Robinson's smile intrigues me. It seems so spontaneous and genuine, so open and generous. For those of us who remember Jackie Robinson we recall best his smile. Younger folk who don't recognize him also don't know that his smile is a cultural icon of sorts. I hereby declare it so. Did Jackie Robinson's smile not merely affect but effectively change the course of American culture? If today hundreds of dark-skinned males can play major league baseball, can sit next to light-skinned females in public schools and walk hand-in-hand with them without being lynched; if our current President is a dark-skinned male, and if Republicans, rightly smarting from accusations that their politics are loaded with racist undertones, has a dark-skinned male running as one of their candidates for the presidency—is this why Jackie Robinson smiled for the camera?

Behind the scenes he spent a lot of time not smiling. When he was a not-invisible minor leaguer he couldn't sleep in certain hotels with his white teammates. When he showed up to play that day's game was sometimes called off by local cops, and the stadium padlocked. When he was brought up to the majors the racial tension in the Dodger dugout was explicit, and he had to turn the other cheek to racial slurs thrown his way by people in the crowds. He had to bite his lip and play the game. His winning smile was a political act.

It's arguable that Jackie Robinson was perhaps the most important catalyst of the civil rights movement. Robinson touched the hearts of millions of baseball fans who had to confront the fact that racial prejudice was directed at a face difficult to hate. His smile softened the cultural glacier frozen with racism, and he changed that culture's course. His smile gained power from the many who had come before—the thousands of activists, most of them nameless, who spent years working on behalf of civil rights, and from individuals like his teammate Pee Wee Reese, who put his arm around him and spoke loudly enough for other teammates to hear, "You can hate a man for many reasons. Color is not one of them." And Jackie Robinson's smile was strengthened by forces irrelevant to racial issues—competence as a baseball player that validated him as a professional, even the improvements in camera technology that allowed his smile to be better appreciated, and, in time, to reveal in close-up and full color the individual faces of many other dark-skinned ballplayers from diverse places in the world. Culture moves in strange and mysterious ways.

Currently other significant cultural shifts are observable. Women's rights and gay rights, for example, have moved our culture in ways that would have been unthinkable fifty years ago, and current discourse about economic inequality seems to be gaining weight. Racism, sexism, greed and homophobia are still with us, of course, and there are still those who throw legal and political roadblocks in front of the movements for positive change. But culture is more powerful than politics, and it has word of mouth and high-tech ways of overwhelming obstacles to what's holding it back. Culture also has a powerful force that politics lacks: Children. Children reinvent cultures by bringing fresh perspectives that speak well for the power of fairness, toleration, and cooperation as powerful moral forces. If given a chance to express their inherent altruism, children will embrace the positive values present in the culture into which they're born. Blessed are the children.

And blessed are those huddled masses, weary of winter and politics, who bite their lip, play the game, and smile as they continue performing the small political acts—at once smart and generous—that add up to weighty cultural shifts.

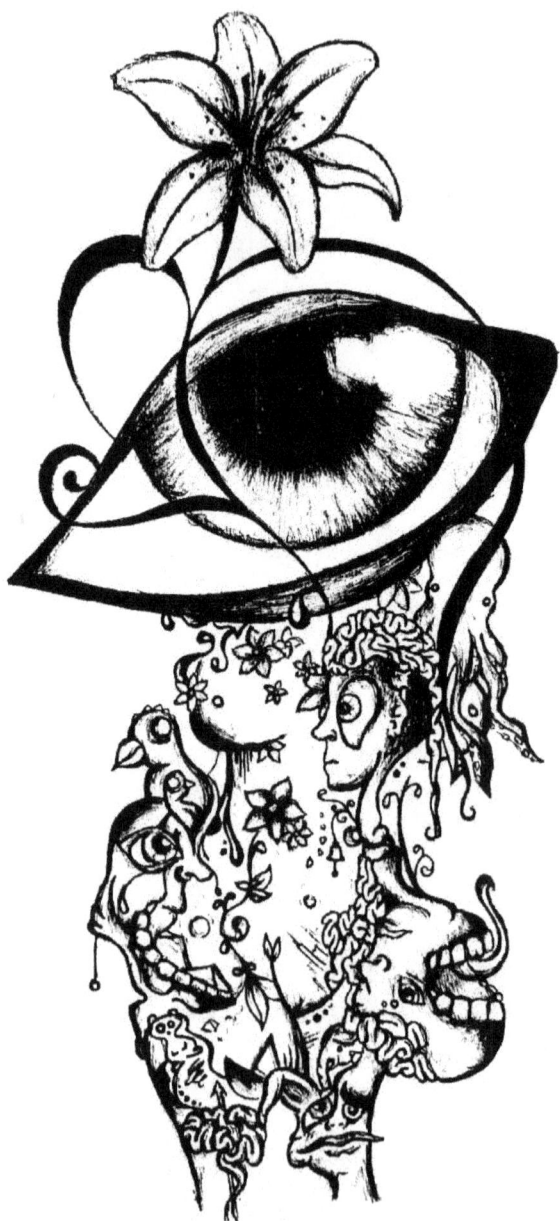

Keeping Score

It's hard not to welcome in a new baseball season with each new spring. Someone like Joe Mauer, homegrown like a ruddy potato in our own back yard, seems so much like a rare innocent teenager we almost feel sorry for the trouble his $78 million will bring his way. We're relieved to know he'll hit $78 million worth of singles to left and still be around to represent us for some years, unlike the stars for whom the green light to hit-and-run toward more millions is always on. Other current local heroes who follow the money trail leading away from home leave us somewhat confused about ourselves. How can turncoat hit-and-runners, loyal only to their bottom line, think of themselves as belonging to our home team?

My confusion swells whenever a new stadium building season comes around. It's always easier to find out who won yesterday's game than it is to keep a running score of who the new stadium winners and losers are. Adding up the costs of our big pro sports franchises can't compete with news thrill-bits about Mauer's latest encounter with the breaking ball, or the depth of some star's latest back spasm or ache.

What's really hard to calculate is what the thrill-bits we get from sports are really worth to us. No one seems to be keeping score of that. While many parents, teachers, and coaches believe that sports build character, it's hard to know if they supply us with more weird characters than people of character. Since the kind of character we associate with moral integrity and steadfastness is hard to measure, and since its expressions often are not in plain view, it's hard to really know for sure whether sports personalities do us more harm than good.

Conventional wisdom normally works well enough to inspire Bob and Mary Taxpayer to get a new stadium built. Pro sports, we're told, are good for the economy. New stadiums put people to work as builders, vendors and managers. The franchise owners and their millionaire athletes pay taxes too. And there's a price to pay in the marketplace of world opinion if a city leaves the impression it's a minor league place. It would hurt the convention industry, and tourism, the bars and restaurants. And imagine the emotional scars that would result from loss of Purple (or maroon or, in Nebraska, red) Pride, a virtue perhaps more invaluable than it is incalculable.

And one other thing is certain too: When Bob and Mary Taxpayer come through with enough funding to get another stadium built, it's the way the ball bounces, not socialism.

So, dear Bob and Mary, give us our slice of your hard-earned bread or we'll cook up our profits in some other major league city. And please, let's not hear any talk about welfare for the rich.

How do we love our Vikings (Twins, Timberwolves, Wild, etc.)? Let us count the ways. We provide them premium property space at premium discount prices. We construct, at public expense, infrastructure that makes access to these properties possible. We add hundreds of millions of pennies to the taxes we pay. We pay bigger and bigger bucks to sit in a seat so far away the players look like ants. We exhaust more than a day's worth of minimum wages for fries, a hot dog, a T-shirt, and a beer. When the good guys win we feel good as we swallow the suspicion we've been had, and the next day at work we have something to say about what everyone's talking about.

We console ourselves: It's fun, clean family fun on family days. Besides, we're sick and tired of talk about deficits. Besides, there are so many troubles and wars we need something to put our minds on hold. Besides, we deserve to be winners too. Besides, even when our team loses it might be good for the economy.

Ask any preacher or shop-keeper whose doors are open on game day. It's hard to dispute that the sale of chips, beer and hot dogs spikes before any game, but what happens in churches, theatres, museums, and retail stores on game day? The traffic flow is sitting on the sofa in front of the TV, and the cash flow is in a one-way funnel leading to the stadium. Has anyone in a school of business bothered to study this phenomenon?

The artists have been better than the athletes at keeping score, and they've scored a lot of points. If Minnesotans need to feel like winners their artists have earned them some bragging rights. According to results of studies reported by Minnesota Citizens for the Arts, Minnesota was named "the most livable state in the nation" for the sixth straight year, "due in part to our citizens' access to the arts." And *Places Rated Almanac* rated the Twin Cities "one of the nation's best art communities," better even than San Francisco. A 2006 study of Minnesota's individual artists and arts organizations puts their total economic impact at over one billion dollars, with the arts providing a return on investment of over $11 to $1. Of the $250.1 million spent on the arts in 2005, 82 per cent went to Minnesota merchants and businesses. the *St. Paul Pioneer Press* reported (1/17/99) that more people (almost 9 million) attended nonprofit arts events than sports events, and that only 2.6 million paid to see the three pro sports teams.

These numbers suggest why pro sports are not shy about asking for donations. Ask anyone who runs a museum, art gallery, food shelter, chemical dependency counseling service, furniture store, service station, or grocery if they'd like to enjoy the same snug relationship that pro (and major college) sports have with newspaper and TV media. As the news in newspapers shrinks into smaller freeze-dried bits, the sports news industry—more and more often heralded on the front pages—routinely offers full sections worth of what amounts to free advertising to free enterprise sports monopolies. TV news, always mindful of the need to provide equal time, plays the same game.

Is the depth of an ageing player's ache to continue playing the game news, or is it free advertising? Are journalism's unwritten rules of the game rigged against ordinary businesses and shopkeepers? Are there winners and losers? Who on a news staff is keeping score?

Tony Judt, historian, does some summing up in his book *Ill Fares the Land*, a work that could be called part of his last will and testament (he died of ALS in 2010). The book's first line doesn't shy away from what many people quietly and deeply feel: "Something is profoundly wrong with the way we live today." His conclusion is grounded on several studies that point to an unfashionable belief:

"The wider the spread between the wealthy few and the impoverished many, the worse the social problems: a statement that appears to be true for rich and poor countries alike. What matters is not how affluent a country is but how unequal it is."

If it could be established that major investments (like a new sports stadium) help ordinary folk pay their bills rather than ensuring that a few will swell their fortunes (often invested in offshore ventures), it would be patriotic, pragmatic and arguably moral to have a new stadium in every small town and city neighborhood.

But the present habit is to think big, to indulge in the wishful thinking that some mystical Hidden Hand will allow concentrated wealth to trickle down to ordinary folk. Those who credibly keep score of this phenomenon have bad news for us: Since the 1970s wealth's Hidden Hand has stealthily and steadily propelled wealth upward instead. As Judt points out, "21.2 percent of U.S. national income accrued to just 1 percent of earners." Since Judt's death the figure has increased to about 33%. And it's often a family affair. "The wealth of the Wal-Mart founder's family in 2005 was estimated at about the same ($90 billion) as that of the bottom 40 percent of the U.S. population: 120 million people."

With family values running this high it's easy to see why so many pro sports owners run their operations as family businesses. While Bob and Mary Taxpayer are free to kick in to guarantee that kickoffs continue and the owners score more profits, one would expect that taxpayers would share in a few extra points. But for profit-sharing purposes they are not part of the family team. The entire NFL corporate establishment, and its enormous profits were, until 2015, classified by the IRS as a tax-exempt non-profit. Money talks as quietly as some politicians vote. So what part of the Vikings or Twins or Timberwolves or Wild does the public "own"?

335

Why do we care so much whether they win or lose, especially when they make big money even when they lose games and make us miserable?

What we maybe mainly learn from the contests we watch is that in the dog-eat-dog (do they?) world of pro sports the winners take all. In that world equality is for losers, even if it is well demonstrated that an equal playing field is better for all of us. As taxpayers and spectators buy into big-time sports they tacitly approve the "winning is everything" premise that makes losers of them. The games themselves constitute advertisements for the premise, and the ads for pro sports work best against ordinary fans when their team wins and they go home feeling good rather than had.

I find it hard to divorce myself from a stadium roar that swells, it seems, out of some underground depth that sends us soaring every time someone hits a home run or throws a touchdown bomb. It's hard not to feel good when we get another hit of deep Purple Pride. But do we confuse Purple Pride with civic pride, and does Purple Pride come at the expense of the important improvements that could be made to neighborhoods, schools, the arts, and small businesses? Is anyone keeping score of what growing inequality is costing us?

The Roman emperors understood well the value of providing *panem* and *circenses* (bread and circuses) as ways of controlling discontented populations. Today's stadium builders are happy enough to provide the circuses, while stashing big bread away in banks.

Privatize

"Have we gone insane?" is what a Minnesota cattle farmer probably not much interested in March Madness asked. His question was a reaction to the news that Jerry Kill, the University of Minnesota football coach, had his $1,2000,000 salary increased by an extra $2,100,000, plus perks, for guiding the Gophers to eight wins and five losses during the 2013 season. Maybe winning isn't everything. It certainly isn't for everyone.

No doubt Coach Kill is a nice enough guy and competent enough at what he does. And he doesn't complain about the salary bump he received. Ohio State's Urban Meyer made $4,600,000 that same year, plus perks, and he's in the same league.

It's hard to imagine anyone in his or her right mind seriously believing that the NCAA Division One big money sports—football, basketball, hockey—have anything but a tendril connection to a university's higher education missions. There are several fine student-athletes who get excellent grades while working very hard at their sports. The graduation rate for athletes and non-athletes is comparable, though the amount of money it takes to get a student-athlete a degree is hidden in a murk of red ink. But it seems obvious that the hazards of football seem well out of line with what health educators teach, and that at the D-1 level one of the hardest lessons students need to learn is how to keep their classes from interfering with their serious sports jobs.

Student-athletes must suspect they're part of an entertainment industry. Coach Kill was honest enough to fess up to it, and he left the impression that as a newcomer to the industry his new salary represented his fair market value.

But some of the people responsible for overseeing the numbers at D-1 higher educational institutions maybe need some refresher courses in elementary arithmetic. Only 23 of the 228 NCAA D-1 sports programs generated enough income to cover expenses in 2012, and 16 of the 23 winners received subsidies by way of student fees and university and state funds. The other 205 were losers, as were the donors and tax payers who picked up the tab. Losing seasons are a financial trend for most NCAA schools.

Meanwhile, the NCAA as an organization quietly showed a profit of $71,000,000 for 2012. The NCAA, like the NFL, until 2015, is also quietly a tax-exempt non-profit, in a nation where state governments noisily try to figure out how to pay their bills.

It's time to turn these big-time sports teams into what they really are: Businesses. Because I'm addicted to thrift I think they should get off an unsustainable welfare system. Privatize them.

I'm not a spoil-sport. I know that millions love to cheer for the logos and colors on the laundry they love. Big time sports are major rituals that stimulate a deep need for community identity, and perhaps distract from it. As a kid in Michigan I grew up loving the Spartans and Wolverines, and I got my graduate degrees as a Buckeye at Ohio State, and when I was married to a Nebraska woman I learned to love Cornhuskers, and because I pay taxes in Wisconsin I have a Badger in me, and because my daughter was a student at the University of Iowa I'm a Hawkeye too. As a

Minnesotan I'm a devout Gopher, for reasons I can't fully explain. I want everyone to win.

A lot of people are not ready to give up big-time collegiate sports yet, even when they go home from a game losers again.

Turning big-time collegiate sports programs into for-profit enterprises should especially appeal to fiscal conservatives who have a passion to cut taxes and privatize the public schools.

Here's my business plan: Turn the big-time intercollegiate sports over to private entrepreneurs willing to invest in new business ventures. Let entrepreneurs, rather than participating schools, run them as private for-profit businesses. They buy the naming, branding, and concessions rights from universities. They lease the cheerleaders and marching bands. They lease university facilities, or construct their own. They pay all travel and advertising expenses. They cut their own TV and bowl game deals. They hire the coaches and other managers. They pay the bills and enjoy the profits that come rolling in. Or not. Private investors could get involved, and maybe Wall Street too.

Could these new business enterprises—let's call them clubs—still be considered intercollegiate sports? A few rules would give them permission to say yes. The players would be recruited from the pool of graduating high school student-athletes, as they are now. They would have five years to fulfill four years of service on the playing field. They would be required to establish student identity by taking at least one class at the university whose logo they wear during games.

Nothing much would change, except the ownership of teams, business plans, and bookkeeping responsibilities.

Gopher fans could continue to cheer for players wearing Gopher uniforms, and everyone could continue to have a good time.

Currently there's some talk about student-athletes unionizing. That's an issue players could work out with management, maybe after some discussion about salaries for coaches and club executives. Clubs, as free enterprise businesses, could make millions. Or not.

And if not, owners could downsize or apply other lean strategies.

Already there are rumors about the University of Minnesota needing $190,000,000 for improved practice facilities. Experts feel that the U of M will not be able to compete without the upgrades. They're very probably right. Why would an eighteen-year-old super athlete high school recruit want anything but the latest and best high-tech facilities? Why not go to Penn State instead?

Tim Dahlberg, sports writer for the AP, says, "That's the way things are in big-time college athletics, where the rich are getting richer. Hard not to profit when the labor is free." Hard not to profit when public university athletic programs are bailed out by student fees and tax dollars.

I'm with the cattle farmer from western Minnesota. Why play this game? "Have we gone insane?"

Four or five times a year I get a call from sweet-voiced students at my alma mater Ohio State. They want me to send OSU money because there's never enough to go around. I plead with them to spread the word: For starters, I tell the voices on the line, cut the coaching salaries in half. Call me again after you begin there.

Endnote: Playing the Game

Because they make the big news that makes winners and losers of us every day, sports, of the pro and varsity varieties, are winning the culture war. Our governments, churches and schools are lagging behind and can't compete. The national government, even with its military wings kept afloat by its several wars waged from the sky, inspires mainly resentment and apathy in its taxpayers, while churches lose ground by insisting on the unbelievable. Meanwhile, the sports entertainment industries of our nation's schools and colleges fill bleachers with screaming silent majorities absent from PTA and school board meetings.

The millions of fans fanatical enough to spend billions on spectator sports are too well-fed to be seriously fed up with the ways well established cultural institutions make losers of them. They convert their religious passion into sports mania. Dominant religious narratives that deem ascetic denial and self-abuse essential to the winning of personal salvation chime well with stories athletes tell themselves about the muscular devotion to self-flagellation (and self-medication) required as training routines for the dramas that make them into hero-saints worthy of adoration from the bleacher seats. They too love to make it hurt.

In the absence of an ethics and aesthetics that make playing the game worthy because it clears the mind, instructs the heart, and makes social life more sociable, athletes turn the other cheek when they bench press improbable loads or run more sprints on their way to a win intended to make a loser of someone else. Because they're sometime losers themselves who believe that "winning is the only thing," they console themselves by repeating the mantra that "winning isn't everything." Lurking, somewhere in dark consciousness, is the fact that somebody loses every time, and that one dark day everyone loses in the end. Few dream that every big win transfers their own eventual little defeat to a loser they've created as the crowds cheer on.

There is no turning the other cheek on the football or other highly competitive field of dreams where the illusion that real men are being made persists. The leaders we deem captains of business and industry know their interests are best served when the cheering is loud in the cheapest seats. From those seats the heroes playing their games on their fields of dreams look puny, but not enough people seem to notice.

VIII. Moral Compass

(from *The Oxymoronic Dictionary*)

Adjective with singular noun

1. In America, a political tool designed to interfere with the normal functioning of the genitals.
2. For those who control the airwaves and ads, polls that determine which way the winds are blowing.
3. For those seeking human relationship, the number of pulses it takes to defrost a human heart.

Antonyms: Speedometer. Accelerator.

Belief Addiction

I'm not sure it's really good news: Dr. Michael M. Miller of the American Society for Addiction Medicine has announced that addictive behaviors are "a result of brain dysfunction." It's troubling to learn that brains are quiet addiction conspirators, especially since brains are supposed to do good things for us. But the numbers hooked on destructive hard-core habits (drugs, alcohol, tobacco, snacks, sex, gambling, and video games) are swelling to epidemic proportions, while soft-core addictions such as exercise, hand-washing, cheerfulness, texting, and Snapchatting gain status via entrepreneurs proffering remedies profitable to them. Taken together these well-known hard and soft-core addictions have been rearing their heads so religiously they crowd out of view the worst brain dysfunction of all—the one currently victimizing guilty and innocent alike as it sweeps across this addiction-infected land.

I refer here to Belief Addiction

What is Belief Addiction? Like any hard-core addiction it is a behavior disorder that subjects individuals to compulsions they perversely enjoy. It requires that individuals surrender their free will and common sense to their compulsion to believe. The brain chemistry of this disease tricks users into becoming convicted addicts. Just as druggies or alcoholics can't resist another hit of meth or rum, Belief Addicts are enslaved by the pleasure provided by belief. Brains shrink under the influence of this pleasure, as brain power concentrates vocabulary to a "high" stimulated by the word "Truth." As each high triggers a desire for more "Truth," the pleasure center in the brain secretes chemical pathogens that momentarily sedate the user while increasing the dosage of "Truth" required for further sedation. Users are known to experience especially voluminous secretions if shouting or firearms are involved in debates, with many of these delusions convincing users that they know the minds of gods, have gods as personal friends or are gods themselves. Several of the ecstatic highs of Belief Addicts have spiraled so far out of control that they die with twisted smiles on their faces. Some of those who long to succumb to the disease are known to gather on hillsides to discuss the rapture they hope to inflict not only on themselves but everyone else.

Since not all beliefs are created equal, with some believers grounded in enough good sense to keep themselves from losing their minds, it is difficult not to conclude that those afflicted by Belief Addiction are communists. This conclusion follows from the tendency Belief Addicts exhibit of wanting everybody to be alike, just like them. Those suspected of deviating from the path of Truth are eligible to return to the fold if they successfully, and audibly, repeat certain phrases approved by the relevant Central Committee of Truth. Those safely within the fold may remain as long as their silence fails to drown out the noise of others in their cult.

What is the inspiration for Belief Addiction, and how do adults become as little children in order to get hooked? As we well know from the effects of drugs and alcohol, delirium has strange power. When we were children we all loved to turn and turn in circles until we all fell down, and most kids derived from that experience lessons on how to grow up into mature adults. As Belief Addicts circle they cling passionately to the "Truth" that inevitably will let them down, leaning dizzily on others to cushion their fall while insisting the world is falling apart.

Circling is a cycle very difficult for Belief Addicts to break. The brain gets in a groove that keeps singing the same round to itself: "My Truth Is True Because I Believe It's True and I Believe It's True Because It's True." The delirium induced by this mantra typically reaches a high a few moments before a crash.

The epidemic spread of Belief Addiction should not be surprising, given the profound and subtle way it infects the human mind. Geneticist Dean Hamer, no doubt aware of the "selfish gene" theories of Richard Dawkins, posits the presence of a "God gene" (VMAT2) that "hardwires" belief in our genes and makes us susceptible to "mystic" experiences and a "spiritual" view of life. Though Hamer falls short of claiming that VMAT2 "encodes" belief in God, he does claim that it empowers humans with a gene-based sense of optimism. Whether this optimism in turn inspires belief in the God of the selfish gene has not yet been scientifically established, but it's easy to see how the good feelings we're hardwired with give Belief Addicts such cheerful and uplifting highs users can't get enough of them.

Especially pernicious are the self-medicating immunities built into the addiction process. When they're especially high Belief Addicts feel like God—omniscient and so invulnerable not even their own suicides will put an end to them. They believe that when they're dead they will become as immortal as their beliefs. Many users also carry the flags useful for waving all argument away. For some American addicts belief is not only a God-given right but it's a natural law protected by the U.S. Constitution and Supreme Court.

Because beliefs are sacred, natural and patriotic, they conclude, nobody has to make sense of them.

It is common for Belief Addicts to deny their addiction. Those who accuse them of being addicts they certify as insane losers. Those who ignore them they accuse of cowardice and excessive civility.

It's well understood by addiction professionals that its cure requires long-range treatments, with programs in place to address the needs of the many who routinely relapse into addictive behaviors. The National Institute on Drug Abuse estimates that there are about 23 million Americans hooked on chemical substances, with only two million getting the treatment they need. Drug dependency complicates the treatment of Belief Addiction. The cravings of Belief Addicts are often profoundly spiritual, and therefore not normally relieved by chemical fixes. Even if a drug were invented to cure the disease its persistent brain secretions would be difficult to purify. It would be much less challenging and more socially useful to redirect the yearnings that seem to be at the heart of the disease toward community-building projects.

New pleasures need to be developed to counter the popularity of Belief Addiction. It seems obvious that these new pleasures will have to satisfy the mind's craving for logic, common sense, scientific knowledge, careful scholarship and intellectual honesty. It's obvious too that the terrible rapture some Belief Addicts want to inflict on those who don't believe the way they do must be taken seriously and addressed at an institutional level, especially by churches.

Home Churching

It's an unusual parent who is not alarmed when a daughter calls home from her college dorm to announce that she's decided to major in unemployment. "Religious Studies, Dad. This class I'm taking on Judaism, Christianity and Islam—I can't get enough of it."

Quietly I was elated. Talk about religion in our household is inversely proportional to church attendance. Now and then my wife Monica and I would take the kids to the neighborhood church, sometimes a few Sundays in a row, but at the dinner table the big questions—about God and the gods, faith and works, free will and predestination, right and wrong, justice and grace—are often part of the meal. Religion is a worldwide bone of contention that has to be chewed over. It isn't enough to just nip at it. It is something to think deeply about. We home church our kids.

Much of religion, naturally, is difficult, even impossible, to swallow. When six year-old Dante, our youngest, paused on our walk home from church one Sunday to ask, "Dad, do you believe what he said?" I was proud of him. The preacher, in his earnest desire to convert mythology into history, had made superstition the basis of belief. Stories about Noah's ark, about Jesus walking on water, the end of the world, and Jonah snoozing three days in the belly of a whale before being spit out didn't go down well with him. Did he have to believe stuff like that to be grown-up? Or would he have to learn to zip his lips and swallow his honest thoughts?

"Well, Dad?" asked my ten-year-old daughter Leah. "Do you believe what he said?"

"No."

I saw the relief in Dante's wide-eyed face. "I didn't either, Dad."

From the mouths of babes, we're told, honesty springs forth in its most innocent purity. As six and ten year-olds my children were testing my intellectual honesty, and their own. And on that Sunday morning on the way home from church everyone passed the test.

Leah lost interest in church after that. Aside from the music it was, she said, boring—a code word for uncool. Does one dare say it was spiritually unsatisfying? Her reluctance—refusal—to attend church spoke for what we, as parents, were feeling too. As Huck Finn unfamously said, "You can't pray a lie."

But I was elated by her decision to pursue a major in Religious Studies at the University of Iowa. All subjects of importance attach themselves to religion—the languages, history, literature, mythology, politics, economics, psychology, science. More than anything I wanted her to major in "unemployment" on her way to getting a well-rounded liberal arts education that would best prepare her to negotiate her way both effectively and meaningfully in the world. She might become a waitress, real estate agent, or office clerk, but she also would have a sound understanding of what is of enduring and vital interest to humans as she worked her way toward a profession she loved. She would not have to live in a boring mental environment that might be cool but sure to leave her spiritually unsatisfied.

Her frustration over the standing of religious studies in the real world surfaced soon after her commitment to the discipline. "Dad," she complained to me, "they're everywhere. They believe everything they hear. They believe everything the Bible says—literally. And most of them have never read any of it. They can't be reasoned with. They don't want dates and facts. They don't want to know. They just want to believe."

Welcome to the world, several regions of which are going up in smoke in part because of the bombshell power of belief. Welcome to present-day U.S.A., where polarized hate wears the masks of the Prince of Peace.

I detect the frustration and disillusion in her voice: "They won't carry on a reasonable conversation with me. What can I do?" she asks.

Your college major makes you unemployable, I say to myself, in a world that desperately needs your services right now.

Knowing comes in last.

And here she is, a life-long student (I hope) trying—above all—to know. How can all the hard-earned knowledge she achieves—the result of research, experiment, skeptical analysis, careful scholarship, creative intuition, and honest reasoning—compete with innocent belief?

It can't.

It takes no genius to suspect that in this revolutionary new information age knowledge is losing out. The concept of "knowledge" itself seems to be shrinking, overwhelmed by zillions of information bits, reduced to vocation-promising residencies in merely technical and momentarily profitable fields, and divorced from "wisdom," its ancient godfather, and "Sophia," its great-grandmother. The de-institutionalization of knowledge from schools and colleges seems imminent, and perhaps deserved, even as superstitious belief, like a jackal, lurks to feed on its remains.

What do I say to my knowledge-hungry daughter? That it's merely cool, and also spiritually unsatisfying, to subscribe to blind belief. That blind belief has trouble turning away from passionate belief, one grounded on generosity, fairness, toleration, hard-earned knowledge, and intellectual honesty.

Exegesis Saves

I was pleased when legislators added the word "civil" to the gay marriage legislation approved by the Minnesota legislature and governor. Marriage has a long history of being on the rocks, so it could use a little civility.

Those strongly against gay marriage are hard to argue with, in part because belief has congealed their hearts and minds. One of the beliefs held by opponents of gay marriages is that their version of marriage—a union between one female and one male—has been sanctioned by their version of God for over two thousand years. They have old time religion to prove their point, and bumper stickers all over town proclaiming their view as profound gospel truth.

So I decided to go to the original source, Genesis and other early books of the Bible, to see how marriage fared before it became a part of their new-fangled old time religion. What I found in these early books of the Bible is that it's easy to conclude that God had little interest in having His own wife and family. One thing is certain: He was a committed bachelor forever. He was not married to any queen of heaven. Nor did God take a traditional view of marriages made in heaven. A proper conjugal relationship between one male and one female married to each other is not how family life got its start. When God got around to creating Adam, his first-born, he preferred red clay—some call it dirt or dust—rather than a female as his incubator. From Adam's rib (in one version) He then fashioned Eve, thus freeing Himself from the obligation to have an actual heavenly wife. A postmodernist artist He might have become. A husband He is not.

Marriage as a divinely sanctioned union between one human male and one human female also did not seem to be part of God's original plan. Were Adam and Eve really ever married? Were they husband and wife, or brother and sister? More likely the latter, it seems, since Eve (in one version) was engineered from Adam's rib. And if they are our first parents are we all offspring of an incestuous marriage that it would be hard to conceive as traditional? And after Cain and Abel grew up whose children—Cain's sisters?—did they make into wives with whom they could exchange the vows requiring them to honor and obey?

That God somehow had sons (by whom? Himself?) whose unusual relations with females conjured more sons is apparent in Genesis 6:2-4, where we are told that "the sons of God saw that the daughters of men were fair, and they took to wife such of them as they chose." So, "the sons of God came into the daughters of men, and they bore children to them … mighty men." This exclusive baby-making of mighty men by God's sons is extraordinary. These unions apparently did not result in baby girls, a circumstance that would make future one-male, one-female marriages difficult to come by, and would result in a lot of leftover unmarried men. Or plenty of girls were born but they were not worth mentioning. It's hard to be sure.

The biological prowess of Biblical patriarchs is so extraordinary that our current human condition seems outdated in comparison. Adam was a hundred and five when he fathered Seth, so Eve—if she was the mom—had to be less than one hundred and four. And then Adam has more children until he's eight hundred years old, so Eve, or other women, also must have been biologically able to stay with him. Enosh, Kenan, Mahalalel, Jared, Enoch, Methuselah, and Lamech had children while they were each several hundred years old, though the names of their wives and/or slave-concubines are lost to us. By Noah's time we see a decline. He was only about five hundred years old when he fathers Shem, Ham and Japheth.

These extraordinary family-making feats are impossible to live up to today. Even with Viagra widely marketed, times and people do change. These exploits also make it understandable why some Bible believers find Darwin unbelievable. Men were sexual giants in those early Biblical days, so any talk about "evolution" as "progress" is, indeed, foolishness that makes us seem small. Biology appears to have been different then, and more virulent, especially for males.

Marriage relationships get so bizarre in subsequent generations that most wives today would prefer to be married to my cat than to some of the Biblical patriarchs. That many of these patriarchs practiced polygamy is a fact many Bible-believing politicians can't wish away. If a Biblical marriage is a union between one man and one woman, a lot of Biblical patriarchs have some explaining to do. How can Jacob, for example, justify telling his wife Rachel that she's so old her older sister Leah will have his child instead? What kind of example does this set for modern believers, especially since God approves this unusual family set-up? Jacob's example suggests that traditional family life in the future, if based on Biblical precedent, will not be what it used to be. Why then should we think that future marriages will be what they used to be, especially when so many end in divorce?

It would be wrong not to give some thought to the moral standards of some versions of Biblical family life. In

Leviticus 18:22 homosexuality is openly declared an abomination and therefore contrary to God's law, but that law has features that would inspire terrorism against some of our current laws. Leviticus (25:44) and Exodus (21:7) both say that slavery is legitimate, with Leviticus restricting the practice to slaves taken from foreign lands only. Exodus 35:2 would doom most of us. It declares that anyone who works on the Sabbath should be put to death. The fact that football is played on the Sabbath perhaps saves most of us. Eating shellfish would doom millions. Leviticus (11:10) tells us that it's not as bad an abomination as being gay, but says nothing about whether it's worse to be gay than it is to be a runaway slave or concubine.

There are a lot of other "Laws of God" that the very best Christians wouldn't blame on God. Among the abominations are planting two different crops in the same field (Leviticus, 19:19), allowing a wife to wear garments from two kinds of thread, and touching the skin of a dead pig, a rule that would lead to the execution of thousands of fathers and sons playing catch with a football in the yard. Those who commit these abominations are to be stoned to death.

So who will throw the first stone?

Who has the courage to admit that some of the behaviors deemed "abominations" reflect silly and narrow-minded views, and that the penalties for them are brutal, criminal, and immoral?

Who reads the Bible literally throughout, without noticing that many passages violate the Ten Commandments?

Who hasn't cherry-picked verses from the Bible to conjure an interpretation that conveniently serves emotional and political needs?

Who will not agree that many Biblical commandments violate the commandment that we love our neighbors as ourselves?

Who are those so righteous and moral that they would prohibit the civil institutionalization of loving relationships?

And who would deny those opposed to gay marriages the right to worship as they please?

Saving the Butterflies

Call me a bleeding heart liberal. I try not to step on ants, and I go dangerously out of my way to avoid making roadkill of any caterpillar trying to cross a freeway on its quiet peaceful way to becoming a butterfly. I'm aware that in the Greek myths Psyche, the soul, is personified as a butterfly, and I've also read about a few scientists who have calculated that when a butterfly tilts its wings in Minnesota the stir may cause the marriage of lovers in Thailand or the hurricane that destroys whole towns in Trinidad. Then too I've paused to wonder what it must be like to be happily legging it across warm freeway concrete toward some call of the wildly beautiful grassy knoll when suddenly, without my having a pipsqueak say, a massive machine I never see erases my tiny life.

I also see the billboards informing me that the unborn—call it fetus and/or child in the making—feels pain and is in other ways truly alive. And I'm mindful of the bumper stickers that insist that the abortion issue is mainly about a woman's right to choose. We all travel through a traffic of opinions that frame the question in these confrontational terms.

Before you read on I want to make clear where I stand as male presuming to speak out on a public issue that mainly concerns women, and one that often makes pawns of women in the public debates controlled mainly by males. I fully support Roe vs. Wade and a woman's right to choose. And I sometimes find myself sympathetic to the moral passion of right-to-lifers. Many are bleeding hearts too. In my butterfly world not one abortion would occur.

I also try to be a realist. In a perfect world women would become pregnant only when they choose. But it's not a perfect world, and I have to make sense of that very big fact. Thousands of young women conceive every day because they are raped, coerced, or seduced, or because they are sexually innocent or ignorant, and because accidents occur. Many thousands have limited access to contraceptives and face church sanctions for using them. Many girls and women who face abortion issues are unable to provide homes, fathers, futures, and proper care for newborns. And in the real world thousands of abortions, legal or not, will be performed, either by doctors in medical facilities or by shady characters eager to make a few bucks in some back room.

Bleeding hearts are not always easily fooled. What's seldom talked about is that some key features of right-wing politics are shaped by cunning and cynical opinion makers who, as masters of spin and self-deception, feast on the abortion issue and bleed it to keep it alive and screaming. They know that if the problem is resolved as a public health issue a lot of anti-abortion votes will go to liberals. On their way to getting more tax breaks for their powerful self-interest groups they need anti-abortion votes to fulfill their agenda of privatizing Social Security, gutting Medicare and Medicaid, and repealing the national health care plan. Quietly they subscribe to the Social Darwinist theory that the underprivileged and poor are losers who hurt us all, so why should government help losers out? God rewards success, they say, and losers get what they deserve. Nature's "selfish gene" and their righteous God have established an unholy alliance that sanctions their beliefs.

"I do not believe that just because you're opposed to abortion," says Sister Joan Chittister, a Benedictine nun, "that that makes you pro-life. In fact, I think in many cases your morality is deeply lacking if all you want is a child born but not a child fed, not a child educated, not a child housed. And why would I think that you don't? Because you don't want any tax money to go there ... We need a much broader conversation on what the morality of pro-life is."

One of the tragedies of recent American politics is that many anti-abortion activists exploit the genuine compassion of ordinary folk who are anti-abortion. The unborn are held hostage in voting booths by those mainly interested in advancing their self-interest agendas. Right-to-lifers routinely give their votes to those who oppose the interests of the underprivileged and poor. Many right-to-lifers do this as a matter of conscience, insisting that moral concerns they have about abortion override the economic benefits they stand to achieve by supporting public programs in education, health, welfare, and jobs sponsored by liberals. Because the abortion issue looms large in public debate, it also conveniently shrinks the visibility of the life and death issues at the heart of the dirty business of war. The conspicuous visibility of the abortion debate divides right-to-lifers from peace and justice activists. Both sides abhor waste and death, and both have a deep faith in human potential. Who can blame them?

Liberals also have been trapped by the way the national conversation about abortion has been framed as a conflict between "the right to choose" and "right to life." Advocates for women's rights, struggling for viability that is continuously under assault, insist on the woman's "right to choose" as the most important factor in the debate. The right to life groups argue that the rights of the unborn trump those of women. This framing of the issue artificially pits women against women, and liberal women against the unborn. It unfairly requires individuals to weigh in the scales of justice a woman's "right to choose" with an unborn creature's helplessness. This framing falsifies the realities and seems to cede to right-wing politicians an emotional moral high ground that stands at the center of the abortion debate.

The issues need to be reframed so that realistic national conversation can go forward. For this conversation to develop it will not be useful, or accurate, to equate being against abortion with being against women's rights. Some maybe are, but certainly not all. Conversely, it is unfair to accuse those who support Roe vs. Wade with not having deep moral concerns focused on saving lives. The issues are less troubling for those who justify abortion when a woman's life is endangered. The moral questions on that issue are easy enough. The moral arguments for the right of the unborn to be born are more vexing, as are those for supporting Roe vs. Wade as a legal and moral imperative.

The debate, currently framed as a conflict between slogans, fails to reflect the moral issues at the center of the problem.

How can we, in good conscience, have it both ways?

We begin by ignoring the slogans on bumper stickers. There are more important things to focus on. I'm doing 70 MPH on the freeway again and a caterpillar is slowly making its way toward my front tires. I want it to fulfill its destiny as a butterfly. My wife is in the seat next to me and my three children are in the back seat. A huge truck is breathing down my neck and a fat SUV is crowding me on my immediate left. I can't change lanes without risking a lot of lives. Do I cut in front of the SUV to avoid the caterpillar? Do I take a chance? Certain inevitable probabilities are about to play themselves out.

I know what I would do, and have done. I opt for the greater good. I swallow hard and plow straight ahead. In my rear-view mirror the caterpillar has disappeared, but the huge truck still breathes down my neck.

The comparison is less phony than it seems. I know the difference between a human fetus and a caterpillar. Thousands of women have to make very difficult and morally complex choices every day, often in the absence of the males who do not care about the pregnancy and who will not take care of them or the baby that is born. Many women (and men) make mistakes, as we also would if we, from our distances, were imposing right-to-life consequences on them while being wholly ignorant of the individual circumstances of their personal lives.

In real life we seldom have a rear-view mirror or the time to gaze into it for hints that enable us to make sense of our actions, especially when both private and public institutions fail to address the dysfunctional family, and social and economic systems that make unwanted pregnancies more probable. Those not facing difficult abortion choices imagine themselves breezily free to choose while quietly knowing that their choices are limited by personal and public facts of life. For ourselves we do the best we can, given the circumstances we face, basing our choices, if we take pride in behaving as moral agents, on the best available evidence, probable outcomes, and the direction provided by conscientious ethical reasoning.

Nations, governments, and politicians routinely, more often it seems, do not. They honor power. They torture, conduct suicide missions, indiscriminately kill civilians, drop thousands of tons of bombs, and ask for our approval in churches, mosques, and voting booths. They compel us to pay taxes for wars we don't want, they promote policies that ruin the environment, they stack the deck in favor of the rich and powerful—and we, still hoping for the best, vote for the lesser evils. By voting we routinely participate in and empower actions that are morally repugnant and in violation of our belief in the sanctity of life. Many of us look the other way when capital punishment is exacted, and we send our own children, or those of our neighbors, to fight in wars we don't believe in, and we support pro-gun legislation while knowing that permissive gun use is directly related to increased violence and deaths. We subscribe to these behaviors while believing in the sanctity of human life. Our votes empower us as a collective to take the lives of people we would not dream of harming individually. We make moral decisions about civic matters in swamps full of crocodiles. Then we thank our stars, and our government, for giving us the right to choose with our votes the actions that will best allow us to survive as individuals.

The abortion issue is both a personal (and "religious") and a civic (and "political") issue, one that makes us uneasy when we try to reconcile personal and public morality. Moreover, we are discouraged from reconciling the two. Because the issue is so intensely personal and political, we find ourselves tempted to separate ourselves from the issue's public implications and to find comfort, refuge and moral righteousness in personal religious dogmas that become the basis for decisions we make as citizens. Reducing the issue to a personal religious or moral choice allow us the freedom to enjoy the private privileges conferred by separation of church and state, while conferring on the state the freedom to impose its will on those who disagree with us. In this way a nation built on tolerance, diversity, and individual pathways becomes a toll road full of one-way signs everyone has to obey.

The continuation of civil society demands that we arrive at negotiated settlements between conflicting moral claims. As citizens we pay our taxes to support wars we hate because failure to do so might lead to something worse, the dissolution of all law and order. We vote for the least disagreeable politician because we want to hang onto the democratic process that may allow us to vote the worst ones out next time, particularly those who stack the deck in favor of the rich and powerful. We compromise our moral "purity" because it's what a reasonable citizen would do. Some—I am one of them—support Roe vs. Wade because it helps define a moral position on the abortion issue that more effectively addresses the question of how to decrease abortions.

Decreasing abortions depends on seeing that the right to moral autonomy is also a core American value. While some women facing the difficult abortion choice may be in a moral limbo, the elimination of Roe vs. Wade puts them in a legal quagmire too. When the public is divided on whether a fetus is a "human being" and the judiciary has not proclaimed that abortion constitutes "murder" of a human being, the individual becomes the standard for resolving the issue. Roe vs. Wade does not require abortion. It allows for personal moral choice. A law prohibiting abortion requires wholesale obedience. It eliminates the individual's moral choice. When a moral imperative does not admit to the ambiguities surrounding the individual circumstances involved in abortion decisions, individuals are denied the option to exercise personal moral choice. It also conveniently allows the millions not facing abortion decisions to avoid the problem's complex realities. In these ways moral autonomy as a core American value is jeopardized.

As a nation we celebrate law and order—personal behavior that does not undermine democratically established laws. Obviously preferable are choices that are made in full consciousness of relevant facts, and those that favor both personal and social stability. But in reality the abortion issue is driven by murky private circumstances, examples of women victimized by rape and by pregnancies that result from carelessness, innocence, mental illness and ignorance. Public problems are hard to ignore, and addressing these problems institutionally gives their moral basis weight.

The issue is complicated by widespread acceptance of abortion outside the U.S. On a planet where populations are swelling geometrically while they are making a worn-out hag of Mother Earth, we collectively face a looming worldwide crisis that locks us into three options: Sexual abstinence, birth control and abortion prevention, or sex and childbirth as usual, with abortion permitted.

Abstinence is unrealistic, not likely to be practiced on a scale that will significantly affect the looming problem. Abstinence is also not likely to have wholesale success in an economy driven by steady streams of sex-centered ads. Sex as a way to sell is at the core of American business as usual. This business model, a cultural norm, has liberated sexuality from its traditional restraints and has made active sexuality morally ambiguous, divisive, and exploitable by self-interest individuals and companies with profit motives driving their morality, or lack of it. The "rhythm method" and self-control practices are proving too weak to counter the force of sex that sells.

To focus attention narrowly on outlawing individual abortions takes attention away from big picture issues. Population control is only one. The other—much more immediate and local—is active discussion of what programs are in place to prevent unwanted pregnancies. The media's lack of responsibility—and the cultural conditioning the media create—leaves birth control, sex education, and abortion counseling as the only viable ways to rein in both abortion and population growth. They are also important moral forces because they are the only genuinely practical ones likely to decrease abortion rates.

Liberals must not allow themselves to be fooled: The right-wing political schemers—not to be confused with many of their public supporters taken in by their schemes– –will continue to target Roe vs. Wade, even if many of their constituents quietly support it. The issue's political usefulness is in exploiting the Supreme Court's decision by keeping it alive as a public controversy. Overturning it would criminalize abortion, make "murderers" of women with unwanted pregnancies and of doctors who perform abortions safely. A lot more jails or similar institutions, presumably at public expense, would have to be built, many for teenage girls who abort their pregnancies. While women would be forced to give birth to unwanted children, they would have little assurance that the state would provide either for them or for their newborns. The public mood seems to be against doing just that.

If anti-abortion politicians enjoy accusing defenders of Roe vs. Wade of supporting an immoral law, the time has come to question the public morality of their stance. Many, if not most, of those opposed to abortion routinely oppose family planning initiatives that provide low income Americans with birth control and contraceptives designed to reduce unintended pregnancies. They routinely oppose sex education programs in public schools. Nor do politicians see any immorality in refusing to fund public health, mental health, wellness, and educational programs that most certainly would reduce abortions. They seem to prefer to build more jails, and to privatize them.

A right-to-lifer understandably is more likely to heed practical arguments than legal fine points, especially if these practical arguments have sound moral grounding. It is important to emphasize that the right-wing abortion agenda is on shaky grounds because it is punitive rather than preventative. It addresses results rather than causes, and as such it will not lead to fewer abortions.

The struggle to diminish abortions is synonymous with the ongoing effort to build economic and social systems that are practical, fair, and sustainable. When these efforts fail we see the results—a widening gap between rich and poor, public demoralization, politics corrupted by money and narrow self-interest groups, a nation divided against itself. A lot of good people who have strong moral objections to abortion need to be convinced that many "pro-choice" advocates also care for the needy and poor, and for the unborn. They will find themselves allied to those likely to oppose torture, capital punishment, war, and the marginalization of the needy. More importantly, honest right-to-lifers need to be convinced that prevention diminishes the abortion rate—that programs designed to educate, employ, counsel, nourish, and provide safety are vital to women and family life.

There is much work to be done, mainly at local levels, to design, develop, fund, and document the invisible benefits of these programs. How do we take notice of, and credit for, the number of abortions that *don't* occur because unwanted pregnancies did *not* occur—because we created and supported a program that *prevented* them? And we also should take credit for supporting women and the difficult and necessary choices they make.

There is work to be done convincing right-to-lifers that we're really on the same side.

A Mindset That's out of Sight

Few recall or know about the first assassination attempt on Martin Luther King's life. On September 20, 1958, a woman named Izola Curry drove a seven-inch letter opener into King's chest as he was signing copies of *Stride Toward Freedom* in a Harlem bookstore. King required elaborate surgery and survived the attack, and Izola Curry, a black woman born in Adrian, Georgia, and working as a cook in New York, disappeared from public view.

A public consensus about Izola Curry's state of mind quickly hardened into a judicial conclusion. She was declared insane. She attacked King, she believed, because he was oppressing her. He had led troubling boycotts against whites, and worse: He was a communist. These same beliefs were commonly held by many whites. Though some folks no doubt quietly cheered the stabbing, it seemed reasonable to conclude that a black woman sharing white prejudices was insane because she was black. Interestingly, when James Earl Ray, a white man, later succeeded in killing Dr. King, no one was declared insane.

One voice spoke out strongly against the insanity ruling. Dr. Karl Menninger, renowned psychiatrist, lamented that the insanity ruling made the causes of Izola Curry's violence invisible. The ruling, in effect, "disappeared" her by secreting her away into a mental institution, where she, with many others unlike her, would no longer complicate the lives of those in the mainstream. If Izola Curry heard voices telling her to stab Martin Luther King, these voices were not those of ordinary folks. She was born and raised on planet earth, but she must have been from somewhere else.

Dr. Menninger was of the opinion that she was indeed like many of us—expressing her sense of oppression in racial terms not unlike those resorted to by blacks and whites alike. The oppressed, he believed, tend to take on the characteristics of their oppressors, and the violent act Izola Curry performed is what any number of individuals not deemed insane predictably do when under unusual stress for reasons they don't fully understand. She, a black woman, believed that the white world was the moral norm. Dr. King challenged that assumption. In attacking him she was doing what she thought was right—protecting the white world moral norm that kept her, as a black woman, in her place but also gave her a place. Dr. Menninger did not look the other way from what was happening in Izola Curry's mind: To declare her insane and to hide her away in a mental institution denied not only her but the public a deeper understanding of why certain kinds of violence occurs.

If what Dr. Menninger said is true, not only of Izola Curry but of the many in society who feel alienated, frustrated, resentful, and depressed, we should expect the level of violence in a society to be proportional to the numbers and intensity levels of those who feel oppressed. In a polarizing society such as ours in which people with clashing belief systems attack each other with righteous disrespect, the sense of oppression is likely to be felt on all sides. When we add to the mix millions of guns we should not be surprised at the spontaneity, destructive power, and frequency of widening outbursts of social suicide. People kill people, and guns kill people, especially since killing is easier to do with guns than with, say, clubs or knives. And because it's easier to kill people with guns it's also easier to do more of it when a lot of people are at each other's throats.

It's easy to demonize perpetrators of violence after the fact, and to label the worst insane. But this label also demonizes the millions of mentally disabled individuals who never perform violence and are often victimized by it. It also gets us off the hook, separating the violent from our personal responsibility for them and from the world we have been making for ourselves and children. Killers are our children too—born naked and innocent into the world we have made for them. This in basic ways is an ugly world—twisted toward the justification of killing and torture in a nation perpetually at war, profiting from entertainments that glorify violence, terrorizing its own citizenry with unrealistic fears, demoralizing it with cynicism and greed, and failing to provide institutional support for the needy and confused.

This ugly culture is pervasive. It is also ours, and some would call it "insane." We have bought and paid for it, and as we complain about tax increases we keep paying the terrible costs we inflict on ourselves by producing and purchasing the products that create the ugliness.

We have not yet developed the wisdom and will needed to minimize the nastiness we continue to purchase and promote. There are other, better, voices too, also ours but too seldom heard. Following Izola Curry's attempt on his life Martin Luther King issued a public statement lamenting that she might have injured herself in seeking to injure him. "I can say, in all sincerity, that I bear no bitterness toward her," he wrote.

What he wanted for her was to "receive the necessary treatment" so that her "disorganized personality need not become a menace to any man."

The Age of Special Effects

I think I now have a name for it—for our era, the brave new world we've made for ourselves. The clue came when I asked a neighbor kid, a college senior, about a blockbuster movie he had just seen.

"It was great," he said.

I nagged him to tell me more. "What made it great?"

"The special effects."

I nagged again. "Anything else?"

"The special effects. They were incredible."

"Incredible?" Not to be believed?

It slowly dawned on me how old-fashioned I am. When I watch a movie I'm still taken—or not—by its story elements, what we used to call plot, character, and theme in those Intro to Lit. classes we were required to take decades ago. Special effects—camera angles and lenses, matte, mirror and stop action shots, slow motion, rear projection and similar tricks of the trade—were nothing much to bother about. Today such tricks look lame next to the computer-generated wizardry that has become the fast-food of Hollywood and video fare. In the old days we were taught that if the tricks were good enough they wouldn't detract from the important stuff—plot, character, theme— by drawing attention to themselves. Until very recently it didn't occur to me that I should go to movies to devote my attention to the special effects. Nor could I imagine that special effects could constitute content.

I plead guilty to innocence. All movies, video games, TV ads, and books—and indeed all objects made by human beings—are engineered artifacts. It is naïve if not perverse to be ignorant of the way this engineering, also called artistry or craft, manipulates our responses to a movie, novel, car, or toothbrush. This is a troubling thought. We've all been deeply moved by certain movies, books and works of art. They change our lives in subtle but powerful ways, we say, because what we think and feel is real about them speaks to what we think and feel is real in us. Though we're usually not good at explaining why, we keep insisting that art is not the same as artifice, and that the difference has something to do with the distinction between authenticity and artificiality.

For old fog-heads like me that distinction hangs on, if only in assisted living programs sponsored by retired liberal arts majors.

It's clear that fog-heads have to move over to make room for a dazzling new era, one produced, directed, and storyboarded by cadres of high-tech masters spawned during the Age of Aquarius. This generation has redefined content by mainstreaming its thinking styles into the base of the new economy, advertising. Though advertising is as old as prostitution, it has managed to give itself an irresistible face-lift by shifting attention from the value of products to its own production values. Advertising is our most important product. It's our new Ford, Chrysler, and GM, and anyone who has seen the Olympic games opening ceremonies or watched a mega-church spectacular on TV knows its content has worldwide market appeal.

What defines any transformative era is its economy's impact on the spirit of the times, its manners, morals, and spirituality. The TV nightly news is a good indicator of how our manners have evolved. The news is well dressed, even tempered, civil, and almost always recited by blonde young women or gray-haired older men. And it's clear that a new moral base has taken root. To be virtuous is to be virtual. If virtuality suggests a certain lack, it bodes well for the widespread acceptance of self-esteem levels the new masses enjoy. If in olden days we were all sinners who fell short in the sight of God, nowadays we are also humbled as we watch unnatural depravity violently playing itself out on the screens of our choosing, while we enjoy the no fault exemptions that result from being distanced from actual depravities.

The spirituality of this new era, stimulated by various screens that project the will of sources at once powerful and invisible, has designs on congregations of faith. Media sources are ubiquitous and mysteriously present, and devotions to them may be expressed via its many incarnations—ordinary TV monitors, cinemascope, and I-MAX screens, but also via smallish hand-held devices destined someday soon to be no bigger than prayer beads. Devotions derived from screens are channeled by three important factoids: 1) high definition, which makes the devotions' relationship to content seem brilliant; 2) interactiveness, a process that minimizes the distractions caused by natural stimuli such as wind, water, sunlight and soil; and 3) speed, which saves ritual from the boredom of vain repetitions and troubling visitations of doubt.

The organic relationship between the new content of our economy and our foreign policy and military challenges is already well established. The Shock and Awe offensive in Iraq, for example, was calculated to produce a war theatre scene so engrossing that the enemy and U.S. taxpayers would be stunned into becoming a captive audience. The deployment of drones into the theaters of

Pakistan and Afghanistan foreshadows strategic re-enactments not unlike those we routinely see in Hollywood action movies and video games. Though the drones as yet fail to provide visuals that have the immediacy and detail of a real-time close-up, what remains to be seen are drone armadas outfitted with sonic and visual displays programmed to win the hearts and minds of entire enemy population types. This technology, able to fly without being required to endure the slow growth the walking stage of human development requires, is ahead of its time in its infancy. We no doubt will be shocked and awed as we watch its offspring take off.

Most fog-heads are certain that these changes are present, pervasive, and unprecedented. Lacking is a name for the new era, something suitable for textbook publication that will speed marketing on its way. Names for eras come and go—consider how passé labels such as Renaissance, Reformation, Age of Reason, Romanticism, and Modernism are—so only something really effective will satisfy the promoters of new virtual realities. Though I'm not sure it has either the right ring or a strong enough visual appeal, I prefer The Age of Special Effects, and I cite as my inspiration Henry David Thoreau's chapter "Economy" from *Walden*. There, as he meditates on the heaps of stuff for sale at the auction of a deceased deacon's effects, Thoreau concludes that the dead man's life had not been ineffectual.

As for a logo, I'm at a loss, even after doing an endless Google search. A logo featuring Madonna and laptop conveys some sense of what the new age is all about, though the image is too loaded down by medieval associations. But I'm sure that some artist, given a proper incentive bonus, will conjure a more effective logo, something slick that grabs us without letting go.

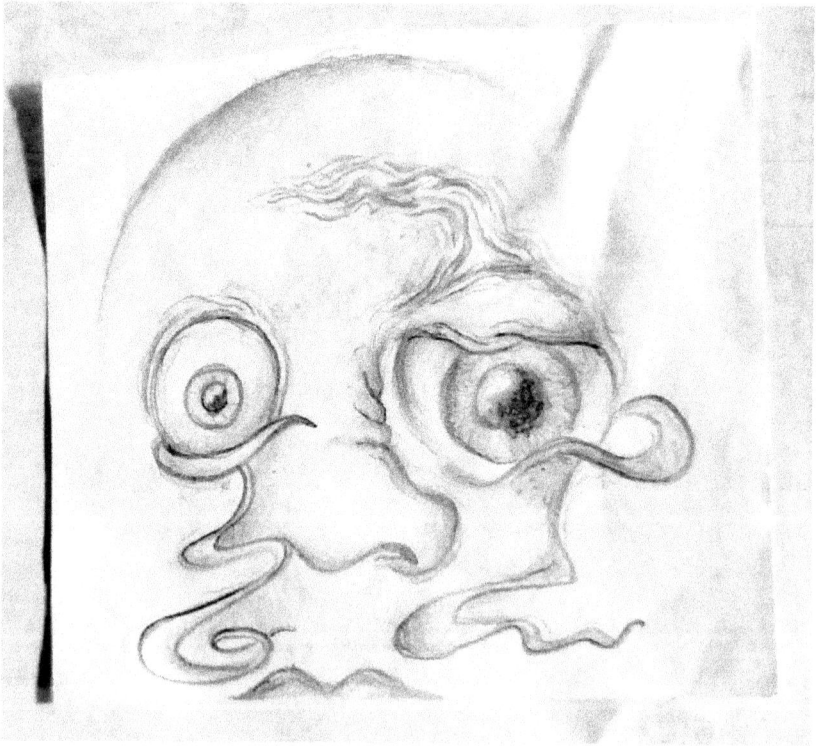

Waste Rituals

My father, an Old Country immigrant, had a ritual. He left the dishwashing to my sisters and the drying to me, but after every meal he routinely escaped to the garden in back with a handful of leftovers—potato peels, eggshells, apple cores, bean tips, and other debris dirt likes to eat. There he'd dig a little hole with his spade and bury the stuff.

It is a sin to waste, he routinely said with a sad little shake of his head. Not only that: The buried stuff would turn into lovely tomatoes, eggplant, and beans next year.

He's gone now, so he won't have to put up with my wasteful ways. One of them is that I keep forgetting to use the reusable cloth bag in the back seat of my car. Again and again I find myself in the grocery store checkout line with the clerk asking me if I want paper or plastic. I always say paper, quietly bewildered by my failure to remember to reach into the back seat for the reusable bag, while feeling morally superior to those lugging their groceries away in plastic bags. The plastic bags disappear, while adding up. By the millions, billions. They're thin but tougher than nails, refusing to rust away when we have no further use for them. They're an invisible and weighty waste problem that, unlike my father's handful of leftovers, don't usefully go away.

Millions—maybe billions—of people would make feasts of our throw-away food. According to the Society of St. Andrew, an organization dedicated to feeding America's hungry, more than twelve billion (12,000,000,000) pounds of food was wasted in the first two months of 2013. If we multiply those two months' worth of waste by ten remaining months we achieve a gross tonnage difficult to find room for in our minds. Of all food harvested in the U.S. less than 50% gets eaten, this in a nation where obesity is a serious health issue.

Waste's ability to increase and multiply makes it a significant growth industry. The EPA reminds us that "food leftovers are the single largest component of the waste stream by weight in the United States." A National Resource Defense Council study (2012) shows that, "Getting food to our tables eats up 10 percent of the total U.S. energy budget, uses 50% of U.S. land, and swallows 80 percent of fresh water consumed in the U.S." And here's another turn of the screw: It costs about one billion dollars per year to get rid of food we don't eat. As talk about the impact of government spending on future generations heats up I wonder if we're feeding our children to the monstrous waste we wallow so neatly in.

Think of what a field day my father's eggplants, tomatoes, and beans would have with all our leftovers.

He had a hard time throwing anything away. He'd find a neat little place in the basement or garage for pieces of pipe and wire, for old boards, engine parts, and used bricks, for coffee cans full of nuts and bolts and bent nails, and for empty coffee cans. When he needed to fix something he knew where to find the part that fit. Meanwhile, the EPA tells us that Americans generate about 250 million tons of Municipal Solid Waste daily, or 4.43 pounds of MSW per person per day.

Researchers at the Lawrence Livermore Laboratory also add their bits of information about the waste Americans pile up. LLL flow charts show that "more than half (58%) of the total energy produced in the U.S. is wasted due to inefficiencies, such as waste heat from power plants, vehicles, and light bulbs…And while residential, commercial and industrial sectors waste about 20% of their energy, the transportation sector wastes a full 75%, making it 25% energy efficient."

It's a lot harder, in short, for oil to move cars made of steel than for humans made of flesh and bones to use their feet. The cars we ride in get a free ride at our expense, and they steer clear of the troubles caused by oil in the Mideast.

We vaguely know these grim facts, if not the actual numbers that are so huge we lose our minds in them. We know enough to turn off the lights, turn the thermostat down, walk or bike or carpool, eat smaller portions, recycle, bury leftovers into a compost pile, and lug our groceries home in a reusable bag.

But in my case there's a disconnect between what I know and what I do. I leave lights on, I drive when I could walk or bike, and I keep forgetting that reusable bag in the back seat of my car.

I wonder if I'm typical. I talk to myself about preventing waste, but my mumbling gets lost in all the noise I hear about "growth" and "jobs." In our national conversations about climate change and environmentalism I seldom hear the word "conservation" used, certainly rarely by "conservatives" whose arguments for fossil fuel growth are underwritten by fossil fuel industries. The case for "growth" and "jobs" is routinely made synonymous with "prosperity," but I seldom hear it linked to the poverty resulting from the expansion of waste. Nor are "growth" and "jobs" linked to the shrinkage of resources on a planet quietly experiencing population explosion. What I don't hear much about is also what I don't want to hear or do much about.

I'm not sure I forget that reusable bag in the back seat of my car because I'm losing my mind. I think that bag is not on my mind enough. When I talk to myself I usually can't remember what I said an hour ago. But when everyone's talking about the same thing it's hard to ignore what's being said. People like me need to tune into a new conversation about food, energy use and waste—call it a national conversation, one with the word *conservation* routinely used in it. Kids should learn to spell the word in their cradles, and older folks should utter it as they begin turning into eggplants, tomatoes, and beans too. Why do all the drilling, fracking, and pipelining to increase fossil fuel energy by 20% in the next ten years when we could reduce it, and much of the waste fossil fuels produce, by 20% in the next five? I don't think it would trouble us much to walk, bike, carpool, turn off some lights, watch less TV, drink from faucets rather than bottles and cans, and carry our groceries out in reusable bags.

The big industries that lobby for business as usual—and more "growth"—have indeed created habits that provide Americans an outstanding materialistic way of life made more enjoyable by sporadic outbursts of religiosity. But are these industries "growing" us to a breaking point, without making waste one of their deadly sins? How can the economy "grow" without turning our neighborhoods into gaseous landfills? The Chinese are wearing protective masks as they stroll down the avenues crowded with exhaustion pipes spewing out toxic fumes the winds are exporting to the U.S.

We need more talk—talk full of smart ideas and urgency—about waste's impact on prosperity. Can we more comprehensively figure the long-term and widespread costs of waste into our business calculations?

How much more stuff do we need, and what can we do better without? Can we cut down on waste and increase prosperity by de-materializing our economy? Can we create both jobs and new wealth by professionalizing the relatively non-toxic and good work done by alternative health and human services providers, by educators and artists, by fix-it-up gurus, and by caretakers of culture and the environment? Would more people actually be happier in this leaner and cleaner economy? Would it save future generations of our children from the disasters business as usual profiteers are warning us about?

Certainly it would help if politicians and celebrities would speak out about this issue in a big way, but they're unlikely to do so until they hear a lot of us talking about it first.

I know I talk too much to myself, and it's one reason I so easily slip out of the habit of lugging my groceries home in a reusable bag. Every time I do that I almost realize that I've failed to translate my mind's preferences into the behaviors of everyday ritual. I've thought about buying more reusable bags and spreading them around the car so they're impossible to ignore, but that somehow rubs me wrong. I need a reusable ritual, not more reusable bags. Proper rituals, which conjure widespread commitment to norms that have special, even sacred, significance, are vital to the survival of a society. If I saw others routinely walking to the front door of the grocery store with reusable bags in hand, I'd be much more inclined to reach for mine in the back seat of my car. And I'd change other habits too, probably getting some good exercise riding the six blocks to the grocery store on my bike instead of in my car.

Chirping in a Room of My Own

Whenever the house gets messy enough I like to retreat to a favorite little space where I hope everyone will just let me be. There, in that small room, I find some quiet ways to come to terms with all the messy troubles in the world. The only sounds I love to hear in that room is the chirping of birds. I wish I could chirp like birds—they sound so spiritual. But I'm suspicious of the way the word "spiritual" is used, so I tell myself my room and my silences are the best I can do toward making my separate peace.

In that room there's a window looking out. So I also call it a room with a view.

That window is small enough to provide me some narrow impressions of how human beings tend to behave. Yesterday, after turning off the TV news and its steady stream of talk about wars and the terrorist potential of four-hour erections, I imagined myself somewhere in the Mideast right after a fellow named Jesus, like many others, was crucified. The region I'm in is teeming with religious cults, rituals, prophets, seers, and devotees. Some of these cults come from Persia and beyond, others from what we now call Israel, Palestine, Lebanon, Syria and Turkey, and beyond. And all these cults compete for attention with the devotees of the various Greek and Roman deities, and the classic philosophers too.

The region is, religiously speaking, untidy, and messy if we disapprove. The Romans, who rule the scene, think it best to let people believe what they want as long as they pay their taxes and behave. A few of the Roman emperors think of themselves as gods, but because there are so many gods all around the emperors secretly know they're not the only ones in a crowded field of minor league god-players.

Anybody with teenagers in the house knows this much: Untidiness gets on the nerves. So many cults, so many deities, so many important things to believe, this way or that. The urge for neatness kicks in, for the sake of order and clarity—and purity. Throw a bunch of stuff out, finally. Get rid of all the cults and gods that clutter the temples, streets and minds. Get back to basics, the god I like.

So polytheism officially lost out, and the great monotheistic religions took over. The woman devoted to chastity no longer has a special goddess, Artemis, to call her own, and the drunken lecher no longer calls on Bacchus to juice him up. The Gnostics, who believe themselves in the special know about most things divine, have to join the Roman church or play dumb, and the Manicheans, with their rival kingdoms of evil and good, become just one more designated minority "heretic" group. The One God—Jewish, Christian, and eventually Muslim too—becomes the acceptable, invariable and eventually required only God.

So why don't we get along? Why all the trouble and fuss in the Mideast and here at home? The troubles are not just about oil and jobs. They're also about dignity and belief and the right to believe and be left alone to get on with the daily chores of life. Trapped by these troubles are ordinary and reasonable people who want zealot politicians and preachers to go mum for a change. These good folk don't like others trying to mind their spiritual business.

The monotheistic leaders agree that they all worship the same God—one and absolute, an invariable. Meanwhile, the other invariables persist—the chaste woman, the lecherous drunk, the mystic knower, the saint who thinks he's living in a black and white, evil and good, world with other believers who look at all things—spirituality, morality, abortion, gay marriage, big corporations, and religion's role in politics—this way and that.

But now there are not countless sacred cults to choose from and to find comfort and community in. So here we are, stuck either inside the monotheistic umbrella, or somewhere outside. If we're inside the One God umbrella it's easy to take potshots at everyone outside, and vice versa.

Things get much worse when those inside the One God umbrella multiply and divide into Godlets. Then they begin taking potshots at each other too. Various types of Catholics and Protestants come to mind, and Sunni and Shia, with many local variations. Things get much worse when the uncivil comments the zealots hurl at each other turn into civil wars. While people stuck in civil wars brutalize each other, they often live in the same town, and sometimes next door.

There's usually no backing down, especially when zealots begin making speeches and when the basic response that results from thinking of the world as good and evil gets on the roll called revenge. You killed my son? Then I'll rape your daughter. That kind of thing.

And when there's no Rome to collect taxes and keep the calm, that is, when people require government to take only one side, things are likely to get worse.

It makes a lot of people wonder where they can find a decent cult to join. They'd probably do much better by clearing space for a little room of their own, but please, everyone, don't bring your messes into my little room.

It's where I try to chirp like a bird, and imagine the little waves my chirping makes in the air.

A World War III Whine

World War III has not been declared, and most of the world's ordinary folk are going about their daily business as usual. Because the word "war" conjures grand military responses and self-fulfilling prophecies of the worst sort, I'm very reluctant to use the word "war" to describe what I think is happening. But the troubles are widespread, profound, and unprecedented, and they leave in their wake the wreckage of millions of lives. The number and diverse locales of conflicts affect us terribly when we're safe and sound and looking the other way. Even with the spread of new technologies making global communications virtually instantaneous, the same technologies pose new problems for organized response, and make new conflicts possible and dangerous.

For me World War III began during the "conflict" in Vietnam. By then World War Two, the black and white "Good War," was being colorized on screens, with its traumas and casualties merged with the spoils that flowed to city and suburban development schemes, as rural areas declined. Meanwhile, the Cold War was heating up, with Good War winners on opposite sides of an imaginary Iron Curtain scheming, mainly through proxies, to do each other harm. The Cold War's closest bastard child of the Good War, the Korean "conflict," turned into a case of arrested development when the division of the Korean peninsula gave that war a long time out that made a runt of it in the litter of twentieth century wars. By the time the Berlin Wall came down in 1989, the Cold War was bleeding its poisons into World War III, the war without borders that now requires new armies of doctors without borders.

Pogo explained it to us best: "We have met the enemy, and he is us." One day, in the middle of a Vietnam war that seemed to have no beginning or end in sight, I realized I was living in my own enemy country. The battle lines were suddenly blurred. Enemies were living next door to each other in the same neighborhoods, profoundly divided by the politics of wealth, gender and belief. As the intensity of the antagonisms spread, the loyalties defined by lines drawn on maps began to dissolve, as if written in invisible ink. Here and there patriots were becoming partisans for competing tribes, fanatical sects, lost causes, and criminal clans within the same national states, many of their chiefs elected to office in order to put down their own citizens.

My optimist friend, a fatalist, tells me to sober up: There have always been wars and rumors of wars. Wars are…natural. And only two were actual "world wars," and they're over and done with now. And we won.

And one of our most popular young historians, Yuval Noah Harari, argues (in his *Sapiens: A Brief History of Humankind*) that, "Most people don't appreciate just how peaceful an era we live in." He cites "mass statistics" to validate his claim that, "we easily forget how much more violent the world used to be." Only—"only"—310,000 individuals died in wars in the year 2000 A.D., and only 172,000 died in 2002's wars. Car accidents and crime took far more lives in both those years.

We should be grateful that our lives are so peaceful we aren't blown to bits by a bomb as we drive down the street?

Well yes, but.

Harari's macro view of history zeroes out the hundreds of thousands of faces victimized by recent wars. His statistics are calculated in the same way the U.S. prefers to wage its wars—from an aerial view. To compare casualties from warring tribes when the whole world's total population was only one hundred million to those suffered when the population approaches seven billion provides percentages that create the illusion that we live in the best of all possible worlds. And conspicuously missing from Harari's count are the millions uncounted for except by the dogs of war—the little tragedies that don't make the TV news.

So what makes me think our current troubles are big enough to qualify as World War III?

The suicide bomber who blows himself up in a crowded marketplace is probably no taller than I am. I don't know where he's from, or his name, or his barber or grocer's name, or the names of any of the fifty-nine shoppers in the marketplace blown to bits by his bomb, or who made the bomb or parts for the bomb, or the names of the dead shoppers' cousins or grandmothers, or much of anything about what was running through the bomber's mind, what was gnawing at him so painfully, or what he hoped others would gain from it, and what will be gained and lost by his gesture crossed by heroism and desperation. It seems that more and more are volunteering to do what he did to scores of ordinary folk going about their business as usual. Suicide bombers and their victims alike represent no single nation, sect, income level, race or tribe. Some of their violence resembles that performed against innocent bystanders by criminal clans, but it's highly unlikely that any of the suicides think of themselves as criminals or psychotics. Nor do we, as perhaps we should. We call them "terrorists."

The war they wage is happening here and there, and most of the world, unless directly hit, doesn't pay much attention to it. As they swell into the thousands the casualties have a wholesale look. It's hard to care about troubles so distant, faceless and widespread they aren't seen.

From an aerial view the suicide bomber's act seems so small it's not on our radar screens. But what gives it world war status is its invisible viral power. If new technologies have managed to contain the spread of Ebola and other plagues, the spread of new technologies also gives the suicide bomber's act global presence. His explosion instantaneously makes the news, and it's known about by everyone with a mobile device, with the results of the explosion rather than its causes getting almost all the coverage. The group claiming credit for the act remains out of sight, as does the history of the grievances the group's act expressed. It's not easy to drop a smart bomb on such uncertainty.

My little World War III gains stature because the bombs are never smart enough, and because there are more and more of them being made, both improvised and carefully engineered in the finest facilities. If the twentieth century's world wars made that century the bloodiest in history, the firepower available worldwide in its final decade made possible what Pulitzer Prize winning historian Samantha Powers called "The Age of Genocide." If knives and machetes did their share of the killing work in Rwanda, plenty of weapons of mass destruction did the dirty work of ethnic cleansing elsewhere. From the gas and chemical weapons used in Syria, to the cluster bombs in Iraq, the technical expertise directed at the art of mass murder is historically unprecedented, and widely available.

The U.S. leadership role in the volatile but highly profitable armaments marketplace should not be understated: The U.S. is Number One worldwide in the sale of weaponry. Many of the weapons we produce come back to haunt us, and the vast profits from their sales inspire exciting but quiet new business opportunities.

The "world leadership" role the U.S. has assumed since the fall of the Berlin Wall and rise of global markets also have allowed worldwide local troubles to swell to the level of our planetary influence. If we don't everywhere wield a big stick, we speak softly in a lot of places. In a one sentence blurb *The Week* magazine proclaimed, in February, 2015, that "U.S. Special Operations forces quietly deployed to 133 countries in 2014—roughly 70 percent of the nations on the planet."

Because our new technologies allow millions to go "viral" with their messages, news and its imagery easily spread worldwide. One suicide bomber's gesture cannot be isolated or contained. Suddenly, unless we play dumb, we're all involved in some threat or war on the other side of the world, and with the disruptions of trade and population migrations that result. The U.S., posturing as "world leader," makes it a usually unwilling but responsible participant, the scapegoat and cause of conflicts everywhere, at once the world's great savior and enemy, the force the survivors and innocent victims should side with or destroy as the leading cause of troubles.

Meanwhile, a nation as small as Israel, with its nuclear bombs, has "balance of terror" capability, while Pakistan, chronically unstable, trusts members of a rogue military with the keys to its nuclear arsenal, and North Korea has nukes controlled, it appears, by kooks. When the World Trade Center towers were attacked on 9-11, World War III came to American turf in an obvious way not well foreshadowed by Vietnam. With it came a realization dimmed by the dust of destruction: Strangers somewhere in the world, more and more of them from places our students can't locate on a map, hate the U.S.

And with a new intensity Americans began blaming each other for everything going wrong. Where were the good old-fashioned wars, with turf battles that could be won and lost? Where were the official declarations of war––rather than "executive actions"—and formal truce ceremonies that ended the wars of yore? Enemies no longer could easily be identified by the colors of their uniforms, and the new battles being fought were "asymmetrical."

While terrorists were targeting Americans and each other, organized crime governed many governments, while internationalized bankers and corporate enterprisers, their enablers and suppliers, looked the other way as rivers of money rolled past computer screens into their vaults. Sects driven by old religious beliefs secured hoards of weapons, their leaders driven by vague resentments deeply associated with the symbols of wealth and vulgar worldliness broadcast worldwide by fancy new technologies. And the hot spots where troubles flared spawned thousands of people feeling angry and alienated––disaffected migrants and refugees for whom "home" had become an empty word. The divisions Americans began feeling during the Vietnam war brought no new unity against a common enemy easy to identify. Enemies were everywhere, both inside and outside the U.S., and everything going wrong was somebody else's fault.

Though it nostalgically remains the war game of choice for most Americans, football, with its ground game battles fought over lines drawn on turf, looks back to the Good

War rather than forward to the untidy fields of force of World War III. The roots of this new war are deep, wide and as cranky as angry young males blowing their minds.

If the Vietnam war brought some attention to the Post-Traumatic Stress problems caused by that war, it drew little attention to the PTS problems abandoned to their fates on obscure battlefields elsewhere in the world. There millions of civilian survivors suffer untold pains and madness. The general malaise caused by two world wars and the Cold War, and the profitable infrastructure of arms profiteering they created, remain terribly alive. If war is a terrible monster gorged with ill will, it has had plenty of illness to feed upon. If a Good War is fought to rectify terrible injustices, the injustices addressed by the new wars go so far back and are so obscured by fanatical belief the injustices can be raged against but not understood or rectified. One obvious feature of World War III is that it will not have a just conclusion, or just conclude.

An aerial view of planet earth makes other features of this new war visible. From the sky we can see the planet's webwork of river dams, oil fields, and mines, its fresh water streams and stretches of desert and fertile lands, even as we view the grey exhaustion hovering over vast cities crowding ocean shores. Individuals are lost in this picture, but not the impression that populations are swelling beyond the planet's ability to support the expansion of human enterprise. Inside village huts and in the narrow alleyways of cities whose names we have yet to learn teeming millions are struggling to find the food and water needed to get through another day. Meanwhile, as fertile soil washes away and water tables drop, new technologies provide millions of poor people glimpses of skyscraping wealth, their resentments gnawing at them from hunger and envy, and more intensely so when conspicuous consumption is compounded by Hollywood vulgarities that spread an infectious cynicism over traditional religious beliefs.

World War III festers in the resentments bred by this cynicism, and in the corruption of politicians and police that follows unnaturally enough from it.

From the aerial view it's also clear that the wealthy few, with their enormous profits secreted away into safe haven accounts, so far have been unmoved by the actual casualties the masses have been inflicting on each other. Each setback for the rule of law will be a multinational win for the planet's free enterprising individualists, whose moral sense urges them, when it is immediately useful to them, to obey their unnatural version of the law of the jungle. What is not entirely clear to them is that their new world trade towers are vulnerable to the clever technologies many of the wealthiest among them have developed and sold to the highest bidders.

Beneath the engine exhaust of the global view what we used to call "home"—an actual apartment or room, a house, a village or town, a city neighborhood—becomes harder to see. Wars destroy homes and makes migrants of masses who no longer have homes. Nations change their ethnic identities as "others" move in, and new classes of outsiders become squatters in the places they happen on. If alienation causes resentment and its often violent outcomes, the new global economy, with its promise to wire people together into social and commercial relationships, generates the alienation those living in lonely crowds deeply feel. As populations concentrate themselves into tighter spaces, the potential for explosions multiply.

The deepest resentments—call them also the main causes of war—have their source in the indignities and injustices that continue to trouble the long and dysfunctional history of male and female. Because women have godlike power to give birth from their own bodies, men have been at a loss about how to make up the difference. At best males use their creative genius as artists, artisans, workers, intellectuals, and engineers—and at their worst they become brilliant when devising clever and more devilish technologies of war. Ongoing war provides males ongoing excuses to make more powerful men of themselves, and it is no accident that their spoils of war so often are women who are raped, abused and locked into subordinated roles. In World War III the rights of women, and the male's right to ownership of women's lives, are the domestic center of the battleground, and old-time religious beliefs help anchor male domination there. World War III is more deeply a battle over sexual roles than it is between the haves and have-nots.

This war's ultimate victim is becoming Mother Earth herself, her rounds of creative processes necessary to natural growth. Nature herself is becoming virtually man-made, and the new technologies are literally getting under our skin as we expend our genius on new ways to get them to do our thinking for us. We are in a bizarre hurry to do this, driven by a curiosity dying to get us somewhere else more exciting than where we now are. As World War III heats up, and as profitable new technologies and weapons proliferate, the atmosphere also will be warmed for more war, and more violently waged against Mother Earth herself.

No Congress of Vienna, Treaty of Versailles, or Yalta Conference will conclude this war by arriving at accords or treaties, by exacting reparations, or by drawing the lines for new spheres of influence. As new conflicts flare here and there, only separate peaces will be possible. They will happen, or not happen, among neighbors and groups living in villages, cities and neighborhoods. The quality of culture—defined mainly by whether its table-talk emphasizes tolerance for diversity and values that dignify––will mainly determine which localities manage to remove themselves from the general strife. When violence, either in its grotesque or shadowy forms, is part of the mission of these institutions good table-talk gets lost in the noise. But if the good table-talk is overheard by established institutions—churches, businesses, schools, governments—it may gain enough weight to diminish the violence.

Thanks for listening. Let's talk. About peace.

Endnote: The Moral Compass, Its Genes

As violence throws its fits and starts here and there if not everywhere on the world map, I'm cursed and blessed to know my moral compass is calibrated to respond to both my selfish and unselfish genes. These genes, like the seeds of ragweed and beans, are living canisters that lie dormant or sprout when exposed to the conditions that make them thrive. To make myself an individual fit to survive I slip easily into the egocentricities my selfish gene requires. Because I've been fortunate, so far, to be merely a civilian casualty of the troubles surrounding me, I feel free to wiggle my moral compass according (in Emerson's words) "to how the wind blows and newspaper directs." While making a spectator of me it needles the artist in me into painting strangers as enemies wearing terrorist black, while I rise above the carnage like an angel singing holy hymns. These hymns have the same refrain line: This terrible war, and its far off troubles, is not mine, and not of my making. My moral duty is to make myself a survivor child on holy retreat from its beheadings, bombings, riots and firefights. By allowing my selfish gene to remove me from violence, I achieve not only a safe retreat but the righteousness that comes from believing I'm in tune with evolution's survival of the fittest law.

Meanwhile, my moral compass keeps quivering, as if it's warning me there's something still terribly awry. A moral compass is a subtle instrument sensitive to outrage and injustice, particularly when ongoing participation in public life—democracy—calls for outward and visible responses to the wrongs. One can be momentarily separate and safe in a lot of places, without having a separate peace, and the silence of holy haunts does not wall out the latest bad news. Who can look the other way without seeing hundreds of boys and men marched into ditches and shot in the back of the head, or the litter of body parts a suicide bomber leaves behind in a crowded marketplace? Or the faces of women and girls kidnapped, raped, and abused by men with black scarves covering their faces? And who lacks enough imagination to ignore what happens when narrow-minded bombs from jets and drones fall from the sky on houses and city neighborhoods? Who can be a holy ghost free of the knowledge that the returns on investments used to buy a condo, college degree, or fuel efficient car come from the companies that manufacture those jets, drones and bombs, perhaps within walking distance of the neighborhood where my selfish gene enjoys its immunity from the violence? How does my moral compass wriggle its way out of complicity for the death and destruction visited on strangers in far off places? My selfish gene easily makes a point of pointing the finger of blame away from me, without pointing a way out of the mess in which I participate.

In a war in which lines are blurred friends and enemies live inside the same enemy lines. If I separate myself from my complicity my separate peace hides within a mind that refuses to actively participate in the democratic society that provides everyone a limited opportunity, at least, to speak and vote. That mind's silence, as a response to the distractions culture uses to sell its goods, belief systems and entertainments, is one form of cheating the selfish gene uses to promote its personal survival agenda. Disengaged silence—the stoic's way of life in the slaughterhouse—resounds with the silence of the lambs.

In a world wired by technologies it is hard for the selfish gene to look the other way. If the Information Age makes the oscillations of the moral compass nervously uncertain, the bad news we stream in keeps the compass quivering. The sheer quantity of bad news makes it hard to know when and how to speak out, and to whom and about what.

It is comforting—and troublesome—to learn we very probably also have an unselfish gene. For decades researchers have been trying to establish a biological basis for altruism, and the probable existence of an unselfish gene is gaining currency among evolutionary geneticists: Survival of the fittest applies to groups rather than merely to individual winners within those groups. Bees work for the queen bee and all bees work for the survival of the hive, not so they can buzz on as self-styled libertarians. A GI throws himself on a grenade in order to save buddies who, as a team, torched a village with their enemies in it. A suicide bomber blows himself up in a crowded market-place to save not just his soul but his sect.

Unselfish genes move individuals to generate collective responses to forces that threaten the survival of groups. Inward moral impulses are projected outward to insure the survival of the fittest groups, and the scope of moral gesture is multiplied when it carries with it the weight of political, educational, business and religious institutions.

Devotees of democratic engagement tie their public morality to evolution of general humanity. This legacy, well-intentioned if not color-blind, has been passed on by Enlightenment philosophers and American Founding

Fathers to generations of Americans who have scant memory of the oppressive tyrants and aristocrats it targeted. It also has been the basis of some of the most doctrinaire crusades for American "exceptionalism"—the assumption that our version of democracy (and its tendencies toward selfish gene capitalism) is a God-sanctioned ideology destined to benefit humanity as a whole. Exceptionalism's missionaries believe they have an unselfish moral sanction based on a higher consciousness that will blossom in unexceptional regions under the influence of American military and economic intervention, and that intervention is necessary if general humanity is to survive threats posed by alien, ignorant, and primitive groups.

My moral compass is prejudiced to object to exceptionalist claims, but my unselfish gene still troubles me: Does its group orientation require me to focus my efforts on the salvation of general humanity, on its American "exceptionalist" brand, or on the survival of one or more smaller, and more local, group varieties?

I take for granted that moral choice depends on the best available consciousness. Ignorance, and the institutions (commercial, political, entertainment, religious, and educational) that promote it, does not seem viable as a survival strategy. Moral judgment obligates us to know as deeply and broadly as we possibly can, while assuring us that knowledge is provisional and linked to probabilities rather than certainties. Such knowledge has little to do with beliefs that scorn evidence and careful reasoning in favor of some wished for Truth.

Knowledge and belief also have an uneasy relationship to what we call "imagination" and "creativity." Creative and imaginative works are more likely to be credible if the acceptance—call it "belief"—they call for derive from sound knowledge. Since it takes us into the unknown, knowledge, when transformed into well-crafted art, takes us toward, and into, the "otherness" that has been alien to us. So imagination, when on high alert for what's truest and most real, has the power to put human faces on the people in the marketplace blown to bits by a suicide bomber. It also may inform us that the bomber had a human face, and parents, and friends, and the personal troubles ordinary individuals encounter in a life. He lives in a house, has a mother and father, cousins, a grocer. He has feelings and thoughts, many of them like ours. Our active consciousness put us in his place, provides us some understanding of why he turned the debate in his mind against himself, and against us. As the source of moral— not moralistic—art, imagination sees the suicide bomber in a complex context that makes him more familiar, if not just like ourselves or someone we know. We begin to understand, if not approve of, the sources of the bomber's decision to blow himself up in the marketplace. He is no longer wholly an outsider; he becomes a member of a group becoming visible, someone perhaps not unlike members of our own group who perhaps is threatening the survival of our group too. As a familiar rather than alien, he commands different attention and different moral gestures from us.

It is only natural that imagination, good art's vital source, moves and can be moved by the moral sense. The best art reveals the common bonds humans share, and exposes as permeable the oppressive limits individuals and groups impose on each other. It reveals the textures and tones of the life and death processes of planet earth, and of the individuals and tribes enduring its hardships and enjoying its offerings. Best of all, good art dissolves the arrogant black lines stereotypes impose on life's complex diversity.

I like to think that good art does the bidding of my unselfish gene. But imagination is a trickster too. It can invent apparitions, make nothingness seem real, and put a false face on things. Its salespersons are often eager to divorce and distract us from sound knowledge and to win our hearts by crafting artworks that mystify without illuminating the strange and unknown. Such works take us away from genuine "otherness." They make the suicide bomber more invisible, more a stranger to be feared. It is also ironic that even the best art, that which takes us to the heart and soul of an unknown, may be so masterfully performed that we wallow in it for its own sake rather than responding to the claims it makes on us as moral agents. If moral choice depends on consciousness, it also wanders in a mental playground where tricksters easily make a fool of it.

I can't keep myself from holding this belief close to my heart: Consciousness has a nose for what stinks, especially in those rare moments when we're breathing fresh air.

So much foulness circulates in the airwaves today it's easy to get demoralized. For me it has not been demoralizing to realize, even late in life, that my Christian heritage, if not all its art, is prejudiced in favor of my selfish gene. Doctrine and practice tell me I am born in sin into a sinful world where I will continue to live, as if morally disabled, in sin. I find both truth and solace in this grim view. It makes dirty business as usual seem inevitable while providing me a scapegoat savior relieving me of responsibility for the complicity the dirty business requires of me. I especially enjoy the true believer's simple and certain beliefs, which nail down my individual salvation while getting me off a lot of moral hooks.

Meanwhile, because I still feel the hooks, and because I must face the limitations of my knowledge—its merely human consciousness and imagination—my moral compass continues to have bouts of the shakes.

Do I favor—not only favor but speak out loudly in favor of—this cause or that? Do I cheer on the drones that zero their bombs in on a potential suicide bomber, while strongly suspecting that bystanders also will be hit? Do I leap forward to imagine how many will die, and where, if the drones do not do their deadly work? My compass requires me to calculate and choose, often between certain destruction and loss of life now, and perhaps worse destruction and loss of life later on. Moral choice's terrible choices live unhappily together in me. In the end I have to choose with some uncertainty, for example, whether my moral compass favors the heroic GI who throws himself on a grenade to save a platoon that has just torched a village with fifty strangers in it who may be unfriendly to American troops, and the suicide bomber who blows up fifty strangers in a marketplace to achieve a heavenly martyrdom.

Choices like this are also made in shadowy certainty that the unselfish gene can play selfish tricks on those who act unselfishly in the name of their special group. My moral compass wavers when it suspects that some groups may swallow us as they use us to destroy other groups. We hope to direct our moral prejudices toward groups that seem more inclusive of others, and more inclined to be reasonable and just. But it is ironic, and one absurd consequence of so-called human "progress," that democracies do not necessarily qualify as the most reasonable and just societies.

I live, then, trying to do the more probable right thing. Moral certainty gives me the shakes, given the violence that predictably results from certainty's dogmatic righteousness. It seems right to favor unselfish gene tendencies. Such a moral sense chimes best with theologian Paul Tillich's words: Sin is separation. This is a simple, and perhaps profound, rule by which to calibrate moral gestures. It is one thing to kill a person who lives in our house or neighborhood; but it is usually easier to kill someone whose face, name, and mother remain separate from us and unknown, especially when powerful weapons—rather than actual hands—do the killing. The differences that divide us, especially when agents arm themselves with weapons of mass destruction, operate most brutally, and mindlessly, when acting anonymously on anonymities. Victimized too is the sympathetic imagination of the agents of destruction, who deny themselves the power to name, see, and allow into their presence the powers they destroy.

Can it be that those willing to die for a cause—by simple obedience to commanders—are possessed by suicidal tendencies? When agents of destruction victimize themselves, do they not also destroy their own powers of imagination and creativity—those urges that provide them the capacity to understand and reshape the powers they wish to destroy? Do they fear the powers within themselves that are strangers to them, masquerading as enemies?

Out of ignorance, arrogance, and confusion the complex choices I face require me to separate myself from some people as I try to find solidarity with others. I have to make terrible compromises if I want to do anything at all. So I speak out against sending American ground troops to Iraq or Syria, and in so doing perhaps empower murderous militias and jihadist fanatics. I support Roe vs. Wade, believing the alternative to be worse for both the living and the unborn. I pay my taxes to the U.S. government, hoping that our democracy as a system has unselfish gene tendencies, even as I face the fact that hundreds of billions go toward an overgrown military establishment with a vested interest in war. Knowing full well that many of its leaders and good folk are selfish and bigoted, I keep alive in myself the dreamy notion that democracy, and the human progress its devotees credit it for, requires me to believe in or speak out in favor of the signals my clumsy morality is sending out.

Until I'm better informed I'm obligated to trust the knowledge some scientists are providing us—that there is an unselfish gene trying to attune us to its ways. When I imagine myself confronting the scale of violence occurring worldwide, I realize that my moral gestures are, well, mainly gestures. I speak out, I vote, I join a protest parade, I write these words. When I'm thinking small—about my family, neighborhood, or town as groups—my moral gestures seem weightier if they gain the support of established institutions. I don't give up easily on churches, schools, social organizations, and arts centers. They too may have unselfish genes lurking in them. On faith, then, rather than on fact I trust that human survival may depend on our helping our unselfish genes point the way.

Meanwhile, I recite the Golden Rule as if it's on a prayer wheel, and keep fine-tuning my nose for what stinks.

Acknowledgments

"Why Humpty Dumpty Fell from the Wall" was presented as an address at the Institute for Theological and Interdisciplinary Studies, in St. Paul, MN (April, 2013).

"Intellectual Honesty" was delivered as a lecture at Winona State University, April, 2008.

"The Woman from Beijing" was published in *Shadow and Light: A Literary Anthology on Memory* (Monadnock Writers' Group, 2011), and was reprinted in *The Green Blade*, 2011.

"Bikini Parade" appeared in *Midwest Gothic*, 2012.

"Horn Lore" first appeared in *The Horn* (2012).

"Privatize" appeared as a guest opinion column in *The Minneapolis Star/Tribune* (2014), *Winona Daily News* (2014), and *Winona Post* (2014).

Most other pieces appeared on "Downstream" blog site with the *Twin Cities Daily Planet*.

The Green Blade reprinted the following "Downstream" pieces: "The Zeroes of the Dogs of War" (2013), "Baronics" as "Entitlements" (2013), and "Belief Addiction" (2014).

"Just Because" was reprinted in *Best Dearborn Stories*, Volume II (2012).

Lost Lake Folk Opera also reprinted "The Zeros of the Dogs of War" and an earlier version of "A World War III Whine" (April 2015).

Thanks

To Mary Turck, who as editor made important suggestions about how to improve several of the pieces before they appeared at the "Downstream" blog site for *The Twin Cities Daily Planet*.

To Tom Driscoll, managing editor of Shipwreckt Books, for his encouragement and editorial expertise.

To Dante DeGrazia, my son, for the cover art and line drawings that adorn this book.

To Monica Drealan DeGrazia, my lovely and brilliant wife, who is the final editorial gatekeeper of all my work.

About the Author

Emilio DeGrazia, a resident of Winona, Minnesota, has authored four books of fiction, including *Seventeen Grams of Soul*, winner of a Minnesota Book Award, and *Enemy Country*, a Writer's Choice Award winner. A founding editor of *Great River Review*, he also has co-edited (with his wife Monica) *26 Minnesota Writers*, *33 Minnesota Poets*, and *The Nodin Poetry Anthology*. His most recent books are a collection of essays entitled *Burying the Tree*, a collage of memoirs called *Walking on Air*, and *Seasonings*, a collection of poetry. He also has served as Winona's Poet Laureate.